Van Gogh Face to Face

THE PORTRAITS

Contributing Authors

ROLAND DORN

GEORGE S. KEYES

JOSEPH J. RISHEL WITH KATHERINE SACHS

GEORGE T.M. SHACKELFORD

LAUREN SOTH

JUDY SUND

WITH A CHRONOLOGY BY KATHERINE SACHS

With 228 illustrations, 204 in color

 Thames & Hudson The Detroit Institute of Arts

This book is published in conjunction with the exhibition
"Van Gogh: Face to Face"

The Detroit Institute of Arts
March 12–June 4, 2000

Museum of Fine Arts, Boston
July 2–September 24, 2000

Philadelphia Museum of Art
October 22, 2000–January 14, 2001

First published in hardcover in the United States of America in 2000
by Thames & Hudson Inc., 500 Fifth Avenue, New York, New York 10110

Library of Congress Catalog Card Number 99–66191
ISBN 0–500–09290–7

Designed by Sarah Praill

Unless otherwise noted, excerpts from the letters of Vincent van Gogh
are reprinted from *The Complete Letters of Vincent van Gogh* (Greenwich, Conn.,
New York Graphic Society, 1958), by permission of the Vincent van Gogh
Foundation, Amsterdam

Frontispieces: Vincent van Gogh, *Self-Portrait with Bandaged Ear and Pipe*
(F 529, JH 1658), detail, first half of January 1889, oil on canvas, 51 x 45 cm,
Private Collection
Detail of fig. 71
Detail of fig. 92

Title page: Detail of fig. 130

Contents page: Detail of fig. 193
Detail of fig. 119
Detail of fig. 152
Detail of fig. 181
Detail of fig. 174

Full credits for reproduction permissions appear in the List of Illustrations in
this book

Printed and bound in Singapore by CS Graphics

Contents

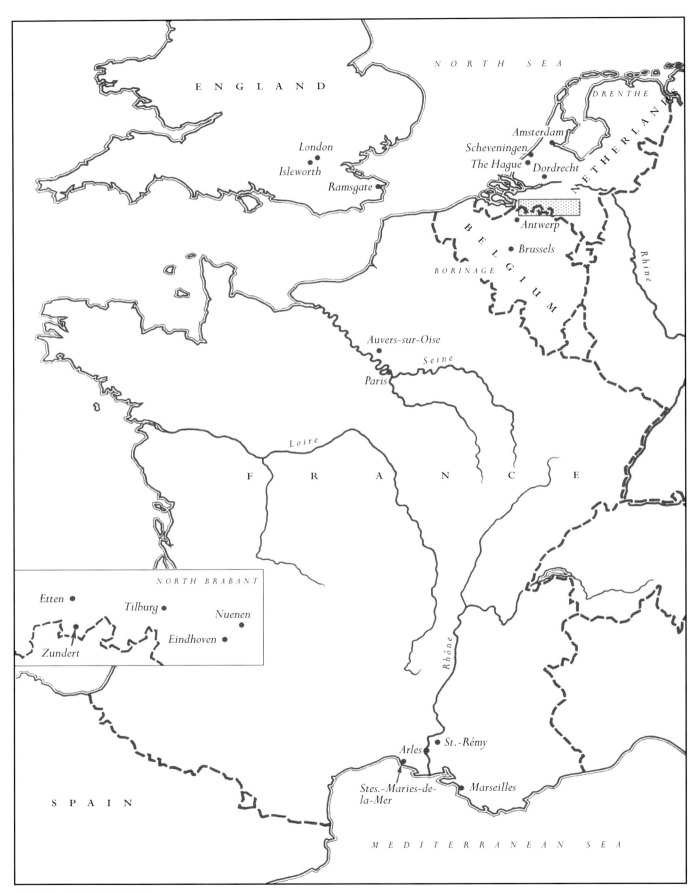

Map of places where van Gogh lived

Foreword

The reasons for yet another collection of van Gogh's works need little explanation. On one level, any sort of project invoking his name, whether book or exhibition, will automatically receive wide attention. Can one actually think, in terms of popular culture, of another name which solicits such an immediate flash of recognition: Mickey Mouse? Marilyn Monroe? Elvis? Vincent is now a phenomenon well beyond the conventional bounds of art history, or art for that matter.

And yet even the most experienced (and sometimes jaded) gallery-goer or book-reader gets caught in the web. The power of van Gogh's images pervades any number of social or cultural barriers. His pictures have the power to renew themselves; there are still discoveries to be made at each new encounter, even against the most formidable odds of overexposure. And for all this exposure and scholarly investigation into van Gogh's life and work, there remains a lot yet to learn and to experience. It is a shock to realize that, until now, his portraiture has not been given serious examination as a coherent body of work, even though it is the one aspect of his art which he himself held most dear. It was with both pride and excitement, therefore, that we undertook *Van Gogh: Face to Face*.

It began with Detroit curator George S. Keyes's idea for an exhibition of the portraits, which quickly developed into a collaboration with George T.M. Shackelford at Boston and Joseph J. Rishel at Philadelphia, each of which has an equally rich collection of van Gogh's portraits. Even so, such a strong and innovative show would not have been possible without the generous response from public and private lenders throughout the world in parting with prized objects from their own collections.

This handsome book reproduces even more pictures than were available for the exhibition. George Keyes, George Shackelford and Joseph Rishel have been joined by other eminent art historians to contribute original essays discussing different aspects of van Gogh's portraiture, and the result is both a major compendium of portraits by the artist and a unique body of scholarship. At a time when there a vast, ongoing, and profoundly self-revealing series of events relating to Vincent van Gogh—with shows, publications, lectures, movies, televisions programs, CD-ROMs, Internet websites, plays and lectures—it is very satisfying to be able to contribute in the process in such a distinctive and innovative way.

Graham W. J. Beal
Director, the Detroit Institute of Arts

Anne d'Harnoncourt
The George D. Widener Director and Chief Executive Officer,
Philadelphia Museum of Art

Malcolm Rogers
Ann and Graham Gund Director, Museum of Fine Arts, Boston

2. *The Baby Marcelle Roulin* (F 441, JH 1641), detail,
early December 1888
Oil on canvas, 35.5 x 24.5 cm
Amsterdam, Van Gogh Museum

Lenders to the Exhibition

Australia
Melbourne, National Gallery of Victoria
Sydney, Art Gallery of New South Wales

Belgium
Brussels, Koninklijke Musea voor Schone Kunsten van België

France
Paris, Musée d'Orsay

Germany
Essen, Museum Folkwang

Italy
Rome, Galleria Nazionale d'Arte Moderna e Arte Contemporanea

The Netherlands
Amsterdam, Rijksmuseum
Amsterdam, Van Gogh Museum (Vincent van Gogh Foundation)
Groningen, Groninger Museum
Heino, Hannema-de Stuers Fundatie
Otterlo, Kröller-Müller Museum
Rotterdam, Museum Boijmans Van Beuningen
Rotterdam, Private Collection

Russia
Moscow, Pushkin State Museum of Fine Arts

Switzerland
Basel, Rudolf Staechelin Foundation
Bern, Kunstmuseum Bern
La Chaux-de-Fonds, Musée des Beaux-Arts
Private Collection
Winterthur, Kunstmuseum Winterthur

United Kingdom
Edinburgh, National Galleries of Scotland
Glasgow, Glasgow Museums

United States
Boston, Museum of Fine Arts, Boston
Cambridge, Harvard University Art Museums
Chicago, The Art Institute of Chicago
Cleveland, The Cleveland Museum of Art
Detroit, The Detroit Institute of Arts
Los Angeles, The J. Paul Getty Museum
Los Angeles, Los Angeles County Museum of Art
New York, The Metropolitan Museum of Art
New York, The Metropolitan Museum of Art (Robert Lehman Collection)
New York, Private Collection
New York, Solomon R. Guggenheim Museum
Philadelphia, Philadelphia Museum of Art
Private Collection
Washington, D.C., National Gallery of Art

Note to the Reader

Catalogues raisonnés of works by Vincent van Gogh used for this book:

J.-B. de la Faille, *The Works of Vincent van Gogh, His Paintings and Drawings* (Amsterdam, 1970); abbreviated as "F."

J. Hulsker, *The New Complete Van Gogh: Paintings, Drawings, Sketches. Revised and Enlarged Edition of the Catalogue Raisonné of the Works of Vincent van Gogh* (Amsterdam and Philadelphia, 1996); abbreviated as "JH."

Sources for quotation of the letters of Vincent van Gogh:

The Complete Letters of Vincent van Gogh: With Reproductions of All the Drawings in the Correspondence, 3 vols. (Greenwich, Conn, 1958; 2nd ed. 1978).

Verzamelde Brieven van Vincent van Gogh, 4 vols. (Amsterdam and Antwerp, 1974).

The Letters of Vincent van Gogh 1886–1890: A Facsimile Edition, 2 vols. (London and Amsterdam, 1977).

The Letters of Vincent van Gogh, ed. R. de Leeuw, trans. Arnold Pomerans (London, 1996).

L	Letters from Vincent van Gogh to his brother Theodorus (Theo)
LW	Letters to his sister Willemina (Wil)
LB	Letters to Emile Bernard
LR	Letters to Anthon van Rappard
LT	Letters from Theo to Vincent

As van Gogh did not give titles to his works, they may vary according to source or author's preference. Likewise, sources differ as to the dating of his works and letters.

The credit line "Amsterdam, Van Gogh Museum, Vincent van Gogh Foundation" has been shortened in the captions to "Amsterdam, Van Gogh Museum."

Van Gogh used canvases in standard French sizes, which were identified by numbers. Each size was divided into three groups —*figure*, *paysage*, and *marine*—that shared the measurements of the long side of the canvas but with successively reduced short sides. Thus, size 15 *figure* measures 65 x 54 cm, *paysage* 50 x 65 cm, and *marine* 46 x 65 cm; size 30 *figure* measures 92 x 73 cm (see P. Mitchell and L. Roberts, *Frameworks: Form, Function & Ornament in European Portrait Frames* [London, 1996]). The current dimensions of certain paintings differ from the original due to the restretching of their canvases.

Introduction

GEORGE S. KEYES

JOSEPH J. RISHEL

GEORGE T.M. SHACKELFORD

Van Gogh: Face to Face is the first comprehensive coverage of the full range of Vincent van Gogh's achievement in portraiture.

Given the artist's own high value of his portraits, it is ironic that for more than a century after his death, this critical aspect of his career was not the subject of much attention. Only a few projects, in fact, have touched on the subject directly. Two exhibitions presented selections of his self-portraits: in 1960, Marlborough Fine Art Ltd. in London showed eighteen paintings in the exhibition "Van Gogh Self-Portraits"; thirty-five years later, the Kunsthalle Hamburg organized an exhibition devoted to the self-portraits painted by van Gogh during his two-year period of residence in Paris. Some scholars —notably Evert van Uitert, Carol Zemel, and Griselda Pollock —have written specifically about van Gogh as a maker of portrait images, but these are in a minority. Until now no single project has addressed the full range of van Gogh's attainment in the realm of portraiture over the course of his brief but intense career.

Van Gogh: Face to Face, which looks back to that decade of concentrated activity and evolution little more than a century ago, has therefore been inexplicably long in coming. And if it serves as only partial explanation of our reasons for launching this ambitious project, we can also call attention to a revived interest in portraiture among scholars in the past decade, when museums in Europe and North America have mounted an impressive series of exhibitions devoted to the subject, and numerous books on portrait-making have appeared. In just the last few years, "Degas: Portraits" was presented in Zurich and Tübingen, "Picasso and Portraiture: Representation and Transformation" at the Museum of Modern Art, New York, and "Rembrandt by Himself " in London and The Hague. Is our fascination with the portraits of these artists a symptom of millennial nostalgia or of a desire to explain ourselves by understanding the past? As Vincent wrote to Theo, referring to the French artists of the previous century, "It is a delightful thing to be able to study that period—from which *so much can be learned* by—to use the expression—*notre fin du siècle* in which we live."

Initially *Van Gogh: Face to Face* was to concentrate on the portraits of the Roulin family, those extraordinary and penetrating images of the postman in Arles, Joseph Roulin, his wife Augustine, their two sons, Armand and Camille, and their infant daughter, Marcelle. It seemed a good choice: after all, the family ensemble was a project that had excited van Gogh himself in the first place ("portraits of *a whole family*" he wrote enthusiastically to his brother Theo from

Arles). This group of works is one of the features of the essay on the portraits of van Gogh's Arles period by Roland Dorn. The idea of portraiture in general, in fact, was central to the artist's plan to start a "Studio of the South": van Gogh envisaged his portraits acquainting the people of Arles, who were "blankly ignorant of painting," with art, and he simultaneously engaged in an exchange of portraits with other painters—Emile Bernard, Paul Gauguin, and Charles Laval—as he strove to bring his own portrait-making to maturity. It is in this period in Arles, 1888–89, that he writes of his ambitions in the form: "I want to paint men and women with that something of the eternal which the halo used to symbolize, and which we seek to convey by the actual radiance, by the vibration of our coloring."

As our discussions about *Van Gogh: Face to Face* continued, then, it became clear that the paintings of the Roulin family (van Gogh's most important sitters, with the exception of the artist himself), constitute only part of the story of his investigation of portrait modes. It was decided to expand the focus to include the full range of van Gogh's portrait activity, from his earliest copies, made in 1881, after Hans Holbein (fig. 76) to the final portraits painted at Auvers just under a decade later.

The fact that this had not been attempted on such a scale before suggested that there would be much to discover in bringing the paintings and drawings together. We were particularly emboldened by our study of the artist's letters, which continually reveal his commitment to portraiture, and, above all, the high esteem in which he held the genre from the beginning of his career to its end. "What impassions me most—much, much more than all the rest of my métier," Vincent wrote in 1889, "is the portrait, the modern portrait."

Following the steps of the artist's engagement with portrait types, we intended from the outset to extend the commonly held definition of the portrait to encompass a range of images that were important to Vincent's conception of the definition of character, expression, and physiognomy. Lauren Soth's essay investigates the less well-known works of his period in The Hague in 1882 where he produced a variety of large, carefully finished pictures, his "heads of the people," depicting fishermen and "workhouse men," whose "ruins of physiognomies" he found so movingly expressive, and his full-length drawings of archetypal characters of the urban poor (figs. 48 and 54, for example). It was in this period that he befriended the prostitute Sien, and the drawings of her,

her mother, and her daughter form a powerful and unified group of work. We also decided to include not only the brightly colored paintings most familiar to the public—the faces by van Gogh known from postcards and calendars—but also the more subtle, more modest monochromatic works of the artist's early career in The Netherlands, rarely seen outside his native land. We wanted to see, as part of the same body of work, the final portraits painted in Auvers, such as the famous images of himself (fig. 174) and Doctor Gachet (fig. 198) who nursed him in his final breakdown, and the portraits of Dutch peasant men and women which occupied him at first, pictures which culminate in his early masterpiece *The Potato Eaters* (fig. 23). From all stages of his career, in fact, in addition to the iconic portraits known to the public from museums in Europe and North America, we sought out works less well-known to our audiences, from both private collections and museums around the world.

Vincent van Gogh is now, without question, the most famous painter in the history of Western art, the subject of mass media fascination, public hero worship, and a vast quantity of more specialized academic scrutiny. It is clear, however, based on the evidence of the number of ongoing exhibitions and forthcoming publications about van Gogh, that there is still a great deal to be discovered.

Van Gogh: Face to Face, in its final form, presents a full picture of the artist's exploration and elaboration of the portrait type in the short span of his career, providing a sense of the artist's position in relation to the art of the past, to his contemporaries, and to the modernist pantheon.

We have, for instance, taken the opportunity to consider van Gogh's own consciousness of the Dutch tradition that reaches back to Rembrandt van Rijn and Frans Hals, influences that are the subject of the essay by George Keyes. The Dutch old masters were important to van Gogh all his life: their naturalism, technical virtuosity, and sense of truth made a lasting impression on him. His Dutch contemporaries influenced him too, especially the artists of the Hague School such as Anton Mauve, for a while van Gogh's teacher. In their choice of subject matter, and their moral tenor, they provided van Gogh with a sharpened sense of his own work.

George Shackelford's essay concentrates on van Gogh's stay in Paris, citing his position as a portrait painter in the context of the movements that van Gogh grouped under the heading of impressionism. This was the period in which he produced not only his celebrated portraits of Père Tanguy (figs. 86, 98, and 99) and Alexander Reid (fig. 93), but also an extraordinary and varied sequence of self-portraits, many of them still unfamiliar to the general public.

Van Gogh's period at St.-Rémy and Auvers is best known for the landscapes he painted such as *Starry Night* and *Crows Over Wheat Field*. But it is also, as Judy Sund explains, the period of the most penetrating portraits. Unflinching self-portraits (figs. 169, 173, and 174, for example) were painted in the aftermath of his breakdowns, and portraits of people around him, such as the attendant Trabuc (fig. 171) and Trabuc's wife (fig. 175) show a similarly intense gaze.

In the final essay in this book, Joseph Rishel examines van Gogh's striking influence on the conception of portraiture well into the twentieth century—as he himself predicted. The effect of his example on painters of the following generation—the painters associated with the Fauves in France, and the German expressionists—is clear. Thereafter, his effect is more subtle, often depending on the ahistorical response of one artist to another, as in the case of Francis Bacon or Chuck Close. Yet his influence remains powerful, and continues up to the present day. Perhaps it should be no surprise. It is Vincent, after all, who wrote of his desire "to do portraits which will appear as revelations to people in a hundred years' time."

All in all, we concluded that, given the relatively limited literature devoted to Vincent as a portraitist, this book should be as inclusive as possible. It therefore acts as an illustrated compendium of all the critical portraits, even ones that could not be included in the exhibition itself.

Art historian Meyer Schapiro noted in 1950 that "The singularity of van Gogh's life lies in the fact that art was for him a personal destiny in the fullest sense." One element of our fascination with his art and his life must be our awareness of this quality of Vincent's transcendence, which affects our appreciation of the ways in which—while remaining deeply conscious of his connection with the past and the present—he created works of art in a way that placed him outside any such context. This phenomenon, so difficult to spell out, was perhaps best described by another painter gifted with a kind of second sight: Pablo Picasso. As Picasso explained to his wife, the artist Françoise Gilot,

> Beginning with van Gogh, however great we may be, we are all, in a measure, autodidacts—you might almost say primitive painters. Painters no longer live within a tradition and so each one of us must recreate an entire language . . . In a certain sense, that's a liberation but at the same time it's an enormous

limitation, because when the individuality of the artist begins to express itself, what the artist gains in the way of liberty he loses in the way of order, and when you're no longer able to attach yourself to an order, basically that's very bad . . . Painting isn't a question of sensibility; it's a matter of seizing the power, taking over from nature, not expecting her to supply you with information and good advice . . . Van Gogh was the first one to find the key to that tension.

Life with Picasso (New York, 1964)

George S. Keyes
Elizabeth and Allan Shelden Curator of European Paintings,
The Detroit Institute of Arts

Joseph J. Rishel
The Gisela and Dennis Alter Senior Curator of European Painting
and Sculpture before 1900, Philadelphia Museum of Art

George T. M. Shackelford
Chair, Art of Europe, Museum of Fine Arts, Boston

4. *Peasant* (F 163, JH 687), March 1885
Oil on canvas, 39 x 30.5 cm
Brussels, Koninklijke Musea voor Schone Kunsten van België

The Dutch Roots of Vincent van Gogh

GEORGE S. KEYES

5. Rembrandt van Rijn, *Pilgrims at Emmaus*, 1648
Oil on panel, 68 x 65 cm
Paris, Musée du Louvre

On the most elementary level, Vincent van Gogh's Dutchness can be encapsulated by his signature, *Vincent*. Van Gogh began signing certain of his works, in particular selected large drawings, while living in The Hague. He signed these with self-conscious style using only his first name, which he underscored with a flourish. Several years later, writing to his brother Theo from Arles, van Gogh declared that his name ought to appear in the catalogue for the Société des Artistes Indépendants as he signed his canvases and not as "van Gogh," because the French did not know how to pronounce his surname.[1] Stylistically this type of signature, underscored from right to left with a long, vigorous flourish, emulates the signatures of several Hague School artists, in particular Anton Mauve, his cousin by marriage, but also that of Hendrik Willem Mesdag and Jan Hendrik Weissenbruch.[2] Vincent's intense involvement with the Hague School immediately after his arrival there in 1881 would partially explain this kind of imitation. However, another Dutch master also comes to mind, Rembrandt Harmensz. van Rijn. Early in his career, Rembrandt signed his works with a monogram that referred to his full family name. After he settled in Amsterdam, Rembrandt progressively dropped the reference to van Rijn and simply signed his canvases with his first name. Van Gogh's lifelong admiration for Rembrandt found early expression in his serious study of Rembrandt's prints in London and Amsterdam.[3] Many of these prints are prominently signed *Rembrandt* and must have inspired Vincent to follow this illustrious antecedent.

As a young man, Vincent van Gogh's relationship to the art world was tempered by his familial and personal connections to the art trade. Three of his uncles ran art galleries, in Amsterdam, The Hague, and Rotterdam. His uncle Vincent (Oom Cent) sold his gallery in The Hague to the Parisian firm Goupil and Company, which maintained these operations as well as galleries in Brussels, Paris, and London. Vincent began his career at the age of sixteen working in the Goupil premises in The Hague, but he was subsequently transferred to London and then to Paris. Goupil carved out a unique niche in the art trade by the commissioning, distribution, and sale of extremely high quality reproductive prints after well-known works of art. These ranged from the old masters to paintings by popular contemporary artists, primarily those of the French school. Not surprisingly van Gogh acquired certain of these images for himself. For example, when working for Goupil's in Paris in 1875, he hung on the walls of his apartment a diverse range of engravings, which he itemized in a letter to Theo.

Among these he describes *Panoramic View of Haarlem from Overveen* (fig. 6) and *The Bush* (fig. 7), after Jacob van Ruisdael, and *Bible Reading*, after Rembrandt.[4] He also acquired a Goupil print after one of his favorite Rembrandt paintings in the Louvre, *Pilgrims at Emmaus* (fig. 5), and added this to his decor.[5]

Vincent was also a voracious reader, which served to reinforce his singular capacity for visual recall. From the vivid descriptions in his letters of paintings he had not seen in years, it is clear that he had something of a photographic memory. As an artist who utilized photographs, van Gogh appreciated the capacities and usefulness of this medium but also recognized its limitations. Writing to his sister Wil (Willemina) from St.-Rémy during the autumn of 1889, he states, "I always think photographs abominable, and I don't like to have them around, particularly not those of persons I know and love. Those photographic portraits wither much sooner than we ourselves do, whereas the painted portrait is a thing which is felt, done with love or respect for the human being that is portrayed. What is left of the old Dutchmen except their portraits?"[6]

Griselda Pollock, in her exhaustive study of the Dutch character of van Gogh's art, stresses the importance of Vincent's ability to maintain an imaginary museum in his head based largely on his access to reproductions after works of art.[7] However, while the number of images available to him expanded his potential sources almost exponentially,[8] the fact that he was forced to interpret much solely from black and white images rather than from the originals they reproduced undoubtedly affected his perceptions. In addition to his study of prints and art manuals, Vincent did visit museums as the opportunity arose. References in his letters demonstrate the importance of visits to the museums in Amsterdam, Haarlem, The Hague, and Rotterdam, as well as to the major museums in Antwerp, Brussels, London, and Paris.

Vincent's father, a minister of the Dutch Reformed Church, provided an example of Calvinist probity that had a great impact on his son. His religious upbringing inculcated in Vincent strong moral convictions that would later find expression during his stay in London. Following his dismissal from Goupil's in 1876, at a time when he was increasingly estranged from his family, Vincent found solace in John Bunyan's *Pilgrim's Progress*.[9] Bunyan believed that those most worthy of God's grace were the lowly workmen and the poor, who were endowed with a natural spiritual advantage because of their humility, self-denial, and renunciation of the trappings of worldly wealth. Bunyan's "Christian workman" galvanized van Gogh resolutely to pursue a degree of social involvement

6. Jacob van Ruisdael, *Panoramic View of Haarlem from Overveen*, ca. 1660
Oil on canvas, 55.5 x 62 cm
The Hague, Mauritshuis

7. Jacob van Ruisdael, *The Bush*, late 1640s
Oil on canvas, 68 x 82 cm
Paris, Musée du Louvre

"Photographic portraits wither much sooner than we ourselves do, whereas the painted portrait is a thing which is felt, done with love or respect."
September 1889

through good works rather than focusing solely on inner spiritual purity. His reading of Bunyan encouraged Vincent to believe that evangelical zeal could give his life a purpose.[10] Van Gogh decided to follow in his father's footsteps as a preacher and went to Amsterdam in 1877 to study theology, but he soon became disillusioned and abandoned his studies. He then pursued a career as an evangelical lay preacher, serving communities of oppressed coal miners in the Borinage region of Belgium. Despite his dedication, van Gogh's appointment was not made permanent, forcing him to seek a new vocation. In 1880, at age twenty-seven, Vincent made the momentous decision to become an artist. Despite all the vicissitudes and mishaps of his subsequent career, he remained true to this new focus for the rest of his short life.

Van Gogh moved to The Hague on Christmas Day 1881 and remained in the city until September 1883. He had already spent time in The Hague during the summer of 1881 and in November of the same year, when he visited Anton Mauve, who briefly offered him instruction, criticism, and encouragement.[11] Mauve introduced Vincent to watercolor and stressed the importance of drawing, a concern already indelibly fixed in van Gogh's mind.[12] Vincent also came into contact with other artists of the recently recognized Hague School, including Weissenbruch and Mesdag. He became friendly with some of the younger artists associated with the Hague School, for example, George Hendrik Breitner and Herman Johannes van der Weele.[13]

In his personal life, Vincent continued to act on his moral convictions. He developed a liaison with Clasina (Sien) Hoornik, a seamstress whose unfortunate circumstances had forced her into prostitution, and he established Sien and her daughter in his household. This situation soon placed him beyond the pale in the eyes of conventional society, including his family, his contacts at Goupil, and certain of the Hague School artists, including Mauve. This isolation caused Vincent much distress, but, in his letters, he stressed his strong belief that by sheltering Sien and her offspring he was saving them from a dismal fate.

It was during his years in The Hague that Vincent's art came to express his deep-seated sense of moral purpose. Even after he had lost his faith in conventional religion, he continued in his letters to refer repeatedly to *quelque chose là-haut* (something on high), and he invested the art that inspired him with an analogous sense of purpose. While in The Hague, van Gogh drew predominantly on the following four sources of inspiration: artists of the Hague School, selected masters of the Barbizon School, contemporary English and Continental wood engravers, and certain Dutch old masters. He admired the realism infused with a sense of moral conviction that was characteristic of the Hague School. He was particularly impressed by the moral tenor of Jozef Israëls's work but also saw a similar degree of integrity in the works of Jacob Maris, Mauve, and Weissenbruch.[14] These Hague School artists were already recognized as deeply inspired by the French realist tradition of the Barbizon School.[15]

Through his involvement with Goupil, van Gogh had been exposed to paintings by the leading masters of the Barbizon School. Among these he particularly admired Jean-François Millet, whose peasant imagery would continue to haunt Vincent throughout his career as an artist (see essay by George Shackelford in this volume). The concept of landscape evidenced in the works of Camille Corot, Jules Dupré, and Théodore Rousseau left an indelible impression on van Gogh. He had the opportunity to see more of their works when he was working at Goupil's in Paris. Moreover, the Hague School painter Mesdag was a serious collector of Barbizon paintings, many of which Vincent had the opportunity to see in a major exhibition held at the Academy of Fine Arts in The Hague in 1882.[16]

Van Gogh was also passionate about the work of the English and Continental wood engravers whose imagery addressed pressing social issues and appeared in serial publications such as *The Graphic* and *The Illustrated London News*.[17] He was particularly fond of British illustrators, such as Henry (Hubert) Herkomer (see fig. 50), Frank Holl, and Lucas Fildes, and of the Frenchman Auguste Lançon, but he collected works by many other illustrators as well.[18] In his letter of 1 November 1882 to Theo, Vincent clearly indicates what he admired in this material:

> What I appreciate in Herkomer, Fildes, Holl and the other founders of the *Graphic*, the reason why they still mean more to me than Gavarni and Daumier, and will continue to, is that while the latter seem to look on society with malice, the former —as well as men like Millet, Breton, De Groux, Israëls—chose subjects which are as true as Gavarni's or Daumier's, but have something noble and a more serious sentiment. That sentiment especially must remain, I think. An artist needn't be a clergyman or a churchwarden, but he certainly must have a warm heart for his fellow men.[19]

Wood engravings by such artists were often used to illustrate modern literature, including the works of Charles Dickens, George Eliot, Victor Hugo, Emile Zola, and Thomas Carlyle.

An avid reader, van Gogh was particularly attracted to novels that focused attention on disturbing issues, such as the disruption of the social order and the displacement of the working class.

Interwoven into van Gogh's experience of modern culture was his keen interest in the Dutch old masters. Above all, he admired Rembrandt as a portraitist and religious painter who uniquely represented the mission of Christ. He marveled at Rembrandt's ability to convey inner feeling in his portraits and his seemingly magical handling of light, with all its associated spiritual symbolism and mystery. Frans Hals's portraits also captivated van Gogh, who admired their virility and the way they mirrored an age of moral conviction and a sense of social connectedness. He appreciated the energy, spontaneity, and sketchiness of Hals's bold painting technique and saw him as the supreme technician.[20] Van Gogh was also attracted to certain of the great seventeenth-century Dutch landscape painters, in particular Ruisdael, Jan van Goyen, Paulus Potter, and Philips Koninck. Specific genre painters also interested him, especially Adriaen van Ostade but also Jan Steen and Gerard Terborch.

Van Gogh's appreciation of the Dutch old masters was deeply influenced by the views of certain contemporary French critics. He was familiar with the writings of Théophile Thoré (Willem Burger), Charles Blanc, and Eugène Fromentin,[21] who had done much to revive interest in these artists, some of whom, like Vermeer, had fallen into almost total obscurity. All these critics admired the naturalism, the sense of truth, and the technical virtuosity of the Dutch old masters, whom they saw as the source for modern naturalist art, especially that of the Barbizon School. Van Gogh identified closely with this assessment. In a letter to Theo he states,

> How much good it does one to see a beautiful Rousseau on which he has drudged to keep it true and honest. How much good it does to think of people like Van Goyen, Old Crome and Michel. How beautiful an Isaac Ostade or a Ruysdael is.
>
> Do I want them back or do I want people to imitate them? No, but I want the honesty, the naïveté, the truth, to remain.[22]

In contradistinction to the eighteenth-century preference for the licked finish and enamel-like precision of the so-called "Dutch little masters," these mid-nineteenth-century French critics particularly admired the bold brushwork, daring painting technique, and even the degree of unfinish in the paintings of Rembrandt and Hals. Rembrandt's unique exploitation of light commanded their highest respect as well.

They equated these painterly qualities with modernism and galvanized artists, van Gogh among them, to appreciate the vitality and even audacity of these Dutch old masters.

For van Gogh these sources of inspiration intermingled and merged as he drew upon them to shape his own art. He could focus on each for its perceived modernity and topicality, yet also recognize how these sources could equally and simultaneously relate to the past. For him the Dutch old masters seemed truly modern, and Vincent conflated them and their supposed naturalism with that of the Barbizon and Hague Schools and with his own endeavors as an artist. The Dutch old masters represented something else of extraordinary significance to van Gogh—a sense of the continuity of Dutch culture and a harking back to a truer, simpler world of shared values as opposed to the fragmented reality of modern, industrialized society. This was a utopian construct superimposed by van Gogh on the tradition as he perceived it. The tradition as he chose to understand it focused on several themes: the edifying portrait; the peasant wedded to the agrarian traditions of the land as a mainstay of the social order; representations of landscape showing mankind in harmony with nature; and a perceived naturalism that expressed truth. These points buttressed van Gogh's assumption that there is a continuum between past and present and enabled him to embrace traditional subject matter as a valid concern for modern art.

As his art evolved, van Gogh's changing choice of subject matter reflected his own intellectual shifts as he sought new strategies in his quest to be a modern artist. During his time in The Hague, van Gogh favored those hapless segments of humanity that to him exemplified the true and eternal human values. His elevation of this underclass as a subject worthy of representation owed much to his interest in Bunyan's *Pilgrim's Progress*, but his choice was also influenced by his strong identification with Jean-François Millet, who, more than any other artist, with the possible exception of Rembrandt, was for van Gogh a kind of spiritual mentor. Millet's and Rembrandt's subjects shared one quality that was of paramount importance—a sense of resignation—a kind of stoicism in response to adversity. Vincent's admiration for Mauve's *Beached Boat with Horses* (fig. 9) indicates the importance this theme held for him:

> There is a Mauve, the large picture of the fishing smack drawn up
> to the dunes; it is a masterpiece . . . That is *the* resignation—the
> real kind, not that of the clergyman. Those nags, those poor, ill-
> treated old nags, black, white and brown; they are standing there

"An artist needn't be a clergyman or a churchwarden, but he certainly must have a warm heart for his fellow men."
November 1882

8. *Peasant Woman* (F 160, JH 722), ca. 1 April 1885
Oil on canvas, 42.5 x 29.5 cm
Amsterdam, Van Gogh Museum

patient, submissive, willing, resigned and quiet . . . They are resigned to living and working somewhat longer, but if they have to go to the knacker tomorrow, well, so be it, they are ready. I find such a mighty, deep, practical, silent philosophy in this picture—it seems to say, "Savoir souffrir sans se plaindre, ça c'est la seule chose pratique, c'est là la grande science, la leçon à apprendre, la solution du problème de la vie [knowing how to suffer without complaining, that is the only practical thing, it is the great science, the lesson to learn, the solution of the problem of life].[23]

Van Gogh's drawn figure studies in The Hague embody a similar sentiment.[24] Ranging from representations of Sien (see fig. 11) and her family (fig. 10) to old pensioners, or orphan men, as Vincent preferred to call them (fig. 12), and the weathered fishermen of Scheveningen (fig. 13),[25] all of these works, despite their subjects' passivity and lack of expression, convey an inherent human dignity. Like Mauve's horses these

9. Anton Mauve, *Beached Boat with Horses,* 1882
Oil on canvas, 115 x 172 cm
The Hague, Haags Gemeentemuseum

unemployable old people, whose poverty is evident in their worn-out clothing and battered shoes, are resigned to their fate as public charity wards.[26] Griselda Pollock and Carol Zemel both call attention to the paradoxical nature of these drawings. Although principally intended as character studies, they also cross over into the realm of portraiture. As such they count among van Gogh's most penetrating studies of actual people.[27] In his correspondence with Theo and his artist friend Anthon van Rappard, Vincent told of how he envisaged using these drawings in a "Series of the People," which he hoped to produce commercially as lithographs in order to make them easily available, at nominal cost, as edifying images for the common man.[28] Shortly thereafter, while still in The Hague, he also conceived another series, "Heads of the People," separate from the full-length images reflected in the lithographs.

Like the peasants of Millet, Vincent's drawn figure studies are generic character types. Millet formulated a concept of the peasant working the land as a metaphor for the traditional bond between humankind and the grudging fecundity of the land. Emotively and spiritually this theme makes inevitable reference to the biblical fall from grace that cast human destiny to perennial labor. While van Gogh certainly shared Millet's views, his images of peasants, unlike Millet's, are distinctly individual. As Pollock indicates, this was partly the result of his own urgent needs as a self-taught artist.[29] Unlike his academically trained peers whose studies of the human figure were prescribed by the formal studio practice of drawing from plaster casts as well as from the nude model, van Gogh initially relied principally on drawing manuals. He soon realized that it was essential to draw from the living form, but, not having access to studio models, he was forced to draw from life whomever he could persuade to sit for him, at nominal cost, in his apartment in The Hague. Van Gogh commenced with the actual and specific, and infused it with a more universal appeal. In this sense he is the opposite of Millet and is fundamentally much closer to Rembrandt, whose drawn and etched representations of beggars and peasants (see fig. 15) also convey the sense of being studied from life.

Pollock has persuasively demonstrated that van Gogh's brief sojourn in the remote province of Drenthe from September to December 1883 was a crucial turning point in his career. During these three months, he rejected the city and the artists of the Hague School as the focus of his inspiration and turned, instead, to the rural landscape. Van Gogh's abiding interest in landscape subjects and his profound admiration for the

10. *Sien's Mother Wearing a Dark Cap* (F 1006, JH 295), December 1882
Graphite, lithographic crayon, and watercolor, 50.1 x 28 cm
Amsterdam, Van Gogh Museum

11. *Sien Seated* (F 937, JH 144), early May 1882
Graphite, ink, and sepia, 58 x 43 cm
Otterlo, Collection Kröller-Müller Museum

12. *Orphan Man with Top Hat* (F 961, JH 284), December 1882
Chalk and graphite, 45 x 24.5 cm
Heino/Wijhe, The Netherlands, Hannema-de Stuers Foundation

13. *Fisherman Wearing a Sou'wester* (F 1011, JH 309), February 1883
Chalk, 43 x 25 cm
Otterlo, Collection Kröller-Müller Museum

14. *Weaver Facing Right* (F 1122, JH 454), 18–23 February 1884
Ink and bister, 26 x 21 cm
Amsterdam, Van Gogh Museum

15. Rembrandt van Rijn, *Peasant in a High Cap*, 1639
Etching, 8.5 x 5 cm
Amsterdam, Rijksmuseum

seventeenth-century Dutch landscape painters whom he so frequently mentions in his letters indicate his unwavering belief in a sense of continuum between his own artistic efforts and the art of the old Dutch school. His interest in landscape, while seeming to be a diversion from the subject of portraiture, is symptomatic of van Gogh's thinking process, which profoundly affected his sense of place within a larger artistic tradition. In Drenthe van Gogh's interest in his Dutch forebears became a sort of dialogue that buoyed his spirits and instilled a new degree of self-confidence. At certain points the great figure painters, especially Hals and Rembrandt, spoke to him most strongly, yet at other times landscape—and more rarely genre—dominated his thoughts. This pattern remains evident throughout his subsequent career in France, despite van Gogh's eager reception of avant-garde ideas when in Paris.

During his short period of activity in Drenthe, the masters of the Barbizon School and the seventeenth-century Dutch landscape painters, above all Ruisdael but also van Goyen and Philips Koninck, served as a potent source for his new initiatives. He describes to Theo his experience of a landscape in Drenthe as if it were Ruisdael's *Panoramic View of Haarlem from Overveen* (fig. 6):

> I saw an effect exactly like Ruysdael's bleaching fields at Overveen: in the foreground a high road overshadowed by clouds, then a low barren meadow, on which the light fell, and down below two houses (one with a slated roof, the other with red tiles) . . . A gray stormy sky over all. I often think of Van Goyen on these misty mornings, the cottages are just like this, that same peaceful and naïve aspect.[30]

His work during this period, with its strong connections to the French realist tradition and seventeenth-century Dutch masters, is charged by a spirit of pantheism that betrays van Gogh's interest in the philosophy of historian and essayist Thomas Carlyle.[31] Carlyle's exalted concept of nature struck a sympathetic chord in van Gogh. For Carlyle nature was a duality—an outward realm of appearance versus an underlying world of truth that reflected the workings of the divine. Each tangible aspect of nature has the capacity to convey a deeper truth to those able to perceive it. Those who could see the deeper truths of nature (and artists were potentially endowed with this insight) were Carlyle's heroes. Carlyle abhorred the adverse impact of the industrial revolution, which had displaced the artisan class and disrupted the traditional patterns of society. Like Bunyan, Carlyle saw the world as fraught with adversity and sympathized with the dispossessed.

16. *Young Peasant* (F 1145, JH 581), December 1884–January 1885
Graphite, 34.7 x 21.6 cm
Amsterdam, Van Gogh Museum

> "In such natural surroundings,
> things can be roused in a heart,
> things which would otherwise
> never have been awakened.
> I mean something of that free,
> cheerful spirit of former times."
>
> Autumn 1883

He also believed that by following a true vocation one could find truth beyond the world of appearances. Carlyle's thesis served to reinforce van Gogh's conviction in his chosen profession as well as his belief that truth is to be perceived by close study of each and every facet of the living world.

The seemingly timeless character of the rural landscape offered van Gogh solace and a sense of well-being. Whereas his experiences in the grim coal-mining region of the Borinage and The Hague had led him to focus on the impoverished, exploited, and dispossessed, his reverence for countryside still unaffected by modern industrial society caused him to see the peasant working the land as the embodiment of the "true human condition." He reinforced his belief in the value of the unchanging world of nature by harking back to the Dutch old masters, whose landscapes were proof that this same landscape had existed for centuries and had nourished a society that did not violate or subvert the natural realm. Van Gogh expressed this sentiment to Theo:

> . . . but if you come to the most remote back country of Drenthe, it will make quite a different impression on you, you will even feel just as if you lived in the time of Van Goyen, Ruysdael, Michel, in short, in what perhaps one hardly feels even in the *present* Barbizon.
>
> That is an important thing, I think, for in such natural surroundings, things can be roused in a heart, things which would otherwise never have been awakened. I mean something of that free, cheerful spirit of former times . . . [32]

For van Gogh the Barbizon painters played a role analogous to that of the Dutch old masters. During his sojourn in Drenthe, he repeatedly mentioned Jules Dupré, admiring his atmospherically evocative, even melancholy, subjects and comparing them to the work of Ruisdael.[33] Vincent saw in the poetic naturalism of the Barbizon painters the same simplicity, sincerity, and truth that he associated with the Dutch old masters.[34]

The ideas that van Gogh formulated in Drenthe shaped his views about the universal nourishing capacity of the land and the significance of the timeless bond that existed between the tiller of the earth and nature's fecundity. Having solidified his view of the peasant as the embodiment of universal human values, when he moved to Nuenen working peasants became his major project, and for the artist, they also became the chosen subject of modern art.[35] By making this commitment, van Gogh allied himself with Millet, Jules Breton, and other French painters of the realist tradition who extolled peasant

17. *Peasant Woman* (F 135, JH 585), December 1884–January 1885
Oil on canvas on panel, 37.5 x 24.5 cm
Cincinnati Art Museum

18. *Head of a Peasant* (F 160a, JH 563), 1884
Oil on canvas, 39.4 x 30.2 cm
Sydney, Art Gallery of New South Wales

subject matter, as well as with Israëls, the Hague School painter whom van Gogh so deeply admired.[36]

During his two years of activity in Nuenen (December 1883–November 1885), van Gogh sought out models from the artisan class of weavers and the local peasants. He began by drawing (see fig. 14) and painting weavers working at their looms but subsequently turned his attention to drawing and painting heads of peasants (fig. 16). He conceived of the latter as a series, which he called "Heads of the People," echoing the similar project that he had begun in The Hague. This was an ambitious project for which the artist wished to paint at least fifty heads.[37] To an even more marked degree than those earlier works, the heads painted in Nuenen are generic character types representing a specific class—the rural peasants of Brabant. These paintings represent heads in close view set before modulated, dark backgrounds (fig. 4). Most are represented full-face, but some appear in profile (fig. 17), and occasionally others are turned three-quarter-view (fig. 18). These studies are broadly painted, with a juicy application of pigment and an evident display of brushwork that recalls the style of Hals.[38]

Van Gogh had long admired Hals, and in October 1885 he made a special journey to Amsterdam to visit the recently opened Rijksmuseum in its new Cuypers building. There he made a close study of Rembrandt and Hals, expressing unreserved admiration for Rembrandt's *The Syndics of the Cloth Guild* (fig. 19) and *The Jewish Bride* (fig. 20) and for Hals's *Isaac Massa and His Wife* (fig. 21), *Merry Toper* (fig. 22), *Meager Company,* and other works by the latter.[39] Vincent particularly admired Hals for his liveliness and sense of truth, his rapid and deft brushwork, the lack of preparatory underdrawing in his works, and the degree to which his paintings seemed unfinished yet visually complete. As he stated to Theo, "I am more convinced than ever that the true painters did not finish their things in the way which is used only too often, namely correct when one scrutinizes it closely. The best pictures, and from a technical point of view the most complete, seen from near by, are but patches of color side by side, and only make an effect at a certain distance."[40]

Van Gogh was impressed by what he perceived to be the rapid execution of the works:

> What struck me most on seeing the old Dutch pictures again is that most of them *were painted quickly*, and that these great masters, such as a Frans Hals, a Rembrandt, a Ruysdael and so many others—dashed off a thing from the first stroke and did not retouch it so very much.

19. Rembrandt van Rijn, *The Syndics of the Cloth Guild*, 1662
Oil on canvas, 191.5 x 279 cm
Amsterdam, Rijksmuseum

20. Rembrandt van Rijn, *The Jewish Bride*, after 1665
Oil on canvas, 121.5 x 166.5 cm
Amsterdam, Rijksmuseum

21. Frans Hals, *Isaac Massa and His Wife*, about 1621
Oil on canvas, 140 x 166.5 cm
Amsterdam, Rijksmuseum

22. Frans Hals, *Merry Toper*, ca. 1629
Oil on canvas, 81 x 66.5 cm
Amsterdam, Rijksmuseum

And please note this too—if it was right, *they left it as it was.*
I have especially admired the hands by Rembrandt and Hals,
certain hands in "The Syndics," even in "The Jewish Bride," and
in Frans Hals, hands that lived, but were not finished in the sense
they demand nowadays.

And heads too—eyes, nose, mouth done with a single stroke
of the brush without any retouching whatever.[41]

For van Gogh, Hals also represented the vitality of a socially
harmonious culture. Hals's burghers interested Vincent not as
members of a patrician elite but rather as the embodiment of
the essential character and truth of an earlier epoch.[42]

Considering the works of Hals and Rembrandt to be the
antecedents of his own character studies, van Gogh noted how
they painted their sitters before a tonally evocative yet
undifferentiated background—a pictorial foil that served to
project attention onto the face of the person represented. The
brushwork, color range, and pictorial language of these old
masters struck Vincent as inherently modern and served to
buttress his own approach to painting likenesses.[43] While in
Nuenen Vincent maintained a continuous discussion about
modern art in his letters to Theo, who informed him about the
French impressionists. At this time Vincent had no firsthand
knowledge of this avant-garde movement. But given what he
did know, he felt the need to defend the more traditional
palette that was the springboard for his own experimentation.
Having recently read, with great enthusiasm, Eugène
Fromentin's 1876 treatise on the seventeenth-century Dutch
old masters, *Les maîtres d'autrefois,* he stated to Theo, "It has
already annoyed me *for a long time*, Theo, that some of the
present-day painters rob us of the bister and the bitumen, with
which surely so many splendid things have been painted, and
which, well applied, make the coloring ripe and mellow and
generous, and at the same time are so distinguished and possess
such very remarkable and peculiar qualities."[44]

Van Gogh also admired Hals's great militia company and
regent group portraits, which he had seen in the Frans Hals
Museum in Haarlem. These and other seventeenth-century
Dutch group portraits were to play a significant role in
the creation and realization of van Gogh's most ambitious
undertaking in Nuenen, his peasant family group, *The Potato
Eaters* (fig. 23) datable to April 1885. This picture required
much effort and provoked great anxiety. It represents
members of the van Rooy and de Groot families at a table by
a hearth in their farmhouse eating boiled potatoes and drinking
a hot, steeped beverage. The painter illuminates the figures by
means of a lamp hanging overhead in an otherwise dark and

23. *The Potato Eaters* (F 82, JH 764), April 1885
Oil on canvas, 82 x 114 cm
Amsterdam, Van Gogh Museum

murky interior. He wished to stress that these peasants eat from the labor of their roughened, gnarled hands. For him, this subject of the laboring peasant was a worthy successor to much earlier representations of dignified seventeenth-century Dutch burghers seated at a table. Rembrandt's celebrated *Syndics of the Cloth Guild* (fig. 19) immediately comes to mind[45] as does Hals's *Regentesses of the Old Men's Almshouse* (fig. 24), two paintings that van Gogh knew and greatly admired. Both of these works represent figures seen three-quarter-length at tables in formal interiors, both include standing servants,[46] and both represent interiors that provide effective foils for their human protagonists. The solemnity that he wished to convey in *The Potato Eaters* actually finds an even more poignant antecedent in Rembrandt's *Pilgrims at Emmaus* (fig. 5). Van Gogh was entranced by this picture, which he first saw in Paris in 1875, and his enthusiasm never waned, as indicated by his memory of it when writing Theo from the asylum in St.-Rémy:

> And so what Rembrandt has alone or almost alone among painters, that tenderness of gaze which we see, whether it's in the "Men of Emmaus" or in the "Jewish Bride" or in some such strange angelic figure as the picture you have had the good fortune to see, that heartbroken tenderness, that glimpse of a superhuman infinitude that seems so natural there—in many places you come upon it in Shakespeare too.[47]

This painting is notable for its subdued palette and mysterious lighting. Rembrandt represents the figures full-length at a table before a wall containing a niche. The architectural setting seems to envelop and isolate the human drama it contains. This lends a further degree of solemnity to the hushed yet revelatory atmosphere of the subject.

By representing peasants gathered in a rustic interior as a modern counterpart to such seventeenth-century antecedents, van Gogh projects his efforts into a much wider context. In essence he conceived of *The Potato Eaters* as a kind of history painting linked to an important artistic tradition.[48] He not only connected his work to representations of the patrician class by Hals and Rembrandt, or to Rembrandt's religious subjects, but also saw a connection to the peasant subjects of Adriaen van Ostade (fig. 25). Ostade's depictions seemed far removed from the urban centers of seventeenth-century Holland and, to van Gogh, projected the heart of rural life.[49]

Although van Gogh was inspired by these seventeenth-century antecedents, this was certainly not to the exclusion of contemporary painters who treated analogous themes. Works well known to van Gogh included *La Bénédicité* by the Belgian painter Charles De Groux[50] and Jozef Israëls's *The Frugal Meal* (fig. 26).[51] Israëls's picture depicts a peasant family in admittedly less oppressive circumstances but is tinged by a sentiment that struck van Gogh as kindred to his own. The pious religious associations in these peasant subjects by Israëls and De Groux were qualities that van Gogh sought to project in *The Potato Eaters*. Israëls's palette, with its tonal range of deep earth tones, evocative shadow-filled interiors, and reliance on the effects of bitumen, linked him closely to Rembrandt. Van Gogh recognized this relationship and formulated in his own mind the triad Rembrandt/Millet/Israëls, which traversed time and fused those qualities that he so admired in the Dutch old masters with French realism and the Hague School.[52] Earlier, writing Theo from The Hague, Vincent discussed another picture by Israëls, *Old Friends* (fig. 27), which he particularly admired. In his imagination he envisaged hanging *Old Friends* at one end of a long empty room with Millet's *Death and the Woodcutter* facing it at the opposite end.[53]

Van Gogh's years in Paris (1885–87) exposed him to the avant-garde and the progressive pictorial tenets of French impressionism. Here, largely for lack of other models, he began to represent himself. The roughly two dozen painted likenesses of himself from this period represent Vincent dressed as a peasant (fig. 96), in city clothes (fig. 73), as an artist before his easel (fig. 28), or simply as a character study. As Zemel has observed, he seems in these works to be exploring his public and professional identity.[54] Such a proliferation of self-portraits finds its greatest antecedent in Rembrandt,[55] who explored his own likeness throughout his career in painted, drawn, and etched images. Rembrandt assumed different roles and personae in his self-portraits.

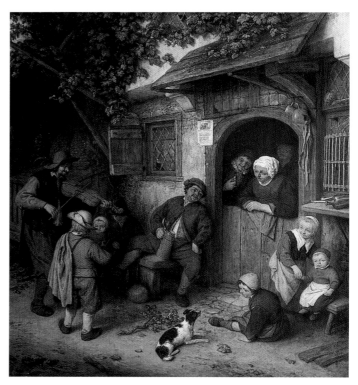

25. Adriaen van Ostade, *The Violinist*, 1673
Oil on panel, 45 x 42 cm
The Hague, Mauritshuis

24. Frans Hals, *Regentesses of the Old Men's Almshouse*, early 1660s
Oil on canvas, 170.5 x 249.5 cm
Haarlem, Frans Hals Museum

26. Jozef Israëls, *The Frugal Meal*, 1876
Oil on canvas, 88.9 x 65 cm
Glasgow, Art Gallery and Museum, Kelvingrove

27. Jozef Israëls, *Old Friends*, before 1882
Oil on canvas, 132.4 x 175.4 cm
Philadelphia Museum of Art

28. *Self-Portrait as an Artist* (F 522, JH 1356), winter 1887–88
Oil on canvas, 65 x 50.5 cm
Amsterdam, Van Gogh Museum

29. Rembrandt van Rijn, *Self-Portrait*, 1660
Oil on canvas, 111 x 90 cm
Paris, Musée du Louvre

"What Rembrandt has alone
or almost alone among painters,
that tenderness of gaze."

Summer 1889

In certain instances he wore chains of honor (a distinction he never received in real life) and attired himself in fantastic costumes. He would also occasionally include himself in his multifigured history subjects.[56] It is doubtful that van Gogh, who so admired Rembrandt's expression of inner self and truthfulness, was cognizant of the calculated artifice that went into Rembrandt's self-portraiture.

In his celebrated *Self-Portrait as an Artist* (fig. 28), van Gogh clearly paid homage to Rembrandt's analogous *Self-Portrait* of 1660 in the Louvre (fig. 29), a picture that Vincent knew and admired. He extolled its virtues in a letter to Emile Bernard in 1888: "He paints a self-portrait, old, toothless, wrinkled, wearing a cotton cap, a picture from nature, in a mirror. He is dreaming, dreaming, and his brush resumes his self-portrait, but only the head, whose expression becomes more tragically sad, more tragically saddening . . ."[57] Pollock stresses that for van Gogh, Rembrandt's portraits expressed a unique depth of feeling and became quasi-religious works, luminous and consoling. Importantly, van Gogh's interpretation of Rembrandt's portraiture as religious in tenor enabled him to use Rembrandt as a model for his own concept of modern art. For Vincent, portraiture was a fully legitimate source of illumination and insight into his own times, a kind of history painting for the modern era.[58] Moreover, the portraits of the past, in particular those by Hals and Rembrandt, could offer consolation and hope for the future.[59]

Pollock has made a cogent argument for the importance of Hals to Vincent in his realization of other Paris period portraits, including that of Alexander Reid (fig. 93), in which she sees van Gogh's sustained admiration for the *Merry Toper* (fig. 22) as a strong counterweight to impressionism, particularly in the way van Gogh employed brushstroke patterns to model the sitter's face.[60] Van Gogh's two celebrated portraits of Père Tanguy (figs. 98 and 99) represent the sitter seated three-quarter length before a background composed of assorted Japanese block prints. Despite the evident modernity of these two portraits, Juleke van Lindert and Evert van Uitert compare the version in the Musée Rodin to Rembrandt's moving *Old Man Seated in a Chair* of 1654 in the Hermitage in St. Petersburg. They stress the analogous frontal pose and the strikingly similar positioning of the clasped hands in both artists' pictures.[61]

During the summer of 1888, the very moment when he began producing his astonishing series of Arles portraits, van Gogh renewed his dialogue with the seventeenth-century Dutch landscape painters he so admired. The resulting

30. Frans Hals, *Jacob Pietersz. Olycan*, 1625
Oil on canvas, 124.6 x 97.3 cm
The Hague, Mauritshuis

31. Frans Hals, *Aletta Hanemans*, 1625
Oil on canvas, 124.2 x 98.2 cm
The Hague, Mauritshuis

paintings express a serenity and sense of well-being that energized van Gogh in all his projects, not least his portraits. In a letter to Theo, Vincent describes the Camargue as looking exactly like a Ruisdael. He then describes another subject, La Crau: "I am working on a new subject, fields green and yellow as far as the eye can reach. I have already drawn it twice, and I am starting it again as a painting; it is exactly like a Salomon Konink [Philips Koninck]—you know, the pupil of Rembrandt who painted vast level plains."[62] The expressive mood of his Arles pictures, their emphasis on the distinctive character of a particular landscape, and the idiosyncratic nature of individual details all find antecedents in his Nuenen landscapes. The locale differed radically but, in spirit, it was the same world of nature finding expression. While the painter does make reference to certain features of the modern world—trains, for example—his choice of subjects brings us back to the world of the peasant. The countryside projects a sense of harmony between the rural laborer and the land. At this point he realizes modernity in representing themes analogous to those that he first explored in Drenthe and Brabant.

32. Adriaen van Ostade, *The Painter's Family* (so-called), 1654
Oil on panel, 70 x 88 cm
Paris, Museé du Louvre

33. Frans Hals, *Catharina Hooft Held by a Nurse*, about 1620
Oil on canvas, 86 x 65 cm
Berlin, Staatliche Museen, Gemäldegalerie

In Arles van Gogh came to know the postman Joseph Roulin and his family and embarked on an ambitious project to paint the entire family. He produced multiple images, including variants and replicas of the postman, his wife, and their children, Armand, Camille, and Marcelle. Pollock has ingeniously argued that among this extended series the painter's three-quarter-length representation of the postman (fig. 145) and a version of *La Berceuse* (fig. 125), considered as a pair, may, in fact, have antecedents in seventeenth-century Dutch marriage portraits.[63] Obvious candidates by Hals that would have been familiar to the artist include such pairs as *Nicolaes Hasselaer* and his wife, *Sara Wolphaerts van Diemen*; *Nicolaes van der Meer* and his wife, *Cornelia Vooght Claesdr.*; *Jacob Pietersz. Olycan* (fig. 30) and his wife, *Aletta Hanemans* (fig. 31); and *Paulus van Beresteyn* and his wife, *Catharina Both van der Hem.*[64]

Pollock notes that the distinctive, attenuated hands of Joseph Roulin seem to recall the hands of the seated woman at the right in Frans Hals's late *Regentesses of the Old Men's Almshouse* (fig. 24).[65] She further notes that a third painting by Hals representing the entire Beresteyn family, which was acquired by the Louvre with the pendant paintings of husband and wife in 1880, could conceivably have been the spark that inspired van Gogh to represent the entire Roulin family, albeit not in a single group portrait.[66] Another family portrait greatly admired by van Gogh was Adriaen van Ostade's so-called *Painter's Family* (fig. 32), which he saw as an example of the potency of this vigorous, naturalistic manner of painting.[67] Finally, van Gogh's *Augustine Roulin with Her Baby* (fig. 149) finds a potential antecedent in *Catharina Hooft Held by a Nurse* by Frans Hals (fig. 33).[68] By the same token, the combination of a mother holding up her child may also derive from Rembrandt's celebrated *Family Portrait* in Braunschweig, which van Gogh could only have known through a print.[69]

More than just a pictorial affinity with the works of the Dutch old masters, van Gogh's portraits project his yearning for a modern counterpart to the Dutch "Golden Age." In depicting members of a society that was simple, truthful, and reflective of a better time, the portraits of Hals and Rembrandt represented consolation and a hope for the future.[70] In his own words he alluded to what this future should mean: "And in a picture I want to say something comforting as music is comforting. I want to paint men and women with that something of the eternal which the halo used to symbolize, and which we seek to convey by the actual radiance and vibration of our coloring."[71]

The Early Years

March 1853–February 1886

CHRONOLOGY

The Early Years

March 1853–February 1886

KATHERINE SACHS

35. Vincent van Gogh, ca. 1866
Amsterdam, Van Gogh Museum

Previous spread
34. *Flower Beds in Holland* (F 186, JH 361),
detail, ca. 1883
Oil on canvas on wood, 48.9 x 66 cm
Washington, D.C., National Gallery of Art

1853

30 March

Vincent Willem van Gogh is born in the
town of Groot-Zundert in Brabant, The
Netherlands, near the Belgian border. He is
the eldest surviving child of Theodorus
van Gogh (1822–85), a pastor in the Dutch
Reformed community, and Anna Cornelia
Carbentus (1819–1907). Their first child,
who would have been named Vincent, had
been stillborn exactly a year earlier.

1857

1 May

Theodorus (1857–91), Vincent's favorite
brother is born. His siblings will ultimately
number five: three sisters, Anna Cornelia
(1855–1930), Elisabeth (Lies) Huberta
(1859–1936), and Willemina (Wil) Jacoba
(1862–1941), as well as another brother,
Cornelius Vincent (1867–1900).

1861–68

Vincent attends the local village school
from 1861 until 1864, when he goes to
a boarding school in Zevenbergen. There
he learns English, French, and German.
In 1866 he begins secondary school in the
nearby town of Tilburg.

1869

30 July

Vincent leaves school to work as a junior
clerk at a branch of the art firm Goupil and
Company in The Hague, under his Uncle
Vincent (Oom Cent), a partner in the firm.
His superior is H.G. Tersteeg, who sends
Vincent's parents good reports about his
abilities and enthusiasm for his job.

1871

January

The van Gogh family moves to Helvoirt in
Brabant after Vincent's father is transferred
to a new parish.

1872

Written correspondence between Vincent
and Theo begins in August with the first
recorded letter from Vincent to his brother,
who had recently visited him in The Hague:

"Dear Theo,
I was glad you arrived home safely. I missed
you the first few days; it was strange not to
find you when I came home in the evening.
Always your loving Vincent" (L 1, August).

In December Theo is taken on as an
apprentice at the Brussels branch of Goupil
and Company. In a letter to Theo, Vincent
congratulates him on his new position:
"I am so glad that we shall both be in the
same profession and in the same firm.
We must be sure to write to each other
regularly . . . Wishing you good luck,
believe me always,
Your loving brother, Vincent"
(L 2, 13 December).

1873

Vincent is transferred with the highest of
recommendations from The Hague to the
London branch of Goupil. On his way to
London in May, he stops in Paris, visiting the
Louvre and the Musée du Luxembourg.
In London Vincent finds his work interesting
and is exposed to a wide variety of art,
including reproductions after old masters
and paintings by French Barbizon artists and
members of the Hague School. He visits
London museums and galleries, gaining
a new appreciation for English artists.
Vincent's first extant drawing is of houses
along the street where he is staying.

Theo is transferred to Goupil's in The
Hague, where he occupies Vincent's former
position.

1874

Vincent's spirits remain high until spring,
when he declares his love for Eugenia

36. Vincent van Gogh, ca. 1872
Amsterdam, Van Gogh Museum

37. Theo Van Gogh
Amsterdam, Van Gogh Museum

Loyer, the daughter of his landlady, and is rejected. He becomes withdrawn and depressed and also more religious. Uncle Cent uses his influence to get his nephew a temporary transfer to Goupil's in Paris, hoping the change will do him good. Vincent stays in Paris from October to December, then returns to his former post in London.

1875

He stays in London until May, when another temporary placement (which is later to turn into a permanent transfer) begins in Paris. There he becomes increasingly religious. In a letter to Theo, he describes spending every evening reading from the Bible (L 42, 11 October).

Vincent is unhappy with the move to Paris and with the art trade in general. He neglects his work and is unpopular with colleagues and customers. He continues to visit museums, but his letters are melancholy and his parents begin to understand that it would be better for him to change his career.

Vincent's father is transferred to the parish at Etten in October, and the family moves there.

1876

January

Having spent the Christmas holiday with his family in Etten without the firm's permission, Vincent returns to Paris and is dismissed from Goupil and Company, effective 1 April.

April–December

Vincent goes to England, where he finds work teaching in Ramsgate. In July he becomes an assistant preacher at a school in Isleworth, near London, and his religious fervor deepens.

1877

January–March

After returning home for Christmas, Vincent decides not to return to England. His parents help him secure a job in a bookstore, Blussé and Van Braam, in Dordrecht. He is not happy there. He writes to Theo of his desire to preach the gospel: "That someone in our family has always been a minister of the gospel . . . it is my prayer and innermost desire that the spirit of my father and grandfather may also rest upon me" (L 89, 22 March).

May–December

In May Vincent moves to Amsterdam to pursue theology but must study for rigorous university entrance examinations first. Vincent reads and draws a great deal and visits the Trippenhuis, the former quarters of the Rijksmuseum, where he sees paintings and prints by Rembrandt. He finds his theological studies difficult and irrelevant because of their emphasis on Greek, Latin, and mathematics.

1878

January

Vincent outlines his belief in the importance of the inner spirit over outward appearance in a letter to Theo (L 264, see essay by Lauren Soth in this volume).

July–December

Vincent abandons his theological studies in Amsterdam, opting for a more practical program that will prepare him to be an evangelical missionary. In August he goes to Brussels and enrolls in a short course but after three months of study is found unsuited for the job of lay preacher and returns to Etten. Undaunted, Vincent hopes to fulfill his calling in the Borinage, a coal-mining district in Belgium. In late December he travels to the village of Wasmes and works without compensation as an evangelist among the poor miners.

38. *Portrait of an Elderly Gentleman* (F 876, JH 14),
July 1881
Graphite, ink, and watercolor, 34.5 x 26.1 cm
Amsterdam, Van Gogh Museum

"I want to create drawings
which *touch* some people."
July 1882

1879

In January Vincent receives a temporary, paid position which allows him to continue giving Bible classes, teaching children, and visiting the sick. He tries to put into practice the Christian ideals that inspire him by giving away all his possessions and choosing to live in a hovel, sleeping on straw. His superiors are displeased with his fanatical behavior, and his appointment is terminated. In August Vincent moves to nearby Cuesmes and works without pay.

He reads a great deal (Charles Dickens, Victor Hugo, and William Shakespeare) but is mainly occupied with drawing the miners. He asks Theo for books on the basic principles of draftsmanship, and he receives a box of paints from Tersteeg, his former supervisor at Goupil's.

It is at this time that Vincent decides to become an artist. It appears likely that he experienced a spiritual crisis that resulted in his giving up as an evangelist and embracing the idea of becoming an artist.

1880
July

For the first time in almost a year, the correspondence between Vincent and Theo having halted—probably as a result of disagreements between Vincent and his father—Vincent writes to Theo, ostensibly to thank him for sending fifty francs but also to rekindle their friendship: "If ever I can do anything for you, be of some use to you, know that I am at your disposal." Vincent also reveals his uncertainty about the future, wondering "How can I be of use in the world? Can't I serve some purpose and be of any good?" (L 133). Theo begins sending Vincent a share of his monthly salary. These regular remittances provide Vincent with income for the rest of his life.

Theo, who has wanted to move to Paris for several years, is afforded the opportunity in July when Goupil and Company transfers him permanently. Within half a year he becomes manager of the branch.

August–November

Vincent devotes his time to drawing scenes of life in a mining community. Theo sends him reproductions of paintings and woodcuts of *The Labors of the Field* by the French artist Jean-François Millet (1814–75), which Vincent copies. Vincent goes to Brussels in October to study anatomical and perspective drawing. There he meets the Dutch painter Anthon van Rappard (1858–92), and for a while Vincent works in van Rappard's studio.

1881

Because of his desire to return to the countryside, Vincent enlists Theo to help convince their father to let him move home to Etten (L 142, 4 February). On 12 April Vincent leaves Brussels for his parents' home. Vincent's sister Willemina visits Etten for part of the summer and models for Vincent, inspiring him to try portraiture (L 146).

September–October

Vincent goes to The Hague to see Tersteeg and ask him for guidance about becoming a painter. He also sees Anton Mauve (1838–88), an artist who is a member of the Hague School and also a cousin by marriage. Mauve is very encouraging. Vincent writes Theo of his progress: "So what seemed to be impossible before is gradually becoming possible now . . . Diggers, sowers, plowers, male and female, they are what I must draw continually. I have to observe and draw everything that belongs to country life . . . I no longer stand helpless before nature as I used to" (L 150, September 1881).

December

Relations with his parents having become increasingly strained, Vincent moves out of their house after a violent argument on Christmas Day.

> "Diggers, sowers, plowers, male
> and female, they are what
> I must draw continually. I have
> to observe and draw everything
> that belongs to country life . . .
> I no longer stand helpless before
> nature as I used to."
>
> September 1881

THE HAGUE

1882

January

Vincent moves to The Hague, where he rents a studio. Mauve gives him drawing lessons and teaches him the principles of painting in watercolor and in oil.

March

Vincent has difficulty finding models, but in a letter dated 3 March he refers to a family that has been modeling for him: Sien Hoornik, thirty-two; her mother, fifty-three; and her youngest sister, ten.

Vincent receives his first commission, for twelve views of The Hague, from his Uncle Cornelius. He continues his interest in portraying simple working people. A friend lends him Alfred Sensier's 1881 biography of Jean-François Millet, which has a great impact on him, strengthening his resolve to become a painter of peasant life.

April

He creates the drawing *Sorrow* using Sien as his model (for a lithograph of this drawing, see fig. 136) and confides to Theo, "In my opinion the enclosed is the best figure I have drawn yet, therefore I thought I should send it to you" (L 186).

May–June

Both Mauve and Tersteeg eventually turn against Vincent when he takes Sien, a pregnant, unmarried mother, and her small daughter into his house.

Vincent wants to marry Sien and feels that his friends and family should not disown him for it: "let me love and care for my poor, weak, ill-used little wife as well as my poverty permits" (L 201). "She and I are two unhappy people who keep together and carry our burdens together; in this way unhappiness is changed to joy, and the unbearable becomes bearable" (L 204).

July

In a letter to Theo, Vincent writes that he wants "to create drawings which *touch* some people" by expressing deep and profound emotion. "More and more other things lose their interest, and the more I get rid of them, the quicker my eye grasps the picturesque things. Art demands persistent work, work in spite of everything, and continuous observation." He also discusses the difference between modern and old master paintings, preferring the intimacy and expressiveness of modern painters (L 218).

August

The van Gogh family moves to Nuenen in early August. Theo visits Vincent when he is in The Hague on business and, after seeing Vincent's progress, provides him with funds to buy materials for oil painting. Vincent writes,

"I am very glad I have the necessary materials, for already I had often suppressed

39. *Farmer Sitting by the Fireplace, Reading* (F 897, JH 63), October 1881
Charcoal and watercolor, 45 x 56 cm
Otterlo, Collection Kröller-Müller Museum

> "There is soul and life in that crayon . . . [it] knows what I want, it listens with intelligence and obeys."
>
> March 1883

40. *The Public Soup Kitchen* (F 1020a, JH 330), early March 1883
Chalk and watercolor, 56.5 x 44.4 cm
Amsterdam, Van Gogh Museum

> "I am rich—not in money, but because I have found in my work something which I can devote myself to heart and soul, and which inspires me and gives meaning to life."
>
> March 1883

the desire to paint. It opens a much broader horizon . . . but I have attached great value to drawing and will continue to, because it is the backbone of painting, the skeleton that supports all the rest. I like it so much, Theo, that it is only because of the expenses that I shall have to restrain myself rather than urge myself on" (L 224).

He adds in his next letter, "painting is such a joy to me . . . I want to tell you—while painting, I feel a power of color in me that I did not possess before" (L 225, 15 August).

September
Vincent begins to do watercolors and sketches of larger groups of people. He finds a new source for models in the old people's home in The Hague, pensioners whom he refers to as "orphan men" (see, for example, figs. 51, 53, and 54).

November–December
He experiments with lithography in the hope of finding work as an illustrator, inspired by English magazine illustrators. He starts working on a group of lithographs of working men such as *Old Man Drinking Coffee* and *Workman Digging* (figs. 132 and 133).

Vincent writes to Theo, "Before the year is up, I feel I have to thank you again for all your help and friendship . . . I am sorry that I haven't succeeded in making a saleable drawing this year. I really do not know where the fault lies" (L 255).

1883
January
Vincent sends Theo many sketches, which he says are experiments in black and white using lithographic crayon. For the first few months of the year, Vincent draws mostly working people and fishermen. He purchases many issues of *The Graphic*, a journal that contains wood engravings by a number of British artists he admires.

February–March
He writes to Theo about using "mountain chalk," a new medium that produces warm black tones (L 270). "There is soul and life in that crayon . . . [it] knows what I want, it listens with intelligence and obeys" (L 272).

Vincent receives an encouraging letter and twenty-five guilders from his father. In a letter to Theo he wonders if his father sent the money out of pity: "I hope that this was not his motive, for in my opinion . . . I am rich—not in money, but because I have found in my work something which I can devote myself to heart and soul, and which inspires me and gives meaning to life" (L 274).

May
With warmer weather, Vincent is able to work outdoors, and he begins to combine separate studies of figures into larger compositions. He focuses on a large composition of *Peat Diggers in the Dunes*, for which he had done preliminary drawings.

July
He paints in oils and is happy enough with some of his drawings that he makes lithographs of them, something he had not done since November 1882.

August
In a gloomy mood Vincent writes to Theo about the course of his life and career, eerily predicting his future:

"Not only did I begin drawing relatively late in life, but it may also be that I shall not live for so very many years . . . as to the time ahead in which I shall still be able to work, I think . . . a certain number, between 6 and 10 [years] . . . I've walked this earth for thirty years, and, out of gratitude, want to leave some souvenir in the shape of drawings or pictures—not made to please a certain taste in art, but to express a sincere human feeling" (L 309 postscript).

41. *Woman with Dark Cap (Sien's Mother?)*
(F 1005, JH 292), December 1882
Graphite, lithographic crayon, watercolor, 45.4 x 26.3 cm
Amsterdam, Van Gogh Museum

Sien is becoming increasingly difficult to live with. Vincent announces in the second half of August that he is going to move to the countryside, in part because he cannot afford his rent in the city.

DRENTHE AND NUENEN

September–December 1883

On 11 September, Vincent leaves Sien and her children behind and goes to Drenthe—a region suggested by van Rappard. He takes lodgings first in Hoogeveen and later in Nieuw Amsterdam. He explores the unspoiled rural countryside on foot. Many of his letters to his brother are unsuccessful attempts to convince Theo to give up art dealing and become an artist.

The natural beauty of Drenthe and the simple peasant population are much to Vincent's liking, but the bad weather, his loneliness, and the lack of a studio and painting and drawing materials lead him to return to his parents' house in Nuenen on 5 December.

At his parents' home, Vincent encounters problems and writes to Theo of feeling unwanted: "They feel the same dread of taking me into the house as they would about taking a big rough dog" (L 346, December). But encouraging letters from Theo and van Rappard help convince him to persevere. He sets up a small room in the house for a studio.

1884

January

He produces numerous painted and color-washed studies of weavers, a subject that was of great interest to him for several months (fig. 14).

March–April

Vincent is frustrated with his dependency on Theo and expresses doubts about his brother's efforts to promote and sell his work (L 358, 1 March). At the end of April, Vincent makes a deal with Theo that the money he receives will be considered payment for his work and not charity. Vincent, in his own mind, structures this arrangement as a contract in which his art work becomes their joint property, for which Vincent receives monthly payment (L 360, March, and L 364, April).

May

He moves his studio from the cramped space in his parents' house to the Roman Catholic presbytery, where he rents two rooms. His spirits brighten for a while. Van Rappard visits Vincent for about ten days, and the two artists visit the weavers and make trips to the countryside.

June

Theo visits his parents and Vincent in Nuenen. Afterward Vincent writes Theo, describing the visit as pleasant. In the letter he cites a passage about Delacroix's color theory from *Grammaire des arts du dessin* (1867) by Charles Blanc. He also has learned from Theo the names of many of

42. *The Parsonage at Nuenen* (F 182, JH 948), October 1885
Oil on canvas, 33 x 43 cm
Amsterdam, Van Gogh Museum.

> "I've walked this earth for thirty years, and, out of gratitude, want to leave some souvenir in the shape of drawings or pictures."
>
> August 1883

the impressionist painters in Paris, but he has not yet seen their work (L 371, early June).

August–September

Vincent meets Antoon Hermans, an amateur painter who commissions him to design murals for Hermans's dining room. The painted prototypes depict scenes from peasant life, which also symbolize the four seasons. Vincent has photographs made of some of his drawings and sends them to Theo in the hope of finding work as an illustrator.

October–November

Van Rappard visits for ten days in October. During this time Vincent takes on several pupils: "three people in Eindhoven who want to learn to paint, and whom I am teaching to paint still-life." He receives no money from these lessons but plans to ask for tubes of paint in exchange for his effort (L 386). He makes friends with one of the pupils, Anton Kerssemakers.

1885

January

Relations with Theo have been strained, and Vincent's letters in January convey some unhappiness (L 392). However, his excitement about his studies of the peasants is undiminished, and he works diligently. These heads of peasants are rendered forcefully and realistically, and his striving shortly thereafter culminates in *The Potato Eaters* (fig. 23).

"I am very busy painting those heads. I paint in the daytime and draw in the evening. In this way I have already painted at least thirty and drawn as many" (L 394) (see fig. 77).

March

Vincent's father dies suddenly on 26 March.

April

Vincent considers leaving his family home and moving his living space into the studio he has rented nearby. He makes a lithograph of a preliminary version of *The Potato Eaters*. He sends an impression to Theo and asks him to show it to the Parisian art dealer Alphonse Portier. Vincent also sends an impression of the lithograph to van Rappard whose written acknowledgment of the work is critical and causes Vincent much consternation.

May–September

Vincent moves into the rooms he has been using as his studio in Nuenen. He sends the completed painting of *The Potato Eaters* to Theo in Paris. In July he complains of the art critics' narrow academic standards:

"*Nothing seems simpler than painting peasants . . . but—no subjects in painting are so difficult as these commonplace figures! . . . To draw a peasant's figure in action,* I repeat, that's what an essentially modern figure is, the very core of modern art, which neither the Greeks nor the Renaissance nor the old Dutch school have done" (L 418, July; van Gogh's emphasis).

43. *The Potato Eaters*, early version (F 78, JH 734), late April 1885
Oil on canvas on panel, 72 x 93 cm
Otterlo, Collection Kröller-Müller Museum

"I'll admit that when one is working exclusively from nature, something more is needed: the facility of composing, the knowledge of the figure, but, after all, I do not believe I have been drudging absolutely in vain all these years. I feel a certain power within me, because wherever I may be, I shall always have an aim—painting people as I see and know them."

January 1886

Vincent's problem obtaining models becomes more acute in September as the priests discourage the local peasants from posing. As a result, he paints mostly still lifes. He considers leaving Nuenen.

October–November
In October Vincent and Kerssemakers travel to Amsterdam for three days to visit museums, and upon their return Vincent recalls in intricate detail the impact of several paintings by Hals and Rembrandt which he had seen in the recently opened Rijksmuseum: "I seldom saw a more divinely beautiful figure . . . I was literally rooted to the spot" (L 426, October). After this visit, Vincent realizes that he has much to learn from Rubens, who he feels is the greatest baroque artist.

ANTWERP

Late November 1885–end of February 1886
On 24 November Vincent goes to Antwerp, the nearest large city where he can visit museums and study at the academy. He rents a small room above a paint shop and decorates it with Japanese prints.

December
Vincent hopes to generate a source of income by painting portraits. He writes of photographers who do portraits but dismisses them, saying,

"the painted portraits have a life of their own, coming straight from the painter's soul, which the machine cannot reach. The more one looks at photographs, the more one feels this, I think" (L 439).

In an effort to make money, Vincent paints the famous castle of the city, Het Steen, and the Church of Our Lady, hoping that tourists might purchase the scenes. He writes to Theo that he prefers painting portraits, "for there is something in the eyes that is not in the cathedral . . . a human soul, be it that of a poor beggar or of

a streetwalker, is more interesting to me" (L 441, 19 December).

1886
January
Vincent enrolls at the academy. He cannot afford to hire models and wants to work from nude models and plaster casts of antique statues. He writes to Theo of his desire for more formal artistic training: "I'll admit that when one is working exclusively from nature, something more is needed: the facility of composing, the knowledge of the figure, but, after all, I do not believe I have been drudging absolutely in vain all these years. I feel a certain power within me, because wherever I may be, I shall always have an aim—painting people as I see and know them" (L 444).

January–February
At the academy, however, he sees that nude models are rarely used. He takes painting classes, draws from plaster casts of antique statues, and soon finds nude models in sketching clubs, which he visits in the evenings after a full day of classes (L 447).

Vincent indicates to Theo that he is considering returning to Nuenen or coming to Paris. Knowing that living together would be cost efficient, Theo asks Vincent to wait until the summer, when they could rent a larger apartment. In February Vincent begins to write frequently about his urgently felt need to go to Paris.

44. *Beardless Fisherman Wearing a Sou'wester* (F 1014, JH 310), February 1883
Graphite, lithographic crayon, chalk, ink, and watercolor, 50.5 x 31.6 cm
Amsterdam, Van Gogh Museum

Fantasy and Reality in The Hague Drawings

LAUREN SOTH

45. *Sien Seated* (F 935, JH 143), early May 1882
Graphite, ink, and sepia, 58 x 42 cm
Otterlo, Collection Kröller-Müller Museum

In January 1883 Vincent van Gogh made several drawings of fishermen. *Beardless Fisherman Wearing a Sou'wester* (fig. 44) is characteristic. It is a direct, forceful image, close to life-size. The sitter's advanced age is evident in his wrinkled face, sunken cheeks, and tight, seemingly toothless, mouth. Light, falling from the left, defines his strong nose and other features. The graininess created by the black lithographic crayon—van Gogh's favorite medium at this time—gives the skin a mottled effect, and at the left a tuft of white hair (drawn in white chalk) pokes out from under the hat. That hat is a sou'wester, standard headgear for fishermen. With the hat's earflap down and its strap drawn tightly under his jaw, van Gogh's fisherman is prepared for rough weather.

In short, van Gogh has attempted, through artistic skill and correct costume, to convince us of the veracity of his representation. He wants us to believe that this is a real man who lived a real life—a life whose exposure to the elements (suggested by the foul-weather dress) has left its residue on his haggard face. It is a representation that claims the authenticity of lived experience. But the drawing is not what it appears to be. The sitter was not a fisherman, nor did the sou'wester belong to him. It belonged to van Gogh. It was the prop in a scenario that mingled fantasy (the fictive fisherman, product of van Gogh's imagination) with reality (the transcription of the model before him).

Van Gogh's images of fishermen are likenesses but not portraits. To grasp this distinction, turn to a portrait of Joseph Roulin (fig. 46). Van Gogh depicted his friend nine times, in six paintings and three drawings. Each time Roulin is shown in his own uniform of the French postal service, the word *POSTES* emblazoned on his cap. The image bears reference to the sitter's authentic life outside the frame. It is Joseph Roulin, an actual postal worker, not a model masquerading as one, who confronts us. Not only his appearance, which van Gogh likened to that of Socrates,[1] but also something of the character of the man van Gogh described as a "terrible républicain"[2] is communicated through the aggressive pose and direct stare. While the fishermen's heads have character, too, it is a character van Gogh has imposed upon them, not the product of their actual life history or specific personality. These works are "heads," not "portraits." That is exactly the distinction van Gogh makes when he writes about the two series of images. He calls the images of fishermen "heads" and the depictions of Roulin "portraits."[3]

How should we understand *Beardless Fisherman Wearing a Sou'wester,* a likeness of a model that is nonetheless not a

46. *Joseph Roulin Sitting in a Cane Chair* (F 1723, JH 1523), 31 July–3 August 1888
Ink, 32 x 24 cm
Private Collection

portrait? It may be helpful to have recourse to a seventeenth-century concept that has been elucidated in studies of Dutch art: the *tronie*.[4] In the works of Rembrandt and his contemporaries, a tronie was a head or bust-length study taken directly from a sitter. But unlike a portrait, which depicted the sitter in a role that he played or imagined himself playing in his social life, the model for a tronie was cast by the artist in a different, more exotic, role than the one he inhabited in actuality. This was done in part by exaggerating the facial expression but especially by the use of accessories and costume. Dressing the sitter in a gorget suggested he was, or had been, a warrior. Placing a turban on his head implied he was an Oriental potentate. The gorget, turban, and other similar items were supplied by the artist. They were literally his stock in trade.

Right from the start of his career as an artist, van Gogh planned to acquire his own stock of costumes. Writing his parents from Brussels on 16 February 1881, he declared, "eventually I must have a small collection of workmen's clothes

47. *Fisherman with a Sou'wester Sitting with a Pipe*
(F 1010, JH 306), February 1883
Ink, graphite, and chalk, 46 x 26 cm
Otterlo, Collection Kröller-Müller Museum

48. *Fisherman with a Sou'wester* (F 1017, JH 302), February 1883
Graphite, lithographic crayon, ink, and watercolor, 47.2 x 29.4 cm
Amsterdam, Van Gogh Museum

"Eventually I must have a small collection of workmen's clothes in which to dress the models for my drawings. For instance, a Brabant blue smock, the gray linen suit that the miners wear and their leather hat, then a straw hat and wooden shoes, a fisherman's outfit of yellow oilskin and a sou'wester."

February 1881

in which to dress the models for my drawings. For instance, a Brabant blue smock, the gray linen suit that the miners wear and their leather hat, then a straw hat and wooden shoes, a fisherman's outfit of yellow oilskin and a sou'wester."[5] Van Gogh continued, listing other items of regional working-class apparel he wanted, including a Scheveningen bonnet. He then concluded, "Drawing the model with the necessary costumes is the only way to succeed."

Costume to van Gogh was not just a theatrical prop, as it had been in the seventeenth century, but a badge of authenticity. Here, in his blue smock, is a genuine Brabant peasant; here, in his sou'wester, is a real fisherman. The "necessary costumes" were a visible guarantee of the truthfulness of the image.

So it is understandable that van Gogh did not draw fishermen until he actually owned a sou'wester. This finally occurred in January 1883, two years after he expressed his desire for one in the letter just quoted and one year after he had moved to The Hague. During that year in The Hague, he had several times sketched and painted fishing scenes on the beach of nearby Scheveningen but did not have the "necessary costume" to draw an individual figure. Around 13 January, however, he wrote his brother Theo that "Tomorrow I get a sou'wester for the heads. Heads of fishermen, old and young, that's what I have been thinking of for a long time, and I have made one already, then afterward I couldn't get a sou'wester. Now I shall have one of my own, an old one over which many storms and seas have passed."[6]

The series of fishermen's heads was done immediately upon the acquisition of the "necessary costume." Six months later the process was repeated. As van Gogh described it, "Today the almshouse man again posed for a thing that I suddenly felt I had to make . . . Last evening I received a present which pleased me enormously . . . namely a very characteristic Scheveningen jacket with high turn-up collar, picturesque, faded and patched."[7] The result was the full-length *Fisherman with a Sou'wester Sitting with a Pipe* (fig. 47), in which the new acquisition (jacket) joined the old one (sou'wester) in transforming an almshouse man into a fisherman.

Proper costume was essential. But there was more than a desire to be anthropologically correct in van Gogh's use of costume. The articles of clothing exerted an almost magical power over him. Receiving the jacket compelled him to draw "a thing that I suddenly felt I had to make." The sou'wester was "an old one which many storms and seas have passed." If we did not have the context, we could easily imagine van Gogh was describing in this passage not the sou'wester but the fisherman himself. The hat stood for the man. Indeed, the sou'wester was the constant in his fisherman images. The model might change (compare fig. 48 and fig. 44), but the sou'wester remained the same. It, not the human sitter, was the signifier that denoted "fisherman." It, not the model, was what ignited van Gogh's emotional response. "Boy," he wrote Theo, "I have been drawing with such delight—fishermen's heads with that sou'wester I told you about; the fish scales were still sticking to it when I got it."[8]

How enthralled Vincent must have been by the fish scales. Like a shard unearthed by an archaeologist, they were both a mark of authenticity and an emotionally evocative remnant of the fisherman's life. The sou'wester took on an almost mystical significance for van Gogh, as his excited comments on it indicate. And yet it is unlikely that the young artist would have even thought of producing images of fishermen had such subjects not been already a staple of the artistic milieu he had so recently entered. "The painter who gives me lessons now is making a very good picture of a Blankenberg fisherman."[9] That sentence was his postscript to the 16 February 1881 letter from Brussels to his parents, the one in which he listed the costumes he needed.

Coincidentally, his next teacher, Anton Mauve, was working on a major canvas of a fishing scene when he advised van Gogh (fig. 9). Vincent mentions it in letters of 26 January and about 11 March 1882.[10] In the latter he declared it a masterpiece and found in it "a mighty, deep, practical, silent philosophy." What impressed him was the resignation of the horses who were shown resting from their labor of pulling the fishing boat onto the beach.

This subject requires some explanation. Scheveningen, the fishing village near The Hague, had no harbor until one was built in 1904. Incoming boats were roped to teams of horses who pulled them onto the beach. This picturesque activity was a popular subject for painters of the Hague School. Mauve himself made several variations of it. And indeed it was the subject of one of van Gogh's very earliest canvases, in August 1882 (fig. 49).[11]

In January 1883, however, when van Gogh again took up fishing subjects, it was not narrative paintings that he produced but drawings of fishermen's heads. As we have seen, this project materialized only when van Gogh acquired a sou'wester. But there was another acquisition that he found equally stimulating. When he worked for the art dealer Goupil and Company in London in 1873, van Gogh had

49. *Scheveningen Beach in Stormy Weather* (F 4, JH 187), late August 1882
Oil on canvas on cardboard, 34.5 x 51 cm
Amsterdam, Van Gogh Museum

50. Hubert Herkomer, *The Coast Guardsman* ("Heads of the People")
Wood engraving
The Graphic, 20 September 1879

become acquainted with English illustrated journals such as *The Illustrated London News* and *The Graphic*. He continued to admire them and collected individual issues when he could. Then, just at the time he was drawing fishermen's heads, he purchased from a local bookseller a complete run of *The Graphic* from 1870 to 1880.[12]

Beginning in 1875 *The Graphic* had published a series of ten illustrations it called "Heads of the People" (fig. 50). By different artists, these showed individual figures of various occupations—miner, drayman, agricultural laborer—in their characteristic costume. These illustrations were clearly van Gogh's immediate inspiration for his fishermen's heads. He even used the English phrase in referring to his own work: "Waar ik dezen laatsen tijd bejzonder op gesjouwd heb is koppen—Heads of the people—o.a. visscherskoppen met zuidwesters [What I have been working at especially of late is heads—heads of the people—fishermen's heads with sou'westers, among other things]."[13]

In summary, van Gogh's heads were inspired in form by a specific example of English engraved illustration, while their subject, fishermen, was related to contemporary Netherlandish artistic practice. Like the painters of tronies in the seventeenth century, he used costume for expressive purposes even as he drew the model from life. But, if they were not actual fishermen, who were van Gogh's models?

The men who sat for van Gogh were pensioners of the Dutch Reformed Old People's Home.[14] At least six different individuals from that institution posed for him. In fact, van Gogh rarely had them pose as fishermen; he usually drew them in the clothes the Home required them to wear: a top hat and either a long overcoat with wide lapels and a double row of buttons (see fig. 53) or a similar, shorter jacket with tails (fig. 51). Van Gogh wrote of drawing "old men in their Sunday and in their everyday clothes."[15] Probably the shorter jacket, which appears only three times in his extant drawings,[16] was for Sunday and the longer overcoat for weekdays.

Without this knowledge of the pensioners' uniform, a depiction such as *Orphan Man in Sunday Clothes with Eye Bandage* (fig. 54) could easily be mistaken for a product of van Gogh's imagination—a tronie like his fishermen's heads. In fact, everything shown is legitimate in that it belonged to the sitter. The coat and top hat were his prescribed dress, and the medal he wears is one that was awarded to veterans of the 1830–31 war of Belgian independence.[17] Even the eye patch is genuine, not a prop. Van Gogh refers to it in his letters and even mentions the "Sunday-clean bandage around his blind eye."[18]

51. *Orphan Man with Top Hat and Stick*
(F 977, JH 243), September–October 1882
Graphite, 47.2 x 23.5 cm
Amsterdam, Van Gogh Museum

Above right
52. *Man with Pipe and Eye Bandage*
(F 1004, JH 289), late December 1882
Lithographic crayon and graphite, 45 x 27.5 cm
Otterlo, Collection Kröller-Müller Museum

Right
53. *Orphan Man with Top Hat and Umbrella under His Arm*
(F 972, JH 237), September–October 1882
Graphite, 48.5 x 24.5 cm
Otterlo, Collection Kröller-Müller Museum

54. *Orphan Man in Sunday Clothes with Eye Bandage* (F 1003, JH 285), late December 1882
Graphite and lithographic crayon, 46.5 x 27.5 cm
Cambridge, Massachusetts, Fogg Art Museum, Harvard University

Another version of the drawing (fig. 52) shows the sitter in his weekday bandage.

A month after this pensioner sat for him, van Gogh recollected the experience in a passage in a letter that is particularly revealing. He quoted a statement by the Norwegian painter Hans Heyerdahl stressing idealization of the figure: "I don't like a figure to be too misshapen." Drawing the "old man with a bandaged eye" made van Gogh realize that that statement was "*not* true" (van Gogh's emphasis). He concluded, "There are some ruins of physiognomies which are full of expression, as, for instance, 'Malle Babbe' by Frans Hals or some heads by Rembrandt."[19]

Ruins, not perfection. Expressiveness, not idealism.[20] These were what spoke to van Gogh, what he sought in his models, and what he found in the pensioners of the Old People's Home. Poor old men, at the end of their lives, dressed in distinctive and picturesque costume—they were all van Gogh could ask for in the way of models. He never identified any of them—not even the one who sat for him most frequently, Adrianus Jacobus Zuyderland,[21] easily recognizable in the drawings by his distinctive muttonchop whiskers (see fig. 55)—but he seems to have held them in some affection,[22] often using the Dutch suffix for "little" (*tje*) in describing them. They were "little workhouse men" (*diakoniemannetjes*);[23] one was a "little fellow" (*kereltje*).[24] More frequently he called them by the evocative local term "orphan man" (*weesman*),[25] a term that he found both "expressive" (*expressief*)[26] and "the real thing" (*echt*).[27] It can be assumed that it was not just the word *weesman* but the orphan men themselves that van Gogh viewed in such terms. With their aged carriage and visage, they embodied an authenticity and expressiveness comparable even to the figures of Hals and Rembrandt. Wearing their unique costume, they needed no props from van Gogh's stock. (How could he improve upon an eye patch?) Indeed, once he received the sou'wester and started posing the orphan men as fishermen, van Gogh seems to have stopped drawing them in their own top hats and coats. It is as though, having cast them in a role in his fantasy, he could not bring them back to their own reality.

His valuing of expressive character, even ugliness, over ideal beauty was a constant in van Gogh's life. It pre-dated his artistic career, as the following account written early in 1878 makes clear. Van Gogh was then living in Amsterdam, preparing to study theology at the university (this goal was later abandoned). He wrote Theo about a conversation with their uncle, the art dealer Cornelius Marinus van Gogh about a painting by Jean-Léon Gérôme (fig. 56):

55. *Orphan Man with Top Hat* (F 954, JH 287), late December 1882
Graphite, 40 x 24.5 cm
Massachusetts, Worcester Art Museum

Uncle Cor asked me today if I didn't like "Phryne" by Gérôme. I told him that I would rather see a homely woman by Israëls or Millet, or an old woman by Edouard Frère: for what's the use of a beautiful body such as Phryne's? Animals have it too, perhaps even more than men; but the soul, as it lives in the people painted by Israëls or Millet or Frère, that is what animals never have. Is not life given us to become richer in spirit, even though the outward appearance may suffer? I feel very little sympathy for the figure by Gérôme. I can find no sign of spirituality in it, and a pair of hands which show they have worked are more beautiful than those of this figure.

As in art, so in life:

Uncle Cor then asked me if I should feel no attraction for a beautiful woman or girl. I answered that I would feel more attraction for, and would rather come in contact with, one who was ugly or old or poor or in some way unhappy but who, through experience and sorrow, had gained a mind and a soul. [28]

Four years later in The Hague, that scenario became reality. Predisposed to honor homeliness, poverty, experience, and sorrow, van Gogh found them all in the prostitute Sien Hoornik and her family. She became the "one who was ugly or old or poor or in some way unhappy" that he had thrown up to his uncle. Further, where he had cited in opposition to the beauty of Gérôme's *Phryne* "an old woman by Edouard Frère," now he described Sien's mother as "like a figure by Edouard Frère" (see fig. 57).[29] No wonder both women became models for him, and Sien became much more.

Sien (whose full name was Clasina Maria Hoornik)[30] was three years older than van Gogh. When they met in late January 1882, she was four months pregnant. She also had a five-year-old daughter; the fathers of both children had deserted her.[31] "[H]er life has been rough," van Gogh later wrote, "and sorrow and adversity have put their marks upon her—now I can do something with her."[32] Those very marks of adversity were in van Gogh's mind a prerequisite for any artistic achievement on his part. As with the orphan men, Sien's conventional unattractiveness was the very thing that Vincent found attractive. Shortly after their meeting, she appeared in his art as a personification of sorrow (for a lithograph of this image, see fig. 136). Then she moved in with him.

Carol Zemel has argued that, in his personal relationship with Sien, van Gogh was acting out a "favorite Victorian fantasy: charity, forgiveness and rescue."[33] It was the fantasy implied in his earlier response to his uncle, but it ended in a

56. Jean-Léon Gérôme, *Phryne before the Areopagus*, 1861
Oil on canvas
Hamburg, Kunsthalle

57. After Edouard Frère, *Seamstresses*
Engraving
Amsterdam, Van Gogh Museum

reality Sien was all too familiar with when van Gogh left her in September 1883. In the months before his departure from The Hague, however, Sien posed regularly for him (see fig. 59). So did her mother (fig. 60) and, to a much lesser extent, her younger sister (fig. 62), and her daughter (fig. 61).

The Hoornik family, especially Sien and her mother, were the female counterparts of the orphan men. They, too, had experienced and suffered; they, too, had validating "ruins of physiognomies." Sien was, in fact, "marked by small pox." And they, too, had "the right clothes. Black merino and a nice style of bonnets and a beautiful shawl, etc."[34]

A black merino dress in ruffled layers is worn by two different sitters in five drawings (two of which are recto and verso of the same sheet; JH 140, 143, 144 [and verso] and 145). Sien is depicted four times (see figs. 11 and 45) and her mother once (fig. 60). It is undoubtedly the same dress that they wear.

These drawings form a unified group. Not only is the dress the same, but in each work the sitter is shown full-length, seated, and in profile. The drawings are of similar dimensions and were all done on thick Ingres paper, a support infrequently used by van Gogh in The Hague and never with such consistency as here. They can be dated between late April and early May 1882.[35]

The four images of Sien encapsulate the double role she played in van Gogh's life: helpmate and muse. Seamstress was her nominal occupation, and she did repair Vincent's clothes.[36] In her capacity as muse, Sien evoked those qualities of poverty and sadness that van Gogh valued. Thus, on the one hand, he posed her sewing and, on the other, with her head bent over, resting on her palm, in the traditional image of melancholy.

In another full-length drawing (fig. 64), also on Ingres paper and probably done at the same time, van Gogh attempted to capture another aspect of Sien. The sheet is about the same size as the four drawings showing her in the black merino dress, but it has been turned ninety degrees, giving the figure a horizontal orientation. Sien is seated on the floor, not in a chair, and instead of black merino she is dressed in a more informal white costume. She holds a cigar. It is not a prop; Sien in fact smoked cigars.[37] Perhaps we see here a hint of the vulgarity that eventually caused van Gogh to realize that the "experience and sorrow" of Sien's life did not necessarily mean that she "had gained a mind and soul." The fantasy he had adumbrated to his uncle in 1878 would eventually be abandoned—and so would the woman he had made its protagonist.

58. *Woman, Bareheaded (Sien's Mother?)* (F 1009, JH 335), March 1883
Graphite and lithographic crayon, 39.5 x 24.7 cm
Amsterdam, Van Gogh Museum

59. *Sien Sewing* (F 1025, JH 346), 31 March 1883
Graphite and chalk, 53 x 37.5 cm
Rotterdam, Museum Boijmans Van Beuningen

60. *Sien's Mother in a Dark Dress* (F 936, JH 140), April 1882
Graphite, ink, and sepia, 61 x 37 cm
Otterlo, Collection Kröller-Müller Museum

61. *Sien's Daughter with Pinafore* (F 1685, JH 300), first half January 1883
Charcoal and graphite, 48.5 x 25.5 cm
Museum of Fine Arts, Boston

62. *Sien's Sister with Shawl* (F 1007, JH 299), first half January 1883
Chalk and graphite, 43.3. x 25 cm
Otterlo, Collection Kröller-Müller Museum

Before that happened, the Hoornik women served van Gogh well as models. Besides the black merino dress, they had bonnets and a beautiful shawl that also appealed to the artist. It appears that these items were, or became, associated with particular family members. With one exception, as noted above, it was Sien who posed in the dress. Her sister posed in the shawl (figs. 62 and 63), and her mother was the bonnet model (fig. 66).[38]

Many of the most impressive images of the Hoornik women were done in December 1882 as part of the "Heads of the People" series that culminated in the fishermen heads the following month. By my count this series comprises twenty-two drawings, broken down as follows:

6 of orphan men (JH 284–89)
5 of Sien's mother (JH 292–96)
2 of Sien (JH 290 and 291)
2 of Sien's sister (JH 299 and 301)
1 of Sien's daughter (JH 300)
6 of fishermen (JH 302, 304, 307–10)

Using black lithographic crayon or chalk for the first time, van Gogh usually drew the heads on thick watercolor paper. The resistance of the paper to the grainy chalk allowed him, by varying the pressure on the chalk, to create the range of tones—from deep black to white highlights—that is the most striking aspect of these drawings. Through tonal gradation the idiosyncratic features of individual sitters are made clear so that we are able to recognize, for example, the three different orphan men who posed for van Gogh.[39]

Still, as powerful as these images are, they are not portraits in the conventional sense. They were conceived as part of a generic series, "Heads of the People," and it is telling that van Gogh drew a hat on each head (with the exception of the two girls [figs. 61–63], whose unkempt, tousled hair serves a similar denotative purpose). The orphan men all have their top hats, the fishermen all have their (actually van Gogh's) sou'westers, Sien's mother has her bonnets, and Sien wears a white cap of the kind worn by women doing tasks indoors (see figs. 65 and 67); that is, she is portrayed as a housewife.[40]

The "necessary costume" was still the true signifier for van Gogh. No matter how well he captured the likeness of his sitter—and he succeeded at this time and again—it was the costume that carried the stronger denotative power, the keener ring of authenticity. In van Gogh's imagination it could turn an

63. *Sien's Sister with Shawl* (F 1008, JH 301), first half January 1883
Graphite and lithographic crayon, 51 x 31.3 cm
Amsterdam, Van Gogh Museum

orphan man into a fisherman or a prostitute into
a housewife. And, just as he could not retrieve the orphan men
once he had made them fishermen in his fantasy world,
neither could he accept Sien's slipping back into the reality
of the demimondaine once he had portrayed her as his helpmate
and muse.

Van Gogh's depictions of his models in The Hague are so
vigorously drawn and so clearly based upon close observation
that they have been called "virtual portraits."[41] They transmit
powerfully the reality of everyday existence. Yet they are even
more compelling when seen as elements of the artist's fantasy
world, as I have tried to describe it here.

64. *Sien with Cigar Sitting on the Floor near Stove* (F 898, JH 141), late April 1882
Graphite, chalk, ink, and sepia, 45.5 x 56 cm
Otterlo, Collection Kröller-Müller Museum

65. *Sien with White Cap* (F1055, JH 290), late December 1882
Graphite and ink, 43.3 x 27.1 cm
Amsterdam, Van Gogh Museum

66. *Sien's Mother with Bonnet* (F 1054, JH 293), December 1882
Chalk and ink, 46.7 x 26.6 cm
Bern, Kunstmuseum

67. *Sien with White Cap* (F 931, JH 291), December 1882
Graphite and lithographic crayon, 47.6 x 26.3 cm
Amsterdam, Van Gogh Museum

Paris
March 1886–February 1888

CHRONOLOGY

Paris

March 1886–February 1888

KATHERINE SACHS

1886

March

Vincent's desire to go to Paris increases. Not having received a clear plan from Theo other than being told to wait, Vincent boards a train in Antwerp, arriving in Paris unannounced about : March. Upon arrival at the train station, he writes the following to Theo to be hand-delivered by messenger:

"Do not be cross with me for having come all at once like this; I have thought about it so much, and I believe in this way we shall save time. Shall be at the Louvre from midday or sooner if you like . . . As for the expenses, I tell you again, this comes to the same thing. I have some money left, of course, and I want to speak to you before I spend any of it. We'll fix things up, you'll see. So, come as soon as possible.
I shake your hand
Ever yours, Vincent" (L 459)

69. Letter from Vincent van Gogh to Theo (L 459), 1 March 1887
Amsterdam, Van Gogh Museum

Vincent and Theo later (in June) move to an apartment with a studio in the rue Lepic in Montmartre. Theo manages a branch of Boussod, Valadon, and Company (Goupil's successor) on the boulevard Montmartre, dealing in Barbizon and impressionist paintings.

In his first few months in Paris, Vincent paints self-portraits, still lifes, and views of Paris, including cityscapes and the scenic hill of Montmartre.

Theo writes to a family friend, "The remarkable thing about our dwelling is that one has a magnificent view of the whole town from its windows . . . With the different effects produced by the various changes in the sky it is a subject for I don't know how many pictures, and if you saw it . . . it might furnish a subject for poetry too" (LT 1a, 10 July 1887).

April–May

Vincent enrolls at the studio of Fernand Cormon, where he meets Emile Bernard (1868–1941) and John Russell (1858–1931) and comes into contact with Henri de Toulouse-Lautrec (1864–1901) and Louis Anquetin (1861–1932). Theo introduces Vincent to many of the impressionist artists whose work he is attempting to sell. They include Claude Monet, Edgar Degas, Auguste Renoir, Alfred Sisley, and Camille Pissarro, among others.

The eighth impressionist group exhibition is held from 15 May to 15 June. Vincent almost assuredly saw this exhibition, where he would have encountered the new style of pointillism in Georges Seurat's *A Sunday Afternoon on the Island of the Grand Jatte*, as well as paintings by Paul Gauguin and others.

In May Vincent's mother and sisters leave Nuenen and move to Breda (L 462a, 17 March).

June

Adolphe-Joseph-Thomas Monticelli (1824–86), an artist Vincent greatly admires, dies in June. Monticelli's use of a heavy impasto influenced Vincent, as is evident in the many still lifes of flowers he painted throughout the summer. He also experiments with the pointillist style.

70. *View from Vincent's Window* (F 341, JH 1242), spring 1887
Oil on canvas, 46 x 38 cm
Amsterdam, Van Gogh Museum

"The remarkable thing about our dwelling is that one has a magnificent view of the whole town from its windows."

Theo van Gogh, July 1887

July

Theo writes to his mother,

"We are fortunately all right in our new apartment. You wouldn't recognize Vincent, so much has he changed, and it strikes others even more than me. He has had a major operation to his mouth, for he had lost nearly all his teeth as a result of his bad stomach . . . He is making tremendous progress in his work and this is proved by the fact that he is becoming successful. He has not yet sold any paintings for money, but is exchanging his work for other pictures. In this way we are building up a fine collection which, of course, also has a certain value. An art dealer [A. Portier] has now taken four of his paintings and has promised to arrange an exhibition of his work next year. He is mainly painting flowers—with the aim of putting more color into his pictures. He is also much more cheerful than in the past and people like him here. To give you proof: hardly a day passes without his being invited to the studios of well-known painters or else they come to see him. He also has acquaintances who give him flowers every week to serve as models. If they are able to keep it up I think his difficult times are over and he will be able to make it by himself" (Hulsker 1996, p. 234).

August–October

The second "Exposition de la Société des Artistes Indépendants" is held from 21 August to 21 September 1886.

It is unclear exactly how long Vincent studies at Cormon's studio, but in a letter to a friend written between August and October, he writes, "I was in Cormon's studio for three or four months but I didn't find that as useful as I'd expected it to be. But that may be my fault. Anyhow I left there too, just as I left Antwerp. Since then I've been working alone and fancy that I feel more like myself" (L 459a; from R. de Leeuw, *Van Gogh at the Van Gogh Museum* [Amsterdam, 1997]).

October–December

Vincent frequents the shop of Père Tanguy, an unofficial meeting place for artists. Tanguy sells art supplies and paintings, which he often purchases from artists in exchange for materials. After a meeting at Tanguy's shop, Vincent and Bernard become better acquainted. Theo and Vincent see a great deal of the Scottish painter and art

71. *Two Self-Portraits and Several Details* (F 1378r, JH 1197), autumn 1886
Graphite and ink, 32 x 24 cm
Amsterdam, Van Gogh Museum

"The thing I hope to achieve
is to paint a good portrait."

Summer or Autumn 1887

dealer Alexander Reid, whom Vincent had initially met in London. Reid stays with the brothers in October and November, and Vincent paints his portrait (fig. 93). Partially because of inclement weather, Vincent concentrates on portraits, including self-portraits, during the winter months.

1887

January–February

Theo writes to their mother that Vincent is working on portraits. Vincent executes the first of what will be several portraits of Père Tanguy in January. He meets Paul Signac (1863–1935) in Tanguy's shop and often visits the store of Siegfried Bing, a seller of Japanese woodcuts, where he admires and acquires quantities of Japanese prints. The effects of color and perspective in these prints, particularly the simple, linear forms and flat areas of color are of great interest to Vincent. He makes copies of prints and uses them as background motifs in several portraits.

Vincent regularly eats at the Café du Tambourin and begins a relationship with Agostina Segatori, the proprietress of the café (fig. 88). He often hangs his works there, where they appear along with those of Bernard, Gauguin, and Toulouse-Lautrec.

March

Theo, whose health has been poor, complains that life with Vincent is becoming difficult because of his violent mood swings and his disorderliness. His patience endures, however, and on 14 March, Theo writes to his sister Wil,

"I cannot do anything but continue. It is certain that he is an artist and what he makes now may sometimes not be beautiful, but it will surely be of use to him later and then it may possibly be sublime and it would be a shame if one kept him from his regular studies . . . It seems as if there are two different beings in him, the one marvelously gifted, fine and delicate and the other selfish and heartless" (Hulsker 1996, p. 248).

March–June

An exhibition of Japanese blockprints, organized by Vincent, is on view at the Café du Tambourin in March and April. The third annual exhibition of the Société des Artistes Indépendants is held from 26 March to 31 May. During this time

> "When I left Paris, seriously sick at heart and in body, and nearly an alcoholic because of my rising fury at my strength failing me—then I shut myself up within myself, without having the courage to hope."
>
> October 1888

72. Emile Bernard, *Portrait of Père Tanguy*, 1887
Oil on canvas, 36 x 31 cm
Oeffentliche Kunstsammlung, Basel, Kunstmuseum

Bernard becomes a good friend of Vincent and frequents the brothers' apartment. Vincent's interest in Japanese prints influences Bernard and Anquetin.

Vincent and Signac frequently visit Asnières, which is within walking distance of Montmartre. There, on the banks of the Seine, they paint with Bernard.

The official Salon exhibition is held from 1 May to 30 June.

July–August

Vincent works on landscapes of Montmartre and Asnières and also paints self-portraits. In late July Theo goes on a short vacation to Amsterdam and courts Johanna Bonger. About the same time, Vincent ends his relationship with Segatori after a disagreement. He writes to his sister Wil of his desire to leave Paris and go south in search of more color and sun. He also stresses, "the thing I hope to achieve is to paint a good portrait" (LW 1).

September

Vincent and Bernard work on portraits of Père Tanguy (figs. 98 and 99) in the studio constructed in the garden of Bernard's parents' new house in Asnières.

October

Vincent often visits the studio of Armand Guillaumin (1841–1927) and continues to frequent Siegfried Bing's shop, adding to his collection of Japanese prints in the fall and winter.

November–December

"Impressionists of the Petit Boulevard," so called because it comprises the work of younger artists, as compared to the first generation of impressionists, those of the "Grands Boulevards," is on view at the Grand Bouillon, Restaurant du Chalet, on the avenue de Clichy. Organized by Vincent, the exhibition includes fifty to a hundred works by Bernard, van Gogh, Anquetin, Toulouse-Lautrec, Koning, and perhaps Armand Guillaumin. Georges Seurat sees the exhibition and meets Vincent for the first time. Gauguin, who has recently returned from Martinique, sees the exhibition and trades pictures with Vincent.

Vincent exhibits at least one painting in the Salle de répétition of the Théâtre Libre d'Antoine along with Seurat and Signac.

1888

January

Vincent suffers mental and physical strain from the tensions and frantic pace of life in Paris. By early 1888 he has had enough of the city. He later recalls in a letter to Gauguin: "When I left Paris, seriously sick at heart and in body, and nearly an alcoholic because of my rising fury at my strength failing me—then I shut myself up within myself, without having the courage to hope" (L 544a).

February

Gauguin departs for Pont-Aven. Vincent and Theo frequent the artists' studios and cafés of the Petit Boulevard with Guillaumin, Camille and Lucien Pissarro, and Seurat.

14 February

Vincent sees an exhibition at the Louvre of 104 self-portraits by artists including Rembrandt, Jacques-Louis David, Gustave Courbet, Eugène Delacroix, and others. Shortly thereafter, he depicts himself in the role of artist in a self-portrait (fig. 28).

18 February

Having decided to leave Paris and move to the south of France, Vincent, with the help of Bernard, decorates Theo's apartment with Japanese woodcuts and oil paintings, which are intended to symbolize Vincent's presence when he is gone. The next day, Vincent and Theo visit the studio of Seurat. Vincent then boards a train for Arles.

73. *Self-Portrait with Felt Hat* (F 344, JH 1353), winter 1887–88
Oil on canvas, 44 x 37.5 cm
Amsterdam, Van Gogh Museum

Van Gogh in Paris

Between the Past and the Future

GEORGE T.M. SHACKELFORD

74. *Self-Portrait with Straw Hat* (F 294, JH 1209), winter 1886–87
Oil on cardboard, 19 x 14 cm
Amsterdam, Van Gogh Museum

In early February 1886, Vincent van Gogh sent a letter from Antwerp to his brother Theo in Paris. "I am longing terribly for the Louvre, the Luxembourg, etc., where everything will be new to me. All my life I shall regret not having seen the Cent chefs-d'oeuvre, the Delacroix exhibition and the Meissonier exhibition," he wrote, referring to three recent events of which he had read and heard great reports. "But," he consoled himself, "there are other things left."[1] Indeed there were. Less than a month later, Vincent descended without warning to Paris: "Shall be at the Louvre from midday on or sooner if you like. Please let me know at what time you can come to the Salle Carrée," he wrote to Theo in a hastily composed note.[2]

Between the beginning of March 1886 and the end of February 1888, Vincent remained in Paris, at first settling in with Theo in his apartment on the rue Laval, and later moving with him to a larger flat at 54, rue Lepic, up Montmartre from the boulevard de Clichy. During this two-year residence in Paris, he was to transform himself and his art, emerging from the self-imposed gloom of his Netherlandish manner into the full sunlight of his modern French style and changing himself from an unsure and untutored painter of peasant life into a radical—if still not wholly self-confident—member of the avant-garde. Van Gogh's years in Paris are critical ones in his development as a portraitist, moreover, for it was in Paris that he was exposed to the greatest variety of both traditional and modern examples of painting in general and portraits in particular, and in Paris that he first formulated the notions of portraiture that he was to refine and develop in Arles, in St.-Rémy, and finally in Auvers.[3]

On the morning of his first day in the capital of art, Vincent set as his meeting place with his beloved younger brother the Salle Carré of the Louvre, the museum that he had been dreaming of for the last few months, ever since the idea of coming to study in Paris had been broached between them. Although it was his initial stop in Paris, it was not, of course, his first visit to the museum, since he had spent the better part of a year in the city in the mid-1870s, as a young employee of Goupil and Company, the art dealers and publishers. (The successors to Goupil in Paris, Boussod, Valadon, and Company, now had a branch office in Montmartre that was managed by Theo.)[4] In May 1875 Vincent had been sent from his post in London to the Paris offices of Goupil, where he worked until he was dismissed in early 1876. During that time visits to the Louvre and the Musée du Luxembourg—where, as at the Salon, he could see the latest examples of officially sanctioned contemporary art—opened his eyes. At the Louvre he admired not only the masters of the Dutch school, in particular the landscapes of Jacob van Ruisdael and figure paintings by Rembrandt, but also portrait paintings by Philippe de Champaigne; at the Salon he saw works by Camille Corot and Jules Breton, whose paintings he also noted at the Luxembourg; and in June 1875 he visited the salesrooms at the Hôtel Drouot, where he was marked forever by his first significant experience of original works by the artist who was to become his lifelong mentor: Jean-François Millet.[5] He soon procured copies of works by these artists and decorated the walls of his rented Montmartre room with prints after Ruisdael, Rembrandt, and Champaigne, as well as with reproductions of modern pictures by Corot, Millet, Constant Troyon, Jules Dupré, Charles-François Daubigny, and Edouard Frère (fig. 57).[6] So that his younger brother could appreciate what he was learning about art from his time in Paris, Vincent called his attention to prints and photographs that were being sent from France to the Goupil branch in The Hague, where Theo was then working; "How I should like to have you here and show you the Luxembourg and the Louvre," he wrote.[7]

The study of the art of the past and the emulation of modern masters combine in some of van Gogh's earliest drawings, works undertaken in the course of 1880 and 1881, when he had at last abandoned all thoughts of becoming an evangelical minister and had turned seriously to the study of drawing and painting. Among these early works is the *Daughter of Jacob Meyer* (fig. 76) after a drawing by the sixteenth-century portraitist Hans Holbein, a composition that Vincent had found reproduced as plate 10 in the first segment of the painter Charles Bargue's *Cours de dessin* (fig. 75).[8] Bargue's portfolio of reproductions offered examples for the student draftsman, including a substantial number of drawings by Holbein, but also drawings by or after works by Michelangelo, Raphael, and Andrea del Sarto and by the masters of the modern French school, including the works of Bargue's collaborator Jean-Léon Gérôme. Although van Gogh had been familiar with Bargue's collection as early as 1874, it was only in 1880 that his family's friend, H. G. Tersteeg, who ran the Hague branch of Goupil, lent him the large-format, high-quality lithographs in order that he might copy them.[9] "I work regularly on the 'Cours de Dessin Bargue,'" he wrote to Theo in September of that year, "and intend to finish it before I undertake anything else, for day by day it makes my hand as well as my mind more supple and strong, and I cannot be grateful enough to Mr. Tersteeg for having lent it to me so generously."[10] Another section of the *Cours* comprised schematic drawings after the antique, and

75. After Hans Holbein, *Daughter of Jacob Meyer* as reproduced in C. Bargue, *Cours de dessin* (Paris, 1868–70)

76. *Daughter of Jacob Meyer, after Holbein* (F 833, JH 13), July 1881
Graphite and ink, 42 x 30 cm
Otterlo, Collection Kröller-Müller Museum

"Speaking of expression in a figure, I am increasingly coming round to the idea that it lies less in the features than in the whole tournure. There are few things I detest more than most of the academic têtes d'expression."

July 1883

Bargue had also published a series of "exercises au fusain" (studies in charcoal); van Gogh had started out by copying these with great dedication and enthusiasm, before going on to the plates from the *Cours*.[11] The exercise of copying reproductions after these acknowledged masters, artists sanctioned by the academy, was surely for Vincent a way of simulating—alone, and from afar—the time-honored methods of learning to draw and to obtain a likeness that he would have learned under the tutelage of an experienced painter.

At the same time, however, and "with no less, but rather more eagerness," Vincent was at work on copying prints after Millet. "As to 'The Sower,'" he wrote, "I have already drawn it five times, twice in small size, three times in large, and I will take it up again, I am so entirely absorbed by that figure."[12] Vincent's absorption in the art of Millet was only to be intensified by his reading, in 1882, the biography of the painter published by Millet's friend Alfred Sensier in 1881.[13] Sensier's romanticized vision of Millet as the epic painter-peasant, a man deeply attached to his native soil and to the working classes, moved Vincent profoundly and encouraged him in his natural predilection for humble subjects. But he saw Millet as only the most important exemplar of a broader anticlassical tradition: the drawings of "heads of the people" that he produced in The Hague in 1882 and 1883 were equally influenced by his admiration for the work of British popular illustrators such as Hubert Herkomer, whose work he avidly collected through mass-produced wood engravings (see essays by George Keyes and Lauren Soth in this volume).[14]

He recognized that these head studies were, ironically, related to the academic cliché of the *tête d'expression*, the "expressive head," which students were required to master. Nonetheless, as he wrote to Theo,

> Speaking of expression in a figure, I am increasingly coming round to the idea that it lies less in the features than in the whole tournure. There are few things I detest more than most of the academic têtes d'expression—I would sooner look at Michelangelo's Night or a drunkard by Daumier or Millet's diggers and that well-known big woodcut of his, La bergère —or at an old horse by Mauve, &c.[15]

Vincent here places Millet in the company of a giant of the Renaissance and a modern caricaturist who he suspected was a great creator, in opposition to the time-honored traditions of the academy. His consciousness of Millet as a great mentor was to pervade the works he created at The Hague and in Nuenen, where, at the same time, he began to study seriously the color theories of Eugène Delacroix, as described by the historian and theorist Charles Blanc, and to apply them to portraiture.[16] Delacroix's notions of color informed the research that led to *The Potato Eaters* (fig. 23): initially conceived as exercises, these "expressive heads" (fig. 77) in the realist tradition must also recall the drawings—now presumably lost—that Vincent told Theo he was making after lithographs in Bargue's *Cours,* most notably those of women wearing elaborate coifs, the originals drawn by Holbein in the early sixteenth century.[17] The Nuenen studies, therefore, were not wholly divorced, as Vincent had noted, from studio practice, although the caricatural exaggeration of the drawings and the roughshod facture of the painted heads were distinctly anti-academic; he wanted, surely, to avoid taking "realism in the sense of *literal* truth, namely *exact* drawing and local color."[18]

Upon its completion, Vincent dispatched *The Potato Eaters* to Theo, eager to know what his brother and other Parisian viewers would think of the painting. He was hopeful that the dealer Alphonse Portier—who sold works by the impressionists, of whom Vincent was beginning to hear vague things—would take it on consignment and that Portier would, above all, exhibit it. He instructed Theo to remember that it should be shown in a gold or copper-colored frame or against "a wall papered in a deep shade of ripe corn."[19] Thus, in the spring of 1885, from a Brabant village, Vincent was orchestrating his exhibition debut in Paris.

In between the extensive work he completed in 1883–85 in Nuenen and his arrival in Paris in March 1886 lay a short but important period of three months in late 1885 and early 1886 spent in Antwerp, where van Gogh first began to contemplate the making of portraits *per se.* In a city with an art academy (where he briefly took lessons) and an art museum (where he avidly studied the paintings of Peter Paul Rubens and Jacob Jordaens, as well as more recent portraits by Jacques-Louis David, Jean-Auguste Dominique Ingres, and Paul Delaroche), he had occasion to compare his own portraits to the work of other artists and to other kinds of likenesses. "I am working on my portraits all the time," he wrote his brother,

> and at last I have made two which are decidedly good "likenesses" (one profile and one three-quarter) . . . I am getting more and more fond of making portraits. Now, for instance, some of those very famous Rubenses—"Vierge au Perroquet," "Christ à la Paille," etc. I personally prefer to ignore them and look rather at that boldly painted portrait of a man—painted with such a remarkably firm hand—still sketchy here and there, which is hanging not far from Rembrandt's "Saskia" . . . And an Ingres,

77. *Gordina de Groot* (F 140, JH 745), April 1885
Oil on canvas on cardboard, 47.5 x 35.5 cm
Edinburgh, National Gallery of Scotland

"When I compare a study of mine with those of the other fellows, it is curious to see that they have almost nothing in common."

January–February 1886

a David, who as painters certainly did not always paint beautifully, yet how remarkable.[20]

In Antwerp Vincent also began to see further possibilities for the study of color, taking Rubens, with "his way of drawing the lines in a face with streaks of pure red," as his inspiration and lamenting that "the canvases which I brought with me were too small for the heads, because by using other colors I need more space for the surroundings."[21]

For the first time, he commented on the difference between the likeness created by a painter or a draftsman and that which the photograph could produce, a theme on which he was to write again some years later. He mentioned that he had "noticed the great number of photographers here, who are just about the same as everywhere, and seem to be pretty busy." But he argued that "painted portraits have a life of their own, coming straight from the painter's soul, which the machine cannot reach."[22] Perhaps, he wrote, the photographers would hire him to paint over their photographs in color, from the living model. He began to take great pleasure in the new fluency with which he worked and in the new range of paints that was available to him. When he worked side by side with other art students at the academy in January 1886, he noted the difference between his way of painting and theirs, and it was in the treatment of color that he saw his own distinction:

> When I compare a study of mine with those of the other fellows, it is curious to see that they have almost nothing in common. Theirs have about the same color as the flesh, so, seen close up, they are very correct—but if one stands back a little, they appear painfully flat—all that pink and delicate yellow, etc., etc., soft in itself, produces a harsh effect. The way I do it, from near by it is greenish-red, yellowish-gray, white-black and many neutral tints and most of them colors one cannot define. But when one stands back a little it emerges from the paint, and there is airiness around it, and a certain vibrating light falls on it. At the same time, the least little touch of color which one may use as high light is effective in it.[23]

In his letters to Theo in Paris, van Gogh often talks of the many portraits or head studies he is painting in Antwerp— portraits of a singer from a *café-chantant,* whose boyfriend objects to her sitting for Vincent, or studies of other young women of the demimonde. Surprisingly few of Vincent's Antwerp portraits can be securely identified today; we know that he may have been obliged, from time to time, to give the finished portrait to his sitter, in order to pay him or her for the time spent posing, keeping only a "study" for himself.[24] Among the portraits almost certainly made in Antwerp are the extraordinary full-face drawing of a woman in charcoal and black and red chalk (fig. 78), which might relate to the painted portrait Vincent described as "somewhat 'ecce-homo' like," and the swiftly painted profile head of a flush-faced woman (fig. 79), her face as coarse as a Nuenen peasant's, but the red of her cheeks and lips and her flowing hair, tied in a red bow, more suggestive of a beauty by Rubens. Painting such a woman, van Gogh said that he had "tried to produce something voluptuous and at the same time heart-rending." In his portraits of Antwerp women, in fact, Vincent wondered whether "one should start from the soul or from the clothes" and spoke of his ambition to capture the true expression of a woman's character, "the more so as I've felt the infinite beauty of the study of women by the giants of literature—Zola, Daudet, de Goncourt, Balzac—in the very marrow of my bones."[25]

Vincent's self-transformation into a modern painter took a major step forward in his final weeks in Antwerp. He wrote repeatedly to Theo about matters of art and art history. Since October 1885 he had been fascinated by Edmond and Jules de Goncourt's multivolume history of eighteenth-century French painting, through which he had learned more, in particular, about the painter Jean-Baptiste-Siméon Chardin.[26] "It is a delightful thing to be able to study that period—from which *so much can be learned* by—to use the expression—*notre fin du siècle* in which we live," he wrote.[27] In January and February, his correspondence is peppered with observations on the artists whose works he can see in Antwerp, but increasingly he talks about famous modern French painters, those he admires—Corot, Delacroix, Théodore Géricault, and Millet—and those he scorns—Delaroche, Gérôme, and Ary Scheffer, "who are so little *painters*."[28]

Within weeks, he was himself in Paris, the mecca in the mid-1880s of many young artists of all nations, who came to learn from "the ancients," as Vincent wrote, as well as from modern masters.[29] We are left, however, with relatively little documentation on van Gogh's specific encounters with painters and paintings in the Paris years, for the simple reason that he did not have a regular correspondent during his residence in the capital: sharing an apartment with Theo, he did not write to him, except on the rare occasions when his brother was away from Paris. There is nonetheless every indication that he pursued his artistic education with great enthusiasm; the surviving letters to Theo, to his sister Wil, to his old friend Horace M. Livens, and to his new friend Emile Bernard, and his later correspondence from Arles, all attest to

"The way I do it, from near by it is greenish-red, yellowish-gray, white-black and many neutral tints and most of them colors one cannot define. But when one stands back a little it emerges from the paint, and there is airiness around it, and a certain vibrating light falls on it. At the same time, the least little touch of color which one may use as high light is effective in it."

January-February 1886

78. *Head of a Woman* (F 1357, JH 981), January 1886
Charcoal, black and red chalk, 50.7 x 39.4 cm
Amsterdam, Van Gogh Museum

79. *Young Woman with a Red Bow* (F 207, JH 979), second half December 1885
Oil on canvas, 60 x 50.2 cm
Private Collection

his enthusiasms for traditional and vanguard painting during his two-year Parisian residency.[30]

The evolution of Vincent's painting style during his Paris period is also evidence of his encounters with the work of other artists. His first impressions of the city—views of its streets and rooftops, parks and gardens—were not radically different in palette or facture from his paintings of quasi-urban landscapes in Nuenen or Antwerp in the previous twelve months; likewise a group of humble still lifes of food and drink still have the savor of seventeenth-century Dutch breakfast-pieces or of the still lifes of potatoes that were probably painted in the autumn of 1885.[31] In two ways, at least, just before or just after his move to Paris, van Gogh chose to reaffirm his personal identification with Millet. A drawn self-portrait (fig. 81), which probably dates from the moment of his arrival in Paris, is a recasting into a modern, urban mode of the self-portrait drawing by Millet that Vincent knew from Sensier's biography (fig. 80), which he had described to Theo as "a portrait by Millet of Millet himself which I love, nothing more than a head with a kind of shepherd's cap, but the look—with eyes half closed and squinting, the intense gaze of the painter—how beautiful it is, he resembles a cockerel, one might say."[32]

Far left
80. Jean-François Millet, *Self-Portrait*, as illustrated in A. Sensier,
La vie et l'oeuvre de J.F. Millet
(Paris, 1881), p. 101

Left
81. *Self-Portrait* (F 1354av, JH 996), 1885 or early 1886
Chalk, 20 x 11 cm
Amsterdam, Van Gogh Museum

Above
82. *Still Life of Shoes* (F 255, JH 1124), 1886
Oil on canvas, 37.5 x 45.5 cm
Amsterdam, Van Gogh Museum

Right
83. Jean-François Millet, from A. Sensier,
La vie et l'oeuvre de J.F. Millet
(Paris, 1881), p. 183

Similarly, Vincent's Parisian still lifes of boots and shoes
(fig. 82) echo in form and function Millet's drawing of his own
wooden clogs (fig. 83), which was the sort of drawing that,
according to Sensier, Millet would send to admirers as a
souvenir "coat of arms" and a kind of symbolic self-portrait.[33]
In their tonality and somber mood, both van Gogh's brooding
portrait drawing and his haunting still life painting reaffirm his
continuing respect for Millet and the realist tradition in the first
months of his stay in France.[34]

The challenge to this tradition was brought to Vincent's
attention two months after his arrival in Paris. Beginning on
15 May, Vincent would have been able to see the eighth and last
of the impressionist exhibitions, featuring works by artists who
had been with the group since the 1870s, including Mary
Cassatt, Edgar Degas—exhibiting his famous suite of pastel
nudes—Armand Guillaumin, Berthe Morisot, and Camille
Pissarro, as well as artists who were to become better known as
post-impressionists, such as Paul Gauguin, Odilon Redon,
Emile Schuffenecker, Paul Signac, and Georges Seurat—whose
Sunday Afternoon on the Island of the Grande Jatte was displayed.
A month later, the fifth "Exposition Internationale de Peinture
et de Sculpture" opened at the luxurious Galerie Georges Petit,
including works by Auguste Renoir and Claude Monet. And in
August, works by the vanguard painters Charles Angrand,
Henri-Edmond Cross, Albert Dubois-Pillet, Lucien Pissarro,
Seurat, and Signac—artists who formed the core of the neo-
impressionist movement—were exhibited at the second
"Exposition de la Société des Artistes Indépendants."[35]

Over the course of the summer and early autumn, van Gogh
was absorbed by the study of color, reconciling his understanding
of Delacroix with the work of the modern painters he was now
encountering in Paris by painting a series of flower pieces of
great originality and increasing audacity of hue and form.
Writing at this time to his friend Horace Livens, an English
painter he had met in Antwerp, Vincent said, "though *not* being
one of the club yet I have much admired certain Impressionist's
pictures—*Degas* nude figure—*Claude Monet* landscape . . . For
what regards what I myself have been doing," he went on,

> I have lacked money for paying models else I had entirely given
> myself to figure painting. But I have made a series of colour studies
> in painting, simply flowers . . . seeking oppositions of blue with
> orange, red and green, yellow and violet seeking *les tons rompus et*
> *neutres* to harmonize brutal extremes. Trying to render intense
> colour and not a grey harmony.
>
> Now after these gymnastics I lately did two heads which
> I dare say are better in light and colour than those I did before.[36]

84. John Peter Russell, *Vincent van Gogh*, 1886
Oil on canvas, 60 x 45 cm
Amsterdam, Van Gogh Museum

85. *Self-Portrait with Dark Felt Hat* (F 208a, JH 1089), 1886
Oil on canvas, 41.5 x 32.5 cm
Amsterdam, Van Gogh Museum

86. *Portrait of Père Tanguy* (F 263, JH 1202), January 1887
Oil on canvas, 47 x 38.5 cm
Copenhagen, Ny Carlsberg Glyptotek

87. *Portrait of a Man* (F 209, JH 1201), winter 1886–87
Oil on canvas, 31 x 39.5 cm
Melbourne, National Gallery of Victoria

At the same time, landscape studies painted in Paris and its environs showed a gradual lightening of palette and greater variety of touch, so that by the spring of 1887 van Gogh was able to move back and forth between one manner, in which broad patches of luminous color were enlivened by a classic impressionist "comma stroke" derived from Monet or Pissarro's example, and another, in which small dots of color were used in imitation of the "pointillism" of Seurat and Signac.

It is hard to pinpoint which works Vincent was describing when he wrote to Livens of two heads, "better in light and colour" than his previous work, since the chronology of the Parisian portraits is extremely difficult to establish. A series of dark and moody self-portraits, executed in earth tones against brown or deep red backgrounds, are generally thought to be the earliest figure paintings from the Paris period, perhaps

88. *Woman at a Table in the Café du Tambourin* (F 370, JH 1208), spring 1887
Oil on canvas, 55.5 x 46.5 cm
Amsterdam, Van Gogh Museum

executed in the course of 1886 (fig. 85).[37] If these earliest portraits betray a lingering affinity with Rembrandt, perhaps even an emulation of paintings seen at the Louvre (see essay by George Keyes in this volume), they are also close in tone and facture to a portrait of van Gogh painted by his friend from the Atelier Cormon, John Russell, surely in the autumn of 1886 (fig. 84).[38] Evidence of some awareness of impressionism is clear in the portrait of an unidentified man (fig. 87) and in the *Portrait of Père Tanguy*, which is dated January 1887 (fig. 86). Tanguy, the color-merchant who dealt informally in pictures—he is most famous for being the early champion of Paul Cézanne—was at the heart of the artistic scene of Montmartre. His boutique, located at 14, rue Clauzel, was only a block from the apartment that Vincent shared with Theo in early 1886 and was just a few streets away from the rue Fontaine, home to both the painter Degas and van Gogh's friend from Cormon's atelier, Henri de Toulouse-Lautrec.[39] Van Gogh's portrait of Tanguy is marked by its informality: his hair is tousled, his collar is askew, and he wears over his red-brown jacket an apron tinged with green; the painting's sketchlike surface is built up in parallel lines of paint, loosely brushed over a thinly worked ground.

The same facture is more fully developed in two portraits of women that must date from the spring of 1887, works which signal, in no uncertain terms, van Gogh's interaction with the Parisian vanguard. One of these, *Woman at a Table in the Café du Tambourin* (fig. 88), almost certainly shows Agostina Segatori, with whom Vincent had a liaison of some sort in the first half of 1887. A cigarette in her hand, and with a glass of beer beside her, she is seated at one of the tables, decorated to resemble a tambourine, that were in use in Segatori's Montmartre establishment. There, in March and April, Vincent hung a selection of the Japanese prints that he had long admired and which he had been buying, for a few *sous* each, from Siegfried Bing, the promoter of "le Japon artistique."[40] The brightly colored image at the woman's right may refer to these prints—which were to inspire not only Vincent but his friends Louis Anquetin and Emile Bernard. The choice of subject and locale stem from the facts of the painter's life: he spent a great deal of time drinking and smoking in cafés, as is evidenced by Toulouse-Lautrec's pastel portrait of him (fig. 89). But the painting of Segatori also recalls the café imagery of Edouard Manet and Degas and their followers Jean-Louis Forain and Jean-François Rafaëlli. This likewise had an effect on Vincent's friend Toulouse-Lautrec whose *Poudre de riz*, painted later in 1887 (fig. 90), may oddly enough derive

89. Henri de Toulouse-Lautrec, *Portrait of Vincent van Gogh*, 1887
Pastel, 57 x 46.5 cm
Amsterdam, Van Gogh Museum

not so much from these famous forebears as from the more immediate example of Vincent's portrait. The painting of a demimondaine covered with pale rice powder, "a veritable pendant to van Gogh's *Agostina Segatori*," was purchased by Theo for his collection in January 1888.[41]

The vibrant surface effects that mark *Woman at a Table* and *Poudre de riz* alike come from the broken pattern of brushstrokes with which van Gogh and Toulouse-Lautrec built up relatively thin layers of paint. The same effects characterize another painting of a woman from early 1887, the *Woman Sitting by a Cradle* (fig. 91), a portrait of Léonie-Rose Davy-Charbuy, the niece of Pierre-Firmin Martin, an art dealer who was a friend of Theo van Gogh. Perched on a delicate chair in a bedroom decorated with gilt-framed paintings, Madame Davy-Charbuy clasps her hands demurely in her lap and gazes at the artist with large, dark eyes, the very image of maternal probity. In type, she is radically different from Segatori—so much so that her portrait, too, might be seen as a pendant to the *Woman at a Table*. But both paintings reveal Vincent's flirtation with impressionist subject matter on the one hand, and neo-impressionist painting methods on the other. *Woman Sitting by a Cradle*, in particular, is marked by the subtle, recurring patterns of dots with which the artist depicts the reflection of light on the pale bed linens, on the black silk of Madame Davy-Charbuy's gown, and on the trim at its neck and sleeve, a technique that, under the sway of Signac, he was to exploit from the late spring through the summer of 1887.

Vincent's personal interpretation of the neo-impressionist or "pointillist" method marks the *Self-Portrait,* now in the Art Institute of Chicago, that he most probably painted in the spring or early summer of that year (fig. 92). Like the *Portrait of Alexander Reid,* who was a Scottish art dealer apprenticed to Boussod and Valadon (fig. 93), the self-portrait is conceived as a study in color contrasts, chiefly between tones of red and green or blue and orange. Both men had orange-red hair and beards, which would suggest the use of the color complement, blue-green. In the portrait of Reid, which is relatively thinly and seemingly quickly painted, the artist balances an orange-red background by employing tones of bright green and dark blue to suggest the sitter's suit and the high back of a chair rising above his shoulder. For the self-portrait, much more "finished" in a conventional sense, Vincent orchestrated a complex series of contrasts, surrounding the luminous face and its bright frame of hair and beard with a swirling pattern of blue, green, orange, and violet dots, which describe the

90. Henri de Toulouse-Lautrec, *Poudre de riz*, 1887–88
Oil on canvas, 65 x 58 cm
Amsterdam, Van Gogh Museum

91. *Woman Sitting by a Cradle* (F 369, JH 1206), spring 1887
Oil on canvas, 61 x 45.5 cm
Amsterdam, Van Gogh Museum

artist's jacket, chiefly painted in tones of dark red and purple, and the wall or background against which he sits, mainly painted in tones of blue.

It is interesting to compare this self-portrait with three others painted in the spring or summer of 1887. The first of these, the *Self-Portrait with Gray Felt Hat* (fig. 94) from the Rijksmuseum, Amsterdam, shows Vincent wearing the same suit that he wears in the Chicago portrait, as well as a stylish hat that brings with it a certain bourgeois respectability. Painted with sweeping, feathery brushstrokes, the Rijksmuseum painting is stylistically close to the portrait of Tanguy (fig. 86) but more assured in its handling of paint. Another *Self-Portrait*, in the Van Gogh Museum (fig. 95), is directly related to the Rijksmuseum and Chicago paintings: of nearly identical dimensions, it is also painted on cardboard and shows the artist wearing the same dark red jacket, trimmed in blue at the collar. It is virtually a mirror image of the Chicago likeness, and its surface surely reveals what that version looked like at an early stage of its development, when the basic outlines of the face and body had been filled with an initial layer of color, but before the complex layers of dots that formed the body and the background had been fully elaborated. Similarly, the *Self-Portrait with Straw Hat* (fig. 96) is a more fully realized rendering of a sketch version, also facing left, in the Van Gogh Museum (fig. 97). Like the Chicago and the two Amsterdam self-portraits, the Detroit canvas shows the painter's characteristic use of roughly parallel brushstrokes, emanating from the center of the face, to describe its skeletal and muscular structure and to suggest the wiry texture of the hair and beard. There is, however, among the four paintings a curious variation in the artist's conception of his own likeness: while the three portraits in which he wears a city suit coat bear a strong resemblance to each other, the face in the Detroit canvas is distorted in its breadth, the eye at left strangely out of plane with that at right, floating in the shadow cast by the rakish straw hat. And when we compare these four portraits with those done in 1886, or another group of 1887 self-portraits brushed quickly onto the backs of canvases held over from 1885, the differences are even more pointed.[42]

Unlike his friend John Russell, who had captured such an apparently credible likeness in the 1886 portrait of van Gogh (fig. 84), Vincent was not seeking to transcribe that which he saw—in this case, his face reflected in a mirror—with any particular degree of "accuracy." As we have seen, he had long believed that "painted portraits have a life of their own, coming straight from the painter's soul," which transcended the would-be

"The best pictures, and, from a technical point of view, the most complete, seen from near by, are but patches of color side by side, and only make an effect at a certain distance."
November 1885

92. *Self-Portrait* (F 345, JH 1249), spring 1887
Oil on cardboard, 41 x 32.5 cm
Art Institute of Chicago

93. *Portrait of Alexander Reid* (F 343, JH 1250), spring 1887
Oil on cardboard, 42 x 33 cm
Glasgow Museums, The Burrell Collection

94. *Self-Portrait with Gray Felt Hat* (F 295, JH 1211), spring or summer 1887
Oil on cardboard, 42 x 34 cm
Amsterdam, Rijksmuseum

95. *Self-Portrait* (F 356, JH 1248), spring or summer 1887
Oil on cardboard, 41 x 33 cm
Amsterdam, Van Gogh Museum

reality of the photographic likeness.[43] The difference in their attitudes toward the relationship between a painting and its nominal subject was made clear, a year later, when Russell wrote to Vincent, then at Arles, describing a luncheon at the home of Auguste Rodin, where he met Monet and saw the paintings of Antibes that Monet was to exhibit with Theo van Gogh in June 1888. These pictures Russell described as "very fine in colour and light of a certain richness of envelop. But like nearly all the so called impressionist work the form is not enough studied. The big mass of form I mean. The trees [have] too much wood in *branches* for the size of the *trunk* and so [are] against fundamental law[s] of nature."[44] Vincent recounted the letter to Theo:

> [Russell] criticizes the Monets very ably, begins by liking them very much, the attack on the problem, the enfolding tinted air, the color. After that he shows what there is to find fault with— the total lack of construction, for instance one of his trees will have far too much foliage for the thickness of the trunk, and so always and everywhere from the standpoint of the reality of things, from the standpoint of lots of natural laws, he is exasperating enough.[45]

By the autumn of 1887, Vincent's disdain for the exasperating "reality of things" and "natural laws," as they were defined by painters like Russell, was a well-established precept of his art. From the beginning of his career, in 1880 and 1881, he had favored exaggeration and stylization as a means toward expressive ends: the almost grotesque heads drawn at The Hague or painted in Nuenen attest to the degree to which his search for a greater emotional truth could lead him to diverge from "the reality of things." In large part, his growing interest in a form of painting in which such distortion and stylizations of form were allied with a heightened awareness of the power of color parallels his discovery of Japanese art through the prints he collected so diligently from 1886. Some of these, either originals or reproductions, became the sources for more-or-less direct transcriptions from color print to painting in the summer or autumn of 1887; still others served as the collagelike backgrounds for the painter's most ambitious portraits to date, two remarkable images of his friend Père Tanguy (figs. 98 and 99).[46] Almost certainly the first of these to be painted is the version in a private collection; its forms are more simply defined, and its surface combines areas of free and liquid paint with patches of impasto. By contrast, the version of the painting at the Musée Rodin, larger in scale, is also more densely worked, the figure of Tanguy, as well as much of the

96. *Self-Portrait with Straw Hat* (F 526, JH 1309), spring or summer 1887
Oil on canvas on panel, 34.9 x 26.7 cm
The Detroit Institute of Arts

97. *Self-Portrait with Straw Hat* (F 469, JH 1310), summer 1887
Oil on cardboard, 41 x 33 cm
Amsterdam, Van Gogh Museum

98. *Portrait of Père Tanguy* (F 363, JH 1351), winter 1887–88
Oil on canvas, 92 x 75 cm
Paris, Musée Rodin

99. *Portrait of Père Tanguy* (F 364, JH 1352), winter 1887–88
Oil on canvas, 65 x 51 cm
Private Collection

background, described in areas of closely juxtaposed and thickly applied strokes of paint, which have often been compared to the wrinkled surfaces of some of Vincent's Japanese originals.[47] In both versions, the head of Tanguy is placed against a print representing the sacred Mount Fuji, while images of landscapes and courtesans are arranged at either side. Manifestly products of the artist's imagination (or perhaps "the painter's soul") as much as they are records of Tanguy's appearance, the portraits—one an *esquisse* (a sketch), the other a *tableau* (finished picture)—also point to a practice of self-repetition and variation that was to become prevalent in the next two years of Vincent's career, notably in the two portraits of *Patience Escalier* (fig. 193 and JH 1563) or the two variant compositions of *L'Arlésienne* (figs. 148 and 181) but also in the five renditions of *La Berceuse* (figs. 125, 150, 155) and the many versions of the head of *Joseph Roulin* (figs. 100 and 153).

Even, or perhaps especially, when painting his own image, Vincent felt free to create variations on an established theme. The four closely related self-portraits from the spring and summer of 1887 (figs. 92 and 94–96) are followed at the end of the year by even more. One of these, *Self-Portrait with Felt Hat* (fig. 73), a reprise of the Rijksmuseum *Self-Portrait with Gray Felt Hat* (fig. 94) of the previous spring, employs an entirely new, percussive rhythm: the feathered strokes that defined the background in the earlier version here create a halo of lines and dots around the head; the radiant hatching that described the face has here become a pattern of stripes of orange mixed with blue, and the red hair of the beard is shot through with touches of green. The effect is even more sensational in a canvas now in Basel (JH 1333), which is roughly analogous to the hatless self-portrait, facing right, from the Van Gogh Museum (fig. 95). Here, however, the painter has abandoned the refined draftsmanship that characterized the earlier version and has made no attempt to integrate the hatched brushstrokes, leaving patches of the pale ground to show through the blue coat or smock. He treats the face almost like a painted mask, through which glow a pair of lurid green eyes, rimmed in red, eyes that eerily resemble the eye sockets of a skull that Vincent painted at the same time (fig. 101).[48]

The distinctive pattern of hatchlike brushstrokes that these portraits display was to become, in the succeeding two years, the hallmark of van Gogh's style, and it is the manner most often associated with his art in the public imagination. It emerges at the end of 1887 and is seen not only in such portraits as these but also in still-life compositions of fruit, flowers, vegetables, or books. Although it may be true that Vincent took inspiration from the crinkled surfaces of Japanese prints to activate the colored forms

100. *Joseph Roulin* (F 1458, JH 1536), 31 July–6 August 1888
Ink and chalk, 32 x 24.4 cm
Los Angeles, The J. Paul Getty Museum

101. *Skull* (F 297a, JH 1347), winter 1887–88
Oil on canvas, 41.5 x 31.5 cm
Amsterdam, Van Gogh Museum

in his paintings by giving them a texture that would reflect or absorb light—in works such as the portraits of Père Tanguy, for example—the nature of the hatchings in other works does not suggest the same intention. In the *Portrait of a Man with a Skullcap* (fig. 102), the vertical strokes that define the background provide a shimmering foil for the stolid form of the sitter, the so-called *patron du restaurant*. And in the *Self-Portrait with Felt Hat* (fig. 73), for example, the combined effect of radiating hatch-strokes that describe the face and the parallel bands of hatchings that encircle the head is to suggest a source of light in the face and a kind of halo, or nimbus, surrounding it. In other words, the hatchings here are meant to convey the action of light, rather than to modify its action.

Vincent's goals were not far from those of the more conventional neo-impressionists, as the pattern of orange-red dots that the painter scattered across the hatched blue background of this self-portrait reminds us. Seurat, for example, in attempting to create in painting an optical sensation akin to the action of light by dividing colors into dots of their component parts, often posed a final layer of points of color over an initial preparation of more or less broadly hatched paint. It should be remembered that van Gogh's understanding of Seurat's methods—and their relationship, for example, to the methods of a painter such as Monet—was extremely cursory: although he had the opportunity to work with Signac, Bernard, and Anquetin, he never adhered strictly to the quasi-scientific rules of doctrinaire divisionism, and hatch-stroke and dot are freely mixed in paintings from Paris and remain in use in both paintings and drawings from Arles.[49] And Vincent felt free to draw technical or stylistic inspiration from a wide variety of sources: in the *Self-Portrait with Felt Hat* (fig. 73), the pattern of hatchings seems as much *drawn* as painted and is related, for example, to the way he had used chalks in his 1886 *Head of a Woman* (fig. 78) or to the way in which Toulouse-Lautrec had used pastel to draw his portrait in a café earlier in 1887 (fig. 89). Van Gogh himself only rarely employed pastel, but many of the artists with whom he associated—particularly Anquetin—were adept in the medium. We know that he had been greatly impressed by the Millet pastels in the Gavet collection that he had seen in 1875 and that he had admired Degas's pastels of bathers at the 1886 impressionist exhibition.[50] And although we cannot document his reaction, we can be certain that he sought out the work of another master of pastel technique: Chardin.

In the months before he left Nuenen for Antwerp, he had first read Edmond de Goncourt's appreciation of Chardin and was greatly interested by it. Goncourt had written at length about the Chardin pastel portraits in the Louvre and pointed to the *Self-Portrait* (fig. 104) where, in Goncourt's words, the artist "achieves truth, the complete illusion of flesh and blood, by bold touches of bright red, pure blue and golden yellow, with unmixed primary colors which, one would have thought, must have conveyed an exaggerated sense of life, a forced impression of reality."[51] To Theo, who had sent him the book, Vincent reported that "pastel is a process which I should like to know. I shall certainly try it some day," adding that he had

> enjoyed immensely what he says about Chardin's technique. I am more convinced than ever that the true painters did not finish their things in the way which is used only too often, namely correct when one scrutinizes it closely.
>
> The best pictures, and, from a technical point of view, the most complete, seen from near by, are but patches of color side by side, and only make an effect at a certain distance.

And he went on to quote Goncourt's description of the pastel portrait of Madame Chardin, in which the mouth was drawn with "nothing more than a few streaks of yellow, a few sweeping strokes of blue."[52] The pastels, then on view continuously in the Louvre, would have been of great interest to Vincent, who knew little of historical French painting and who told Theo, having read Goncourt, that in matters of daring mastery of technique "Chardin is as great as Rembrandt."[53]

Something of Chardin's vivid command of color may be felt in the last of Vincent's Paris self-portraits: the great image of the artist at his easel, his palette and brushes in hand, in the act of observing and painting (figs. 28 and 103). From memory, he reconstructed the portrait in a letter to his sister, written in the summer of 1888, in which he sought "to emphasize the fact that one and the same person may furnish motifs for very different portraits."

> Here I give a conception of mine, which is the result of a portrait I painted in the mirror, and which is now in Theo's possession.
>
> A pinkish-gray face with green eyes, ash-colored hair, wrinkles on the forehead and around the mouth, stiff, wooden, a very red beard, considerably neglected and mournful, but the lips are full, a blue peasant's blouse of coarse linen, and a palette with citron yellow, vermilion, malachite green, cobalt blue, in short all the colors on the palette except the orange beard, but only whole colors. The figure against a grayish-white wall.
>
> You will say that this resembles somewhat, for instance, the face of—Death . . . all right, but it is a figure like this—and it isn't an easy job to paint oneself—at any rate if it is to be different from a photograph.[54]

102. *Portrait of a Man with a Skullcap* (F 289, JH 1203), winter 1886–87
Oil on canvas, 65.5 x 54 cm
Amsterdam, Van Gogh Museum

"A portrait I painted in the mirror . . . a pinkish-gray face with green eyes, ash-colored hair, wrinkles on the forehead and around the mouth, stiff, wooden, a very red beard, considerably neglected and mournful, but the lips are full, a blue peasant's blouse of coarse linen."

June 1888

Opposite
103. *Self-Portrait as an Artist* (F 522, JH 1356), detail, winter 1887–88
Oil on canvas, 65 x 50.5 cm
Amsterdam, Van Gogh Museum

This is the last of some two dozen self-portraits painted by Vincent between his arrival in Paris in the early spring of 1886 and his departure for Arles in February 1888. It is without question the culmination of an intensive if episodic period of self-examination; it is the most resonant of the "very different portraits" made over the course of two years. In these portraits, Vincent had experimented—as Rembrandt had done before him, or as Pablo Picasso would do little more than a decade later—with the creation of a series of identities: painter, worker, bourgeois, bohemian.[55] Although this exploration suggests a desire to understand or to fix his position in the world, it would be misleading to conclude that this period was one of particular psychological introspection; the preponderance of self-portraits in the Paris period may be merely the result of Vincent's need to depend on himself as a model, in the absence of other opportunities. Nonetheless, his description of the last of his Parisian self-portraits—with its reference to the figure of Death—suggests that he was at least aware *in retrospect* of the emotional impact of his paintings, even if, while painting them, he was primarily intent upon honing his skills as a painter.

All the same, the *Self-Portrait as an Artist* evokes, more than any other Vincent had yet painted, the history of painters' self-portraits: it is part of a long line of images that goes back at least to the seventeenth century, to the Golden Age of painting in The Netherlands, in the case of Rembrandt, and in France and Italy, in the case of Nicolas Poussin (fig. 105). At the Louvre, van Gogh would have admired the self-portraits of Rembrandt, of Poussin, and of Chardin, as he had admired the self-portrait of Ingres in the museum at Antwerp. Some of these portraits were included in the important exhibition, "Cent quatre portraits de peintres," which opened at the Louvre on 14 February, 1888, by which time his own self-portrait must have been substantially complete, since he was to leave for Arles on 20 February. He would, therefore, have imagined his own self-portrait in the context of the images of "the ancients" whose work he had come to Paris to study in the first place.

Despite their connections to the art of the past, Vincent's self-portraits also had a contemporary context. It has often been suggested, though it cannot be conclusively demonstrated, that the *Self-Portrait as an Artist* was inspired by a strikingly similar painting by Cézanne (now in the collection of the Bührle Foundation in Zurich). It is equally probable, however, that the older impressionist painter could likewise have found his source of inspiration in Rembrandt's composition, which

Vincent had appropriated as a model as early as 1886.[56] More important is the fact that, in the autumn of 1888, Vincent was to begin to assemble with Theo, primarily through exchange, his own collection of painters' portraits. In addition to a self-portrait by the older artist Armand Guillaumin, in which the painter's palette is clearly shown, Vincent obtained three portraits of his contemporaries. After a series of letters in which he coaxed his friends to sit for each other, in early October he received Gauguin's *Self-Portrait:"Les Misérables"* (fig. 106), which contains a portrait-within-a-portrait image of Bernard at upper right. From Bernard, at the same time, he received a portrait inscribed *à son copaing Vincent* that similarly included an image of Gauguin, as if it were hanging on a wall behind Bernard (fig. 107). Van Gogh sent to Gauguin the astonishing *Self-Portrait* (fig. 129), in which his close-cropped head, with an exaggeratedly wide brow and cheekbone, was placed against a vivid green background; he had completed it a few weeks earlier, when he described it as "a study, in which I look like a Japanese."[57] To Charles Laval, Vincent sent another, decidedly different, self-portrait, painted with less deliberation but greater delicacy (fig. 130); Laval, in exchange, sent a remarkable self-portrait against an open window (fig. 108), which Vincent sketched in a letter to Theo. "You will also be pleased to hear that we have an addition to the collection of portraits of artists," Vincent wrote. "A self-portrait by Laval, extremely good . . . [it] is very bold, very distinguished, and [it] will be just one of the pictures you speak of, those one gets hold of before other people have recognized the talents."[58] The portraits of Gauguin, Bernard, and Laval were intended, then, to join the portrait of van Gogh at his easel in a kind of pantheon of talents as yet unrecognized by the critics and public in Paris, upon which they had turned their backs.

Vincent was to return to Paris only briefly, in 1890, on the way from the asylum at St.-Rémy to the care of Dr. Gachet at Auvers. He arrived on Saturday morning, 17 May, and on that same day had the chance to meet for the first time his sister-in-law Jo and to gaze on his nephew in his cradle. On Sunday, he spent time in Theo's apartment, looking over the canvases that he had sent to his brother over the last two years, and went with Theo to the shop of Père Tanguy where still other of his paintings, as well as works by other artists, were stored. At the Salon du Champ de Mars he admired particularly the great mural composition, *Inter artes et naturam*, painted by Puvis de Chavannes for the staircase of the museum at Rouen, which he described to his sister as "all humanity, all nature simplified."[59] He could not remain long in Paris, which, as he wrote later to

Theo, "had such a bad effect on me that I thought it wise for my head's sake to fly to the country."[60] And so on Tuesday morning he left Paris once more, never to return.

But the experience of his two years' stay in Paris, between 1886 and 1888, had been critical and was to remain so for the whole of his brief subsequent career. In Paris, above all, he had gained some vision of how he might redefine "the modern portrait," building on the achievements of the past, but with the view to painting "portraits which would appear after a century to the people living then as apparitions." As he wrote in 1890, he wanted to render "impassioned expressions, by using our modern knowledge and appreciation of color as a means of rendering and exalting character."[61] That understanding of color, first awakened in Nuenen, advanced still further in Paris, where van Gogh was able for the first time to see paintings by artists who meaningfully applied modern color theory. The full flowering of Vincent's application of the "modern knowledge and appreciation of color" to portraiture took place in Arles (see essay by Roland Dorn in this volume) and in St.-Rémy and Auvers (see essay by Judy Sund); but it first bursts forth in such works as the Chicago *Self-Portrait* (fig. 92) or the *Portrait of Alexander Reid* (fig. 93).

In Paris, too, Vincent first began to organize groups of related portraits, typically as pendants but also in larger groups. Although he had talked of portraits as having complementary relationships while he was still in Nuenen, it was in Paris, with not only the Chicago *Self-Portrait* and the *Portrait of Alexander Reid* but also the portraits of the *Woman at a Table in the Café du Tambourin* and *Woman Sitting by a Cradle* (figs. 88 and 91) that he first explored the notion of complementary pairs. If the former pair—the painter, the dealer—might be seen as a precedent for the portraits of Eugène Boch, *The Poet* (fig. 140), and Paul-Eugène Milliet, *The Lover* (fig. 141), so the contrasting social types of Madame Davy-Charbuy and Agostina Segatori might be seen as precedents for the portraits of the nurturing mother, Madame Roulin (fig. 149), and the modern woman—or at least the reader of modern literature—Madame Ginoux (fig. 181), or even for Marguerite Gachet, playing her piano (fig. 194), and the *Peasant Woman in Wheat Field* (fig. 192).[62]

In Paris, the capital of artistic life, Vincent was able to measure his art against the art of "the ancients" and the art of the modern painters who were his mentors or contemporaries. It was there, having at last experienced the application of academic practice, that he was to have firm grounds for rejecting it forever. It was there that he could reconcile his

108. Charles Laval, *Self-Portrait*, 1888
Oil on canvas, 50 x 60 cm
Amsterdam, Van Gogh Museum

Opposite above
106. Paul Gauguin, *Self-Portrait: "Les Misérables"*, 1888
Oil on canvas, 79 x 91 cm
Amsterdam, Van Gogh Museum

Below
107. Emile Bernard, *Self-Portrait with a Portrait of Gauguin*, 1888
Oil on canvas, 46.5 x 55.5 cm
Amsterdam, Van Gogh Museum

early admiration for the eternal principles he construed in the art of Millet and Delacroix with the creation of an art based in modernity. And it was in Paris, finally, that he came to understand that he was part of a continuum, "a link in the chain of artists," that began in the past and would extend beyond his present to the future of painting. "I'm not sure who called this condition 'being stricken by death and immortality,'" he wrote to Theo a few months after leaving Paris. "The cab one is pulling along must be of some use to people one doesn't know. And so, if we believe in the new art, in the artists of the future, our presentiment will not play false . . . And those of us who are, as I am led to believe, still fairly far from death, nevertheless feel that these things are bigger than we are and will outlive us."[63]

Arles

February 1888–April 1889

CHRONOLOGY

Arles

February 1888–April 1889

KATHERINE SACHS

110. *View of Saintes-Maries* (F 416, JH 1447),
31 May–4 June 1888
Oil on canvas, 64 x 53 cm
Otterlo, Collection Kröller-Müller Museum

"The best thing to do would be to make portraits, all kinds of portraits of women and children . . . I shall go on working and here and there among my work there will be things which will last, but who will be in figure painting what Claude Monet is in landscape? . . . the painter of the future will be *a colorist such as has never yet existed.*"

May 1888

1888

February

Theo records Vincent's move to the south of France in his letter to Wil of 24–26 February:

"Vincent left for the South last Sunday [19 February] . . . Years of worry and adversity have not made him any stronger and he felt a definite need to be in a more temperate climate . . . I believe it will certainly do his health good and will also benefit his work. When he came here two years ago I did not think we would become so attached to each other, but the flat feels decidedly empty now that I am on my own again . . . His knowledge and clear perception of the world are incredible. I am therefore convinced that if he has a few more years to live, he will make a name for himself. Through him, I came into contact with many painters among whom he is greatly respected. He is one of the champions of new ideas . . ." (Hammacher and Hammacher 1982, p. 128).

On about 22 February Vincent moves into a room at the Hôtel-Restaurant Carrel and buys paints and canvas. He begins his time in Arles painting winter landscapes and still lifes.

March

As the weather improves and the fruit trees bloom, Vincent paints the blossoming trees. On 30 March he learns that his friend Mauve has died. Vincent dedicates his favorite study of peach trees to the memory of Mauve.

Theo has arranged for Vincent's work to be shown for the first time at the exhibition of the Artistes Indépendants in Paris (22 March–3 May).

May

Vincent feels he is being overcharged at the hotel and finds a new place to live in Arles, renting rooms in a small house at 2, place Lamartine on 1 May. It is to be his home and his studio, and he hopes to share this "yellow house" with other artists—a dream he has had since the start of his painting career in 1880. The house is uninhabitable, so on 7 May, Vincent moves temporarily to the Café de la Gare until he can afford to furnish it.

Drawn to the beauty of the women of Arles, Vincent writes, "The best thing to do would be to make portraits, all kinds of portraits of women and children . . . I shall go on working and here and there among my work there will be things which will last, but who will be in figure painting what Claude Monet is in landscape? . . . the painter of the future will be *a colorist such as has never yet existed*" (L 482, 5 May; van Gogh's emphasis).

In pursuit of his desire to form an artist's colony in the south of France, Vincent writes to Theo, suggesting that Gauguin might come to Arles. With Theo's financial assistance, this arrangement would help Gauguin, who is in debt and in poor health. Vincent would like Emile Bernard to come too, and they would then all give Theo paintings in return for his support (L 493).

111. *The Mudlark* (F 1507a, JH 1466), ca. 17 June 1888
Ink, 18 x 19.5 cm
New York, The Solomon R. Guggenheim Museum

112. *The Mudlark* (F 535, JH 1467), ca. 17 June 1888
Oil on canvas, 35.5 x 24.5 cm
La Chaux-de-Fonds, Musée des Beaux-Arts

Vincent goes to the fishing village of Stes.-Maries-de-la-Mer from 30 May until 3 June. While there, he paints and sketches fishing boats, seascapes, and scenes of the village.

June

In mid-June Vincent meets the Belgian artist Eugène Boch (fig. 140). He also makes the acquaintance of a Zouave, a French-Algerian infantryman who agrees to sit for him. "I have a model at last—a Zouave—a boy with a small face, a bull-neck and the eye of a tiger, and I began one portrait, and began again with another" (L 501). While painting a landscape outdoors, he also sketches the head of a "dirty little girl" playing outside, whom he refers to as "the mudlark" (L 501a, [17 June?]).

Mid-July

Vincent hears from Theo that Gauguin has accepted their offer to come to Arles (L 507).

25 July

"And now, if you know what a 'mousmé' is (you will know when you have read Loti's *Madame Chrysanthème*), I have just painted one. It took me a whole week, I have not been able to do anything else, not having been well either . . . That makes two portraits now, the Zouave and her" (L 514) (fig. 143).

28 July

Vincent meets Joseph Roulin, a postman, who becomes an important friend and sitter: "I am now at work with another model, a postman in a blue uniform trimmed with gold, a big bearded face, very like Socrates. A violent republican like Tanguy. A man more interesting than most . . ." (L 516).

31 July

In a letter to Wil, Vincent talks about Roulin and his family: "His wife was delivered of a child today, and he is consequently feeling as proud as a peacock, and is aglow with satisfaction . . . I shall also get to paint the baby born today, at least I hope so . . ." (LW 5) (figs. 126 and 149).

In the three months of June, July, and August, Vincent is extremely prolific, completing thirty-five paintings and thirty-seven drawings.

113. *The Zouave* (F 1482a, JH 1535), 31 July–6 August 1888
Ink, 31.9 x 24.3 cm
New York, The Solomon R. Guggenheim Museum

114. *The Zouave* (F 1482, JH 1487), ca. 24 June 1888
Graphite, ink, wax crayon, and watercolor, 30 x 23 cm
New York, The Metropolitan Museum of Art

115. *The Zouave Sitting* (F 1443, JH 1485), detail, 20–23 June 1888, Graphite and ink, 52 x 66 cm
Amsterdam, Van Gogh Museum

116. *Joseph Roulin* (F 1459, JH 1547),
ca. 4–8 August 1888
Ink and chalk, 51.4 x 42.2 cm
Los Angeles County Museum of Art

August

Vincent writes to Theo about a new model, an old gardener named Patience Escalier, whose portrait he is painting. Vincent wants to imbue the painting with more symbolism and mystery, which he hopes to achieve by using color more arbitrarily (see fig. 193). He envisions painting an artist's portrait in this way but doesn't yet have a model (L 520 [August?]). In September he realizes this portrait using Eugène Boch as the model (fig. 140).

September

In a letter to Theo on 3 September, Vincent speaks of portraiture and color:

"And in a picture I want to say something comforting, as music is comforting. I want to paint men and women with that something of the eternal which the halo used to symbolize, and which we seek to convey by the actual radiance and vibration of our coloring . . . Ah! portraiture, portraiture with the thoughts, the soul of the model in it, that is what I think must come" (L 531).

On 18 September Vincent moves into the Yellow House and begins a period of intense production. During this month he paints a portrait of his friend Paul-Eugène Milliet (the Zouave) and a self-portrait, which he describes in a letter to Gauguin: "I have a portrait of myself. All ash colored. The ashen-gray color that is the result of mixing malachite green with an orange hue, on pale malachite ground, all in harmony with the reddish-brown clothes. But as I also exaggerate my personality, I have in the first place aimed at the character of a simple bonze worshipping the Eternal Buddha" (L 544a) (fig. 129).

October

Vincent paints a portrait of his mother from a black and white photograph, adding color.

Vincent had initiated portrait exchanges with Gauguin and Bernard in September. Their paintings arrive in October. Vincent writes,

"I have just received the portrait of Gauguin by himself and the portrait of Bernard by Bernard, and in the background of the portrait of Gauguin there is Bernard's on the wall, and vice versa. So now at last I have a chance to compare my painting with what the comrades are doing. My portrait, which I am sending to Gauguin in exchange, holds its own, I am sure of that" (L 545, 4 October).

23 October

Gauguin finally arrives in Arles. For two months the two artists work productively together.

November

Vincent focuses on portraits, painting many in rapid succession, including Madame Ginoux, a very important person to Vincent in the last few years of his life. The first

117. *The Night Café* (F 463, JH 1575), early September 1888
Oil on canvas, 70 x 89 cm
New Haven, Connecticut, Yale University Art Gallery

118. *Portrait of Van Gogh's Mother* (F 477, JH 1600),
8 October 1888
Oil on canvas, 39.4 x 31.1 cm
Pasadena, California, Norton Simon Art Foundation

120. *The Bedroom* (F 482, JH 1608), mid-October 1888
Oil on canvas, 72 x 90 cm
Amsterdam, Van Gogh Museum

119. *Portrait of Camille Roulin* (F 537, JH 1644),
early December 1888
Oil on canvas, 43 x 35 cm
Philadelphia Museum of Art

"Ah! portraiture, portraiture
with the thoughts, the soul
of the model in it, that is what
I think must come."

September 1888

portrait is mentioned in a letter written on
6 November, where she is referred to as
"The Arlésienne" (L 559) (see fig. 148). He
also paints the postman Roulin and the rest
of his family—his wife, their baby girl, and
two sons (L 560) (see figs. 153–57).

In a letter dated 12 November, Vincent
describes a painting he has just completed
called *The Red Vineyard* (L 561). It is later
exhibited and sold at an exhibition in
Brussels in 1890.

During the second half of November he
finishes two symbolic portraits of Gauguin
and himself in the form of chairs. Vincent's
is "a wooden, rush-bottomed chair all
yellow on red tiles against a wall (daytime).
Then Gauguin's armchair, red and green
night effect, walls and floor red and green
again, on the seat two novels and a candle . . ."
(L 563) (figs. 151–52).

December
Gauguin gives Vincent a portrait he has
made of him as a painter of sunflowers.
Vincent is not pleased with the work.
In early December Theo becomes engaged
to Johanna Bonger, the sister of his good
friend Andries Bonger.

On 17 December Gauguin and Vincent
visit Montpellier for the day to see the
works by Eugène Delacroix and Gustave
Courbet in the Alfred Bruyas collection of
the Musée Fabre. After this time there is
evidence of a strain in Vincent and Gauguin's
relationship. On 23 December Vincent
admits, "I think myself that Gauguin was a
little out of sorts with the good town of
Arles, the little yellow house where we
work, and especially with me" (L 565).

Their strained relationship reaches a
breaking point with an argument later that
day. Gauguin spends the night in a hotel and
is thus unaware of the events that follow
until the next day. According to the local
newspaper, *Le Forum Républicain*:

121 and 122. Theo and Johanna van Gogh
Amsterdam, Van Gogh Museum

"And in a picture I want to say something comforting, as music is comforting."

September 1888

"Last Sunday night at half past eleven a painter named Vincent Vangogh [*sic*], a native of Holland, appeared at the *maison de tolérance* No. 1, asked for a girl called Rachel, and handed her . . . his ear with these words: 'Keep this object like a treasure.' Then he disappeared. The police, informed of the events, which could only be the work of an unfortunate madman, looked the next morning for the individual, whom they found in bed in a critical condition. The poor man was taken to the hospital without delay" (Hulsker 1996, p. 380).

24 December
Gauguin wires Theo, who rushes to Arles. Vincent is treated at the hospital by Dr. Félix Rey (fig. 128). The Reverend Frédéric Salles, from the Dutch Reformed church near the hospital, comes to watch over Vincent, probably at Theo's request.

26–27 December
Gauguin returns to Paris with Theo on 26 December. The next day Madame Roulin visits Vincent in the hospital, and that evening he has another attack.

31 December
The Reverend Salles writes to Theo that Vincent is calm and seems to be himself.

1889
January
On 1 January Vincent assures Theo that he is doing better and is sorry for having made him come to Arles (L 566). He recovers and resumes painting. Joseph Roulin visits often, keeping an eye on the yellow house in Vincent's absence. He escorts Vincent back to the yellow house for a short visit on 4 January. Roulin writes several letters to Theo, keeping him apprised of Vincent's recovery. Vincent leaves the hospital on 7 January and sends his congratulations to Theo on his engagement and requests more money to pay his hospital bills (L 570, 9 January). On 28 January, Vincent informs Theo that his health and work are progressing. He mentions replica paintings he is making, exact copies of *La Berceuse* and his sunflower paintings, of which he is particularly proud (L 574).

Joesph Roulin leaves for a new post in Marseilles on 21 January but cannot afford to move his family with him. During the next few months, he sees Vincent several times while returning to visit his wife and children in Arles. Vincent writes,

"Roulin, though he is not quite old enough to be like a father to me, nevertheless has a silent gravity and a tenderness for me such as an old soldier might have for a young one. All the time—but without a word— a something which seems to say, We do not know what will happen to us tomorrow but whatever it may be, think of me. And it does one good when it comes from a man who is neither embittered, nor sad, nor perfect, nor happy, nor always irreproachably just. But such a good soul and so wise and so full

123. *Portrait of a One-Eyed Man* (F 532, JH 1650),
December 1888
Oil on canvas, 56 x 36 cm
Amsterdam, Van Gogh Museum

of feeling and so trustful" (L 583, about
5 April).

February–March
Vincent has another breakdown involving
hallucinations, and on 7 February he is again
confined to the hospital. He is released
from the hospital on 17 February, but his
worried neighbors sign a petition
demanding that he remain hospitalized or
return home to his family. As a result,
Vincent is readmitted to the hospital on
25 February and confined to a private cell.
He does not leave the hospital until
23 March, when Paul Signac comes to visit.
Signac later writes to Theo, "I found your
brother in perfect health, physically and
mentally . . . He took me along to see his
pictures, many of which are very good, and
all of which are very curious. There is only
one thing he wishes—to be able to work in
tranquillity. So do your best to grant him
this happiness" (L 581a, 23 March).

By the end of March Vincent has completed
five versions of *La Berceuse* (see figs. 125 and
150).

April
On 17 April, Theo marries Johanna Bonger
in Amsterdam.

Vincent experiences attacks of his illness
intermittently in the winter and spring, and
in a letter of 21 April, he proposes going to
the hospital at St.-Rémy for a three-month
trial as suggested by the Reverend Salles.
Vincent feels incapable of living anywhere
alone and realizes that his primary objective
is to recover and paint in peace (L 585).

"Roulin, though he is not quite
old enough to be like a father to
me, nevertheless has a silent
gravity and tenderness for me
such as an old soldier might
have for a young one."

January 1889

124. *The Courtyard of the Hospital* (F 519, JH 1687), April 1889
Oil on canvas, 73 x 92 cm
Winterthur, Switzerland, Oskar Reinhart Collection "Am Römerholz"

125. *La Berceuse (Augustine Roulin)* (F 508, JH 1671), January/March 1889
Oil on canvas, 92.7 x 72.8 cm
Museum of Fine Arts, Boston

The Arles Period
Symbolic Means, Decorative Ends

ROLAND DORN

126. *The Baby Marcelle Roulin* (F 441, JH 1641), early December 1888
Oil on canvas, 35.5 x 24.5 cm
Amsterdam, Van Gogh Museum

The first painting van Gogh mentioned after his arrival in Arles in February 1888 was a study of an old woman, "une vieux Arlésienne" (fig. 127). Ten months later, when "illness came to interrupt his work," as he put it, another portrait stood unfinished on his easel: the postman's wife, which he called *La Berceuse* (fig. 125). After leaving the hospital, he again took up portraits, painting—among others—his physician Dr. Félix Rey (fig. 128) as well as two self-portraits.[1]

Portraits not only hold a prominent place in van Gogh's artistic biography during his stay in Arles, they also play an important role in his plan to start a "Studio of the South." As soon as he had rented the studio at 2, place Lamartine, he had the idea of sharing his "little yellow house" (*la petite maison jaune*) with one or another of his friends and colleagues, or at least using it as a place to exhibit their works. Later on, in the autumn of 1888, he suggested an exchange of portraits and finally received self-portraits from Emile Bernard, Paul Gauguin, and Charles Laval (figs. 106–8), while he himself supplied self-portraits to Gauguin (fig. 129) and Laval (fig. 130).[2]

Van Gogh also considered portraits to be a way of acquainting the people of Arles, who were "blankly ignorant of painting in general," with art. But during the first months of his stay in Arles, he did not dare start along that line. Exhausted by two years of living in Paris, he felt the need to calm down and recover his strength.[3]

So it was not before the end of June 1888, during a period of rainy days, that he turned again to portraiture, and it was almost another month before he expressed the wish to continue with a real series of figures. At this time, "portraits" and "figures"[4] began to occupy an important place in the letters he wrote to his brother Theo, his financier and closest confidant, as well as to others. Therefore, Theo was well informed when he summarized his brother's affinity for this subject matter in a letter to his sister Willemina on 6 December 1888: "In painting figures, he finds the highest expression of his art."[5]

The number of portraits van Gogh painted in Arles remained modest: little more than a dozen "figures" came together by November 1888, another dozen or so date from the last couple of weeks of this same year, and something less than a dozen were added during the first months of the following year. Compared to the total of some 170 paintings executed during the artist's stay in Arles, three dozen portraits does not sound very important.[6]

Examining van Gogh's correspondence, the reasons for this limited number become obvious. Again and again, he referred to his problems in finding models. Eventually, he even acquired a good mirror in order to get some practice by doing self-portraits. Evidently, he was not interested in just anyone who was willing to pose; his problem was, rather, securing the models of his choice.[7]

This interpretation of the artist's statements on portraiture is supported by the artistic and historical context. The year 1888 was decisive for van Gogh and his art, and his portrait series carries considerable weight; it was one of the most important projects in determining the course of his future work. The decisive period began in mid-August, and toward the end of October, when Gauguin arrived, van Gogh had found his way. In June, however, when he set out to work on his portraits and figures, he was anything but sure about either the means or the ends. It took a while before he was able to state, "sometimes I know so well what I want," adding, "I want to paint men or women with that something of the eternal which the halo used to symbolize, and which we seek to convey by the actual radiance, by the vibration of our coloring."[8] But even at the time he wrote this sentence, everything was in flux, nothing had settled.

Together with some related works, the eighteen or so portraits finished by December 1888 provide a key to a set of ideas that were evidently crucial for the artist himself, as he continuously referred to them in his letters. Nevertheless, these ideas were ignored by most of his critics, and almost purposefully neglected by those who tended to worship their hero under headings like "Genius and Disaster" and who preferred to contemplate "the power of the stream welling up from his unconscious self and sweeping him along without any chance of finding calmer waters."[9] A more cautious evaluation of van Gogh's legacy, both of his correspondence and of his oeuvre, seems to require a different approach, from more or less the opposite direction.

Fundamentals

Van Gogh's starting point was the intellect. The conviction that occasionally made him thoroughly and quickly reorient his ideas or suddenly change the appearance and style of his work throughout the ten years of his career was his unshakable belief that creation is based on rational thought. His contemporaries were fully aware of this. Paul Gauguin, for example, congratulated his friend and colleague on his exhibit at the Salon des Artistes Indépendants 1890 in Paris: "For many artists, you are the most remarkable at this exhibition. In

127. *An Old Woman of Arles* (F 390, JH 1357), February 1888
Oil on canvas, 55 x 43 cm
Amsterdam, Van Gogh Museum

128. *Doctor Félix Rey* (F 500, JH 1659), January 1889
Oil on canvas, 64 x 53 cm
Moscow, Pushkin State Museum of Fine Arts

129. *Self-Portrait Dedicated to Paul Gauguin* (F 476, JH 1581), mid-September 1888
Oil on canvas, 59.6 x 48.3 cm
Cambridge, Massachusetts, Fogg Art Museum, Harvard University

130. *Self-Portrait Dedicated to Charles Laval* (F 501, JH 1634), December 1888
Oil on canvas, 46 x 38 cm
Private Collection

things painted after nature, you are the only one who thinks."[10]

Van Gogh's way of thinking, based on chains of associations, was highly creative, but it had its limits. He was not used to controlling his conclusions to the very end and therefore was not immune to circular reasoning and other defects.[11] When defining himself, however, he left not the slightest doubt about what he considered were his individual and artistic intentions: ". . . to think, not to dream, is our duty."[12] For him, painting was intellectual brainwork *(travail mental)* based upon dry calculation *(calcul sec)* and required extreme effort. He saw himself working under conditions similar to those of "an actor on the stage in a difficult part, with a thousand things to think of at once in a single half hour."[13]

To think, not to dream—van Gogh knew why he insisted on this. Before he had definitely decided to become an artist, he had suffered a great deal from his own dreams— and the burnt hand teaches best. No profession could match his expectations as long as he lived under the sway of romanticism. At the age of twenty-six, van Gogh finally had to admit that all his sublime inspirations would remain infertile as long as he was unacquainted with even the most elementary skills. The romantic image of the genius, from whose pen or brush miracles emanate, added to his despair and almost paralyzed him for a whole year, from August 1879 to August 1880.

During that time of "moulting"—*temps de mue* was his own term—van Gogh came across several books that enabled him to overcome his romantic attitudes and to develop an intellectual habitus. After he had read Victor Hugo's comments on William Shakespeare and revisited Thomas Carlyle's *Past and Present,* he considered the artist to be, above all, a thinker and his labor to be a profession like any other profession.[14]

For the next three years, from 1880 to 1883, van Gogh's goal was to become a draftsman (*teekenaar,* the Dutch term van Gogh used, indicates a very modest position); he hoped to find employment at illustrated papers like *The Graphic, The Illustrated London News,* or *Harper's Monthly*. After a period of discouragement at the end of 1883, van Gogh revised his professional aims and reoriented himself toward the craft of a painter (*schilder, artiste-peintre*).

Like every "earthly craftsman" (Carlyle's term), van Gogh consciously developed a couple of working strategies to save time and secure efficiency, which he continued to use years later when he was at the height of his skills. At first glance, the three versions of the portrait of Augustine Roulin, the postman's wife (figs. 149, 150, and 155), appear to be as

"Sheer work and calculation, with one's mind strained to the utmost, like an actor on the stage in a difficult part, with a thousand things to think of at once in a single half hour."
July 1888

131. Tracing of three compositions: portraits of Augustine Roulin
(black: fig. 155, red: fig. 149, green: fig. 150)

independent from each other as they could be. Yet there is one element that links them together: the pose of the head.

A true-to-size redrawing of the three compositions (fig. 131) proves that van Gogh simply transferred the primary contours of the portrait from one canvas to the next: starting with a study in orange, brown, and green on a small size 15 canvas (fig. 155), he elaborated another version showing Mother Roulin with her daughter against a greenish background (fig. 149). On finishing this larger, size 30, canvas, van Gogh repainted the background, covering the green with a layer of yellow, and thus adapted the composition to a color scheme close to that of the smaller version. In a final step, the artist transferred the contours of the portrait to a second size 30 canvas—leaving out the child and concentrating again on just the mother (fig. 150)—and pushed the color scheme in the opposite direction. Basically, van Gogh had altered only one color—he turned the greenish yellow into intense green—to obtain a radical change.[15]

Simple procedures to gain surprising effects: this summary applies even more to a pattern of thinking that must be recognized if one is to understand van Gogh's work process. From the very beginning, he had a tendency to combine two or more items. For example, in the autumn of 1880 he copied two landscapes, which he considered to be counterparts, after Jacob van Ruisdael and Théodore Rousseau. *Pendants* was van Gogh's term for such a juxtaposition of individual works, which for him implied some kind of mutual explanation.[16]

The way in which this pattern is thought to work becomes transparent in the six lithographs of November 1882 (figs. 132–37). Van Gogh started with a standing old man in his best clothes (fig. 134), continued with a seated female nude (fig. 136), and followed this by a workman digging the ground (fig. 133). Thus, the first half of the set is based on simple contrasts of gender, clothing, and gesture: male/female, dressed/undressed, standing/sitting/working. The second half elaborates different aspects of the figures and suggests phases that continue the elements set out in the first part. The old man is now seen drinking a cup of coffee, still in his good clothes (fig. 132); then he takes his coat off and retires to a fireplace (fig. 135); while the workman rests and prepares his frugal lunch, with his shovel lying on the ground (fig. 137).

At this point, van Gogh's money ran out. Forced to stop taking lithographic proofs, he continued to produce drawings in preparation for a popular edition of "Prints for the People" (*volksuitgave, bladen voor het volk*), which he would have loved to publish. He describes this project as "a series of, for instance,

Above left
132. *Old Man Drinking Coffee* (F 1657, JH 266), November 1882
Lithograph, 57 x 37.5 cm
Amsterdam, Van Gogh Museum

Left
133. *Workman Digging* (F 1656, JH 262), November 1882
Lithograph, ink, and watercolor, 52 x 37 cm
Amsterdam, Van Gogh Museum

Above
134. *Old Man Standing* (F 1658, JH 256), November 1882
Lithograph, 61 x 39.5 cm
Amsterdam, Van Gogh Museum

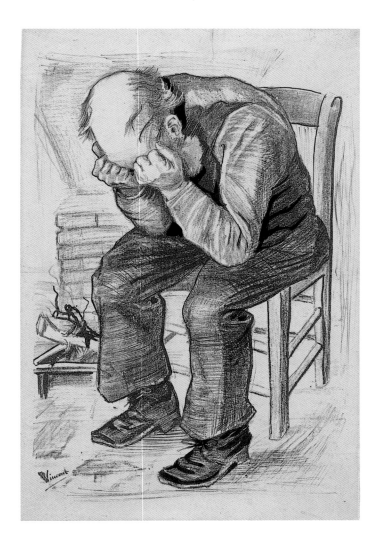

Top left
135. *Worn Out* (F 1662, JH 268), November 1882
Lithograph, 50 x 35 cm
Amsterdam, Van Gogh Museum

Left
136. *Sorrow* (F 1655, JH 259), November 1882
Lithograph, 38. 5 x 29 cm
Amsterdam, Van Gogh Museum

Above
137. *Workman Resting* (F 1663, JH 272), November 1882
Lithograph, 45 x 29 cm
Amsterdam, Van Gogh Museum

thirty sheets of workmen types—sower, digger, woodcutter, plowman, washerwoman, then also a child's cradle or a man from the almshouse," which together should form "some kind of a whole [*een soort geheel, un tout*]," that is, something that is more than the sum of its parts. In 1873 Jules Michelet's *L'Amour* had introduced van Gogh to this pattern of thought. Finally, Victor Hugo's treatise on Shakespeare had definitely confirmed the necessity for every artist to consider antithetical contrasts as conditions of the whole: *totus in antithesi*.[17]

The whole and its parts—pendants linked together by contrast: these are conceptual patterns which continue as a theme throughout van Gogh's work during the period in which he intended to become a draftsman and even for a while after he reoriented his professional aims toward painting. Then, in 1884, this theme was challenged by the academic pattern of the Salon piece, which meant, more or less, that van Gogh now had to tell in one single picture the story that he was used to splitting up into various pieces. So, after having chosen a theme, the next steps were to consider and work out a composition, to study in detail all the necessary parts until the final painting was executed. *The Potato Eaters* (fig. 23), which assumed its definitive form in April 1885, offers the best example of this kind of process.[18]

Although carefully prepared and executed with skill and passion, *The Potato Eaters* was severely criticized for its shortcomings in composition and elaboration, even by his most loyal friends. Self-critical enough to recognize his own weaknesses, van Gogh nevertheless kept this painting and at least some of the preceding studies, while a considerable number of his earlier attempts were granted no such reprieve. By destroying these,[19] he probably added even more to the fame of his first "masterpiece."

"I want to do figures, figures and more figures"—this was van Gogh's ideal.[20] Self-taught and reluctant to adopt academic methods, however, he had problems throughout his lifetime in drawing human hands, heads, and bodies. To remedy these shortcomings, he kept himself constantly busy sketching people in the open air, on the streets, in cafés. Furthermore, he insisted on working from a model and refused to create figure paintings that were not preceded by thorough studies from a model.[21]

In general, van Gogh acknowledged his faults quite frankly, but he was convinced of his right to see and represent things in his own way, especially when his intention was to convey a deeper meaning than one could see at first glance. For the color scheme of *The Potato Eaters,* for instance, he drew on a comment by Théophile Gautier on the work of Jean-François Millet: "His peasants seem to be painted with the earth they are sowing." That is, Millet's choice of color evidently implied meaning. Van Gogh delighted in this metaphorical approach, whether in taking up a pseudo-proletarian pencil (he preferred the carpenter's pencil, *timmermanspotlood*), using a certain kind of paper, which was watermarked *Eendragt maakt Magt* (unity makes force), or bemoaning the fact that bitumen was no longer used in spite of the admirable things that artists had done with it in earlier days.[22]

Metaphorical thought had been familiar to the pastor's son from his childhood days, when he had come across it in the parables of the New Testament as well as in the art of his time. All his life, van Gogh admired and preferred those artists who—like Rembrandt and Millet, or Jozef Israëls and Anton Mauve, the masters of the Hague School—took their subjects from reality but allowed the spectator a metaphoric reading, thus giving everyday objects a deeper meaning. This way of thinking undoubtedly became one of the most important instruments of van Gogh's approach.[23]

"Couleur suggestive"

From the moment van Gogh defined himself as a painter, color became the crucial element in his thinking. In the summer of 1882, when—still fully inspired by the idea of becoming a draftsman—he undertook his first independent attempts at painting on the beach at Scheveningen, he was already acquainted with the basic laws of color. He was, however, unable to apply their theoretical implications and instead, intuitively and innocently, leveled out the colors he perceived in nature with the pigments set on his palette. Two summers later, in 1884, van Gogh finally gained access to an intellectual use of color when the writings of Charles Blanc fell into his hands. In Blanc's *Les artistes de mon temps* and *Grammaire des arts du dessin,* van Gogh found what he needed: not only an instructive presentation of the law of complementary contrasts but also practical advice on its application.

From then onward Charles Blanc's color star served as his guide. This six-pointed star (fig. 138) is formed of the three primary and the three secondary colors. Each of the primary colors, yellow, red, and blue, stands across from its complement, the secondary color derived from the mixture of the two other primaries: yellow opposite violet (red and blue), red opposite green (yellow and blue), blue opposite orange (yellow and red). For about three years, van Gogh

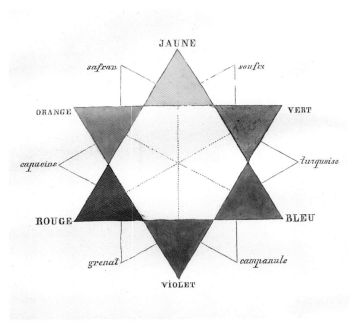

138. Color star from Charles Blanc, *Grammaire des arts du dessin: Architecture, sculpture, peinture* (Paris, 1867)
Reproduced from the second edition (Paris, 1870)

experimented with various palette settings and developed color strategies of his own. Then in 1887 he converted to the palette of the Parisian avant-garde with its pure, unadulterated pigments, which were supposed to be combined only via optical mixture, just like the spectral colors.

Light and pigment, theory and practice, however, did not come together right away. The most serious problem, from van Gogh's point of view, derived from the fact that when he proceeded this way, the complete potential of his palette served only one purpose: to reproduce an effect of light. The first version of the Arlesian *Sunflowers* (fig. 139) gives a brilliant example of such a fully colored impressionist graduation from light to dark. Yellow and orange, their blooms glow in a green vase before a background of turquoise. Light falls onto this arrangement from the front right, creating a shadow behind the vase, rendered with some touches of blue in the red-brown of the table on which the bouquet stands, surrounded by the colorful play of reflections in the glazed surfaces of the vase and the piece of furniture. Van Gogh would probably have considered this "recherche" on the effect of light a mere study, an "étude d'après nature," a proof of skill, a piece of handicraft and nothing else.

But Van Gogh wanted his painting to achieve far more and opted for a more arbitrary use of color, for "color suggesting ardour, temperament, any kind of emotion."[24] Shortly before he executed the "Sunflowers" series, he supplied the following example:

> I should like to paint the portrait of an artist friend, a man who dreams great dreams, who works as the nightingale sings, because it is his nature. He'll be a blond man. I want to put my appreciation, the love I have for him, into the picture.
>
> So I paint him as he is, as faithfully as I can, to begin with. But the picture is not yet finished. To finish it, I am now going to be the arbitrary colorist. I exaggerate the fairness of the hair, I even get to orange tones, chromes and pale citron-yellow.
>
> Behind the head, instead of painting the ordinary wall of the mean room, I paint infinity, a plain background of the richest blue that I can contrive, and by this simple combination the bright head against the rich blue background gets a mysterious effect, like a star in the sky, in the depths of azure.[25]

Van Gogh intended to visualize his feelings, his friendship, and his admiration. As abstractions cannot be copied from nature, he formulated a "poetic idea" to express his meaning, that is, he came upon the metaphor of a star in the night and thereby achieved an effect of light that was to be rendered

139. *Sunflowers*, first version (F 453, JH 1559), late August 1888
Oil on canvas, 73 x 58 cm
Private Collection

with the strongest contrast his palette offered, lightest yellow and deepest blue.

In similar ways, van Gogh intended to visualize other poetic ideas. For example, he wanted "To express the love of two lovers by a marriage of two complementary colors, their mingling and their opposition, the mysterious vibrations of kindred tones. To express the thought of a brow by the radiance of a light tone against a somber background; to express hope by some star, the eagerness of a soul by a sunset radiance."[26] But long before he formulated this metaphorical approach, van Gogh feared he might tumble into "pure metaphysics of color, a mess that is damnably difficult to get out of with honor."[27]

When van Gogh finally decided to take this approach, he was not at all shy of making such metaphors quite conspicuous. In the early days of September 1888, when van Gogh finally found in his fellow artist, Eugène Boch, a model who corresponded to his idea of an artist friend, he indeed placed several stars in the background of his portrait (fig. 140), although he added dark green shades to the hair, instead of making it blond. The head, furthermore, received a "halo" of yellow, which visibly connotes the gleaming of a star, "so that, to the last, everybody who has eyes could understand."[28]

"Décoration"

In October 1888, the portrait of Boch was hanging in van Gogh's bedroom, next to the portrait of his friend Paul-Eugène Milliet (fig. 141), which he had just completed. This arrangement was part of a significantly more comprehensive series of paintings, the *Décoration*, which van Gogh conceived for the Yellow House, his home and atelier in Arles.[29] By this time, the portrait of Boch, "this young man with the look of Dante,"[30] was already labeled *The Poet*, and van Gogh had indicated that Lieutenant Milliet, apparently a heart-throb among the ladies of the Arlesian demimonde, would fit his idea for the painting of lovers.

Poet and Lover, contemplation and activity, *vita contemplativa* and *vita attiva*: this pairing of opposites is well known, indeed, classical. When the two works are displayed side by side, the artist's use of color supports this metaphorical connection. Each of the two portraits is dominated by the contrast of complementary colors which is taken up as a counterpoint in the other one: the yellowish orange and blue in Milliet's uniform cap, the red and green in Boch's tie.

Decoration, considered in this way, was anything but a mere design for walls; rather it offered an opportunity to create meaning by combining individual paintings. In the end,

"To express the thought of
a brow by the radiance of a light
tone against a somber background;
to express hope by some star, the
eagerness of a soul by a sunset
radiance."

September 1888

van Gogh's *Décoration* for the Yellow House comprised the pendants of sunflowers, some portraits, and a series of more than thirty canvases. In addition to color references (applied primarily in portraits), contrasts of form and subject matter served as links between these paintings, all on size 30 canvases: simple contrasts—such as near and far, interior and exterior, open and closed, old and new, day and night, public and private—which by combination served as points of departure for the development of further links, resulting in a kind of pictorial syntax.

Thus the idea of contrast was extended from color to form and became the omnipresent abstract element, the "principe ornemental," which, as van Gogh had learned from Félix Bracquemond's pamphlet *Du dessin et de la couleur,* was essential for every kind of decoration. When van Gogh started work on his *Décoration*, he evidently thought of extending this principle to contrasting room arrangements: a few large paintings were to serve in small rooms, and many small ones in the larger rooms. But even in the early stages, he refrained from doing this and opted for a more balanced solution. Eventually "Toile de 30 figure" became the standard size for the paintings conceived for the *Décoration,* and this standard size further strengthened its visual unity, making it perceivable as a whole *(le tout).*

In its general disposition, van Gogh's *Décoration* adapted strategies from contemporary literature, particularly from such well-known series of novels as *La comédie humaine* by Honoré de Balzac and *Les Rougon-Macquart* by Emile Zola. Both Balzac and Zola were among van Gogh's favorite authors; he referred extensively to both during his stay in Arles, where he even began to re-read Balzac and never ceased to comment on Zola. Van Gogh was convinced, as were Zola and Balzac, that modern reality in all its complexity could not be rendered in one definitive *chef-d'oeuvre,* and when he finally started to work on his *Décoration*, he chose instead a reasoned and analytical approach. Following in their footsteps, he devised a coherent series of images to depict the thoughts, motions, and passions of modern society.

Van Gogh's concept of decoration, therefore, not only mastered the crisis of the *chef-d'oeuvre,* as Hans Belting recently acknowledged,[31] but also established a permanent framework for his future work. Even when, with Gauguin's departure and the end of the Studio of the South, the primary reason for the *Décoration* vanished, its general disposition enabled van Gogh to continue his work on this "series of studies 'Impressions of Provence.'"[32]

140. *The Poet: Eugène Boch* (F 462, JH 1574), early September 1888
Oil on canvas, 60 x 45 cm
Paris, Musée d'Orsay

141. *The Lover: Paul-Eugène Milliet* (F 473, JH 1588), late September 1888
Oil on canvas, 60 x 50 cm
Otterlo, Collection Kröller-Müller Museum

"La série des Figures"

Some of the ideas that van Gogh incorporated, from the end of August 1888 onward, into his concept of decoration are prefigured in his statements on the portraits and figures created in the preceding months. Color symbolism, for example, "a symbolic language of color itself," is first discussed at the end of June 1888, while van Gogh was working on the "portrait" and the "figure" of a Zouave (figs. 142 and 144), and a little later he considered painting landscapes in series linked by the dominant color of each season.[33] Then, closer to the road van Gogh was later to take, he conceived of a portrait which he entitled *La Mousmé* (fig. 143). While his model was a young girl from Arles, the title of the painting is a reference to the female protagonist of *Madame Chrysanthème,* a novel by Pierre Loti (Paris, 1888). Van Gogh's title, however, does not actually refer to Loti's figure, a young Japanese girl, but to her profession, which was, according to Loti, to serve as wife to a member of the colonial troops through a temporary marriage. So, setting *La Mousmé* against *The Zouave,* the French colonial soldier par excellence, obviously echoes the plot of Loti's novel (which at a later date was also to inspire the scenario of van Gogh's *Starry Sky* [F 474]).[34]

Continuing his series of figures, van Gogh chose a local postman—Joseph Roulin (fig. 145)—and a gypsy woman (fig. 146)[35] as models, as well as a former cowherd of the Camargue, then a gardener in Arles, whom he intended to represent "The Old Peasant" (fig. 193). In this way, bringing together the various types of people he met in his neighborhood, he established something similar to *La rue,* a set of illustrations by Jean-François Raffaëlli featuring the crowds and street people of Montmartre (fig. 147). Van Gogh referred to Raffaëlli's illustrations long after their publication in *Le Figaro supplément littéraire* but just at the time when he was busy with his Zouave.[36] Seemingly, in taking up literary as well as pictorial inspirations, van Gogh had in mind a framework similar to his later concept of decoration. The main difference is that there is no standard size to connect this early series of figures.[37]

Significantly, van Gogh's later portraits shift to the size 30 standard of the *Décoration* phase and again reflect already well-known topics. The portrait of Madame Ginoux, posing in the elegant local attire with her gloves and parasol coquettishly spread on the table, was entitled by the artist *L'Arlésienne* (fig. 148), thus reflecting Alphonse Daudet's famous femme fatale,[38] while both portraits of Madame Roulin are references to motherhood. Correspondingly, the pictorial concept of the

"I have a model at last
—a Zouave—a boy with
a small face, a bull-neck
and the eye of a tiger."
June 1888

142. *The Zouave, Bust* (F 423, JH 1486), June 1888
Oil on canvas, 65 x 54 cm
Amsterdam, Van Gogh Museum

143. *La Mousmé* (F 431, JH 1519), July 1888
Oil on canvas, 73.3 x 60.3 cm
Washington, D.C., National Gallery of Art

144. *The Zouave* (F 424, JH 1488), June 1888
Oil on canvas, 81 x 65 cm
Private Collection

145. *The Postman: Joseph Roulin* (F 432, JH 1522), late July/early August 1888
Oil on canvas, 81.2 x 65.3 cm
Museum of Fine Arts, Boston

146. *The Gypsy Woman*, also known as *L'Italienne* (F 381, JH 1355), end of August 1888
Oil on canvas, 81 x 60 cm
Paris, Musée d'Orsay

147. Jean-François Raffaëlli, *La rue*
Title page from *Le Figaro supplément littéraire*, 3 March 1888

first version of the mother with her baby (fig. 149) emphasizes
the bright side, while that of *L'Arlésienne* literally represents
the dark side of woman. Finally, in *La Berceuse* (fig. 150) the
use of contrast expands to include dissonant schemes of color
and light: Mother Roulin's yellow head illuminates a private
interior, while Madame Ginoux is exposed to the light of
a public coffee house.

At about the same time, in mid-November 1888,
van Gogh added to his "Décoration" series a highly ironical
pair of portraits without human figures. In these works,
derived from a conversation piece that he split up into two
complementary compositions (day and night, natural
and artificial light), the artist arranged a symbolic
conversation between his own chair, odd and simple
(fig. 151), and the elegant armchair of his friend Gauguin
(fig. 152).[39] Again, a very simple trick, one which led to
surprising results when van Gogh returned to real portraits,
for which the postman Roulin and his family posed in late
November 1888.

148. *L'Arlésienne (Marie Ginoux)* (F 489, JH 1625), early November 1888
Oil on canvas, 93 x 74 cm
Paris, Musée d'Orsay

149. *Augustine Roulin with Her Baby* (F 490, JH 1637), December 1888
Oil on canvas, 92.4 x 73.3 cm
Philadelphia Museum of Art

150. *La Berceuse (Augustine Roulin)*, first version (F 504, JH 1655), late December 1888
Oil on canvas, 92 × 73 cm
Otterlo, Collection Kröller-Müller Museum

151. *Van Gogh's Chair* (F 498, JH 1635), mid-November 1888
Oil on canvas, 93 x 73.5 cm
London, National Gallery

152. *Gauguin's Arm Chair* (F 499, JH 1636), mid-November 1888
Oil on canvas, 90.5 x 72 cm
Amsterdam, Van Gogh Museum

"La Famille Roulin"

Van Gogh himself confessed that his work from the autumn of 1888 onward could be considered a rebirth of ideas he had already had in his early days in Holland.[40] There is no better proof of this than another set of portraits, which he announced to his brother at the beginning of December 1888:

> I have made portraits of *a whole family*, that of the postman . . . the man, his wife, the baby, the little boy, and the son of sixteen, all characters and very French, though the first has the look of a Russian. Size 15 canvases. You know how I feel about this, how I feel in my element, and that it consoles me up to a certain point for not being a doctor. I hope to get on with this and to be able to get more careful posing, paid for by portraits. And if I manage to do *this whole family* better still, at least I shall have done something to my liking and something individual.[41]

Van Gogh mentioned twice that he was dealing with "a whole family," and in both cases he explicitly underlined his words: *toute une famille, toute cette famille.*

It is surely no coincidence that the complementary colors of Charles Blanc's six-pointed star dominate the five portraits of the family Roulin, although the complementary pairings are spread out among the five paintings (figs. 153–57): Armand Roulin (fig. 154), the eldest son, is painted in a dark blue jacket against a green background; Joseph Roulin (fig. 153), his father, in an ultramarine uniform against yellow; the mother (fig. 155), dressed in green, is set against orange, the baby Marcelle (fig. 157) in white against yellow-orange; and Camille (fig. 156) in blue against red and orange.[42]

There is only one obvious complementary contrast set up between two of these works: that between the backgrounds of the portraits of Camille and Armand. But there is another color

 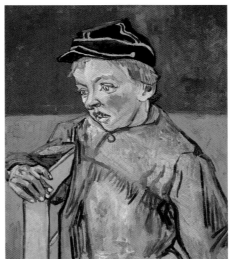 

"I have made portraits of *a whole family*, that of the postman . . . the man, his wife, the baby, the little boy, and the son of sixteen, all characters and very French."

December 1888

setting that evidently implies meaning: the youngest child of the Roulins is dressed in white, the oldest in deep blue-black, and the second-oldest, Camille, in a color derived from a mixture of deep, pure blue and white—a bright light blue.

Furthermore, reference to Blanc's color star allows not only for a reading via complementary colors but also a reading via the neighboring values *(couleurs semblables)*. Thus yellow and orange are allocated to the parents; a third and similar color value links the baby to the parents. Red and green set aside the two elder children and signal their individuality, independence, and—due to the complementary nature of these colors—their relationship to each other. The orange in the background of the baby's portrait indicates her still-close relationship to the core of the family.

What else? Does van Gogh's choice of a vertical format for the portrait of the father and a horizontal format for that of the mother refer to the individuality of the parents? Or would that be a step too far toward over-interpretation? The peril of metaphorizing pictorial means becomes obvious: interpretation must, in the end, be left to the discretion of the beholder.

Van Gogh wanted to paint in a way "that, to the last, everybody who has eyes could understand." It is up to us to learn to read his pictorial means. In this case, the color scheme leaves no doubt that the five Roulin portraits constitute a related whole, a five-fold portrait of a family. This brings these five canvases of modest size into close relationship to *The Potato Eaters* of 1885, which van Gogh recalled in August 1888 when he had the idea for *The Poet*. Some time later, in St.-Rémy, he even considered redoing the composition from memory *(de tête)*.[43]

In *The Potato Eaters* van Gogh had represented another five-strong family: peasants gathered around a modest meal

153. *The Father: Joseph Roulin* (F 434, JH 1647),
last week of November and prior to 2 December 1888
Oil on canvas, 65 x 54 cm
Winterthur, Switzerland, Kunstmuseum

154. *The Older Son: Armand Roulin* (F 493, JH 1643),
last week of November and prior to 2 December 1888
Oil on canvas, 65 x 54 cm
Rotterdam, Museum Boijmans Van Beuningen

155. *The Mother: Augustine Roulin* (F 503, JH 1646),
last week of November and prior to 2 December 1888
Oil on canvas, 55 x 65 cm
Winterthur, Switzerland, Oskar Reinhart Collection "Am Römerholz"

consisting of potatoes and malt coffee. The light of a single gas
flame reveals more of the interior, the table, and the objects on
the walls of the cottage than of its inhabitants. Shadows
dominate dull faces, work-worn hands, eloquent gestures,
depressing silence. Darkness has obscured almost everything
individual in these figures. The light they catch distorts their
profiles, heads, and limbs so that they almost become
caricatures. Van Gogh himself likened such faces to animals
such as cows, crows, and pigs rather than human beings,[44] and,
even more significantly, he did not even mention the name of
this family from the Dutch province of Brabant.

156. *The Young Boy: Camille Roulin* (F 665, JH 1879),
last week of November and prior to 2 December 1888
Oil on canvas, 63.5 x 54 cm
Museo de arte de São Paulo Assis Chateaubriand

Compared to the artist, the Roulins were poor. While van Gogh could not manage to live on the 250 francs a month he received from Theo (although he did not even have to pay for painting materials out of this), Joseph Roulin housed and fed a wife and three children on 135 francs, the salary he received as *Entreposeur des postes* at the railway station of Arles.[45] Roulin was "a man of sorrow" and he and his family were "acquainted with grief."[46] But now van Gogh allowed his compassion, which had thoroughly darkened *The Potato Eaters,* to manifest itself only verbally—in just half a sentence referring to the "Russian" appearance of the Roulins. Theo was expected to connect this remark with a newspaper clipping his brother had sent him in September 1888, deeply impressed by the description of Dostoyevsky it contained: "Dostoievsky's face was that of a Russian peasant: flat nose, small flashing eyes, a broad forehead furrowed by scars and pimples, the temples dented as if shaped with a hammer. Never have I seen, Monsieur de Vogüé says, a similar expression of accumulated suffering on a human face."[47]

In portraying Roulin and his family, van Gogh took an approach that allowed them to retain their individuality, dignity, and self-confidence. Each of them is shown in a different pose: the mother simply rests in her armchair, while the father leans back slightly; the elder son turns aside; his younger brother squirms on his chair; and the baby—unable to pose without help—gets assistance from her mother. *Il reste à être vrai,* surely.[48]

Painted within the space of a few days, late in November 1888, the original set of five portraits shows a certain degree of unevenness in execution. Van Gogh frankly admitted the need for "more serious poses," and someday he hoped to improve "this whole family." Evidently, he did record more poses of each member of the family in the course of December 1888, but then there was no time left to re-edit "the whole."[49]

Nevertheless, when he announced completion of the first set, van Gogh was well aware that he had already succeeded in contributing "something personal" to his oeuvre and to art in general. As unconditionally as Emile Zola had dissected a family of the Second Empire in his famous series of novels,[50] so, soberly and in such modern terms, did van Gogh illuminate—to paraphrase Zola's subtitle—the "natural and social history of a family under the Third Republic" in a simple set of five modest portraits, linked by a metaphorical setting of color which transcribes the fundamental relations, the inner unity of a family. A blast of fresh air, of modern color, modern theory, and modern thought has taken away the smell of "poor-people-portrayed" from this reprise of *The Potato Eaters*: in the Roulin Family, van Gogh gave us his own Rougon-Macquarts.

157. *The Baby: Marcelle Roulin* (F 491, JH 1638), detail, last week of November and prior to 2 December 1888
Oil on canvas, 63.5 x 51 cm
New York. The Metropolitan Museum of Art

St.-Rémy and Auvers

May 1889–October 1890

CHRONOLOGY

St.-Rémy and Auvers

May 1889–October 1890

KATHERINE SACHS

159. The asylum of St.-Paul-de Mausole, ca. 1950s
Amsterdam, Van Gogh Museum

"I think I have done well to come here . . . I am losing the . . . fear of the thing. And little by little I can come to look upon madness as a disease like any other. Then the change of surroundings does me good, I think."

May 1889

Previous spread
158. *Enclosed Field in the Rain* (F 650, JH 1839), detail, ca. 2 November 1889
Oil on canvas, 73.3 x 92.4 cm
Philadelphia Museum of Art

1889

May

Vincent leaves Arles on 8 May for the asylum of St.-Paul-de-Mausole in St.-Rémy-de-Provence, accompanied by the Reverend Salles.

In the hospital, Vincent is given a second room as a studio. He soon begins to paint the enclosed wheat field, the view from his window. About 15 May Vincent writes his first letter to Theo from St.-Rémy: "I think I have done well to come here . . . I am losing the . . . fear of the thing. And little by little I can come to look upon madness as a disease like any other. Then the change of surroundings does me good, I think" (L 591). In a subsequent letter, Vincent asks Theo to give a copy of *La Berceuse* to Paul Gauguin and one to Emile Bernard (L 592).

Vincent suffers periodically from his illness at St.-Rémy but is able to work between episodes. His doctors consider his sickness a form of epilepsy. (There has been much speculation among scholars as to the cause of Vincent's illness, with schizophrenia suggested, as well as other factors that may have exacerbated the epilepsy, such as the consumption of alcohol, particularly absinthe, and the effects of syphilis [McQuillan 1989, p. 9]).

June

Dr. Théophile Peyron, the director of the asylum, allows Vincent to work outside the confines of the hospital. He paints the wheat field and cypresses.

July

Johanna writes Vincent,

"I am now going to tell you a great piece of news, on which we have concentrated a good deal of attention lately—it is that next winter, toward February, probably, we hope to have a baby, a pretty little boy— whom we are going to call Vincent, if you

160. *Window of Vincent's Studio at the Asylum* (F 1528, JH 1807), ca. 5–22 October 1889
Chalk and gouache, 61.5 x 47 cm
Amsterdam, Van Gogh Museum

will kindly consent to be his godfather. Of course . . . it may well be a little girl . . . Do you remember the portrait of the Roulin baby you sent to Theo? Everyone admires it greatly and people have asked me many times, 'Why have you put this portrait into such an out of the way corner?' The reason is that from my place at the table I can just see the big blue eyes and the pretty little hands and the round cheeks of the baby, and I like to imagine that ours will be equally strong . . . and that his uncle will come one day to paint his portrait" (LT 11, 5 July).

On 7 July Vincent goes to Arles for the day to collect some of his paintings and to oversee the storage of his furniture. Possibly the stress caused by this journey triggers another attack about 16 July. This incident occurs while he is outside painting in the fields. He is reported to have eaten some of his paints.

Meanwhile, in Paris, Theo rents a small room from Tanguy in which to store Vincent's paintings.

161. *Hospital at St.-Rémy* (F 643, JH 1799), 5 October 1889
Oil on canvas, 90.2 x 71.1 cm
Los Angeles, The Armand Hammer Museum of Art and Cultural Center

"I am working like one actually possessed, more than ever I am in a dumb fury of work. And I think that this will help cure me . . . I [want to be] capable of doing a portrait that has some character."

September 1889

Theo writes Vincent that his paintings are being well received. Octave Maus, the secretary of the exhibition "Les XX" in Brussels has asked if he would be willing to send in work for the next exhibition. In general, people like the night effect and the sunflowers (LT 12, 16 July).

August

Not having received a letter from Vincent in some time, Theo learns of his mid-July attack from Dr. Peyron. For five weeks the artist's condition is so serious that he is unable to paint. Vincent slowly recovers and in late August is able to paint again, but he still suffers from nightmares.

September

In early September Vincent indicates that he will be happy to participate in "Les XX" in Brussels and writes of what he has been doing: "I am working on two portraits of myself at this moment—for want of another model—because it is more than time I did a little figure work . . . I am working like one actually possessed, more than ever I am in a dumb fury of work. And I think that this will help cure me . . . I [want to be] capable of doing a portrait that has some character" (L 604). He paints a portrait of Trabuc, the head attandant at the asylum (fig. 171), with whom he has regular contact.

On 5 September Theo writes to his brother from Paris to tell him that two of his pictures, *Irises* and *Starry Sky* are being shown at the fifth exhibition of the Artistes Indépendants (LT 16). Vincent writes on 7 or 8 September that he has not been in the open air for two months (L 605). During this time, working indoors, he has produced many copies after Jean-François Millet and Eugène Delacroix.

In a letter to his mother Vincent writes, "As often as I have the chance, I work at portraits, which I myself sometimes think are better and more serious than the rest of my work" (L 606, 19 September).

October

By early October Vincent is again working outside, but his desire to leave the asylum increases. Theo writes that he has learned from Pissarro of a Dr. Gachet in Auvers, a heart specialist who is also a painter. However, "Dr. Peyron came to see me . . . He told me that, seeing that your trip to Arles provoked a crisis, it is necessary to ascertain, before you go to live elsewhere,

162. *Portrait of a Farmer* (F 531, JH 1779), mid-September 1889
Oil on canvas, 61 x 50 cm
Rome, Galleria d'Arte Moderna

De Portefeuille, that speaks highly of Vincent and his work (Hulsker 1996, p. 418). Vincent finds the article unsettling and entreats Theo to tell Isaäcson not to write about him again.

December

Vincent has another violent attack and suffers a relapse in the last week of December. He is confined and allowed to draw but not to paint for fear that he might again eat his paints.

1890

January

In a letter to Madame Ginoux, who is ill, Vincent offers encouraging advice:

"Personally I believe that the adversities one meets with in the ordinary course of life do us as much good as harm. The very complaint that makes one ill today . . . gives us the energy to get up and to want to be completely recovered tomorrow . . . I assure you that last year I almost hated the idea of regaining my health . . . always living in fear of relapses . . . it seems that what matters is that one should learn to go on living, even when suffering . . . In my own case my disease has done me good—it would be ungrateful not to acknowledge it. It has made me easier in my mind, and is wholly different from what I expected and imagined; this year I have had better luck than I dared hope for" (L 622a, early January).

Vincent visits Madame Ginoux in Arles on 19 January. On 21 January he has another attack.

22 January

Theo writes to Vincent from Paris,

"It seems that the exhibition of the 'XX' at Brussels is open; I read in a paper that the canvases which arouse the curiosity of the public the most are the open-air study by Cézanne, the landscapes of Sisley, the

whether you can bear a change. If you can stand these tests, he sees no objection to your leaving" (LT 18). Vincent responds, "What you say of Auvers is nevertheless a very pleasant prospect . . . The main thing is to know the doctor, so that in case of an attack I do not fall into the hands of the police and get carried off to an asylum by force. And I assure you that the North will interest me like a new country" (L 609).

On 22 October Theo sends an article "Opinions about Dutch Art at the Paris World Fair," by J. J. Isaäcson, published in

163. Johanna van Gogh-Bonger and her son,
Vincent Willem
Amsterdam, Van Gogh Museum

symphonies by Van Gogh and the works of Renoir. For the month of March they are preparing a new exhibition of the impressionists at the pavilion of the 'Ville de Paris.' Everyone can send in as many canvases as he likes . . . Please think over whether you will exhibit too, and which pictures you want to send . . . I think we can wait patiently for success to come; you will surely live to see it . . . it will come of its own accord by reason of your beautiful pictures" (LT 25).

31 January

Theo and Johanna's son, named after Vincent, is born.

February

Vincent writes to Theo, "Today I received your good news that you are at last a father . . . I was extremely surprised at the article on my pictures which you sent me . . ." (a reference to the article "Les Isolés: Vincent Van Gogh," written by Albert

Aurier praising Vincent's work) (L 625, 1 February).

Vincent responds to Aurier, saying, "Many thanks for your article in the *Mercure de France*, which greatly surprised me. I like it very much as a work of art in itself, in my opinion your words produce color, in short, I rediscover my canvases in your article, but better than they are, richer, more full of meaning" (L 626a).

15 February

Vincent tells his mother that one of his pictures from "Les XX" sold for four hundred francs. He also describes a painting intended for his nephew: "I started right away to make a picture for him, to hang in their bedroom, big branches of white almond blossom against a blue sky" (L 627).

22 February

Vincent goes to Arles to visit Madame Ginoux. He wants to present her with one of the five portraits he has painted of her

"In my own case my disease has done me good—it would be ungrateful not to acknowledge it. It has made me easier in my mind, and is wholly different from what I expected and imagined; this year I have had better luck than I dared hope for."

January 1890

164. *The Road Menders* (F 658, JH 1861), December 1889
Oil on canvas, 73.6 x 92.7 cm
Washington, D.C., The Phillips Collection

from an 1888 drawing by Gauguin. During this visit he has another attack, and Dr. Peyron sends a carriage to bring him back to the asylum. Recovery takes two months, during which time he is able to paint, mostly people and places from memory.

19 March–27 April

Theo exhibits at least ten of Vincent's paintings at the exhibition of the Artistes Indépendants in Paris.

29 March

Theo writes to wish Vincent a happy birthday. Vincent will be thirty-seven years old on 30 March. Theo tells him that he has met Dr. Gachet, the physician from Auvers, and feels that he is a man of understanding, who may be able to help Vincent (LT 31).

23 April

Theo writes, "Your silence proves to us that you are still suffering, and I feel urgently impelled to tell you, my dear, brother, that Jo and I suffer too because we know that you are ill . . . Monet said that your pictures were the best of all in the exhibition . . ." (LT 32).

29 April

Vincent tells Theo that he is feeling a bit better and very much wants to leave the hospital at St.-Rémy (L 629).

May

"What consoles me is the great, very great desire I have to see you again, you and your wife and child, and the many friends who remembered me in my misfortune, as indeed I too never cease thinking of them. I am almost certain that in the North I shall get well quickly . . . I have more ideas in my head than I could ever carry out, but without it clouding my mind" (L 630).

In his last weeks at St.-Rémy, Vincent paints eleven pictures, including a copy after Rembrandt's *The Raising of Lazarus*

(fig. 180), a copy of Delacroix's *Good Samaritan,* landscapes, and flower paintings.

Vincent leaves St.-Rémy on 16 May and arrives the next day in Paris, where he remains for three days. Theo picks him up at the station. He meets Theo's wife Johanna for the first time and sees his new nephew Vincent. Johanna recalls:

"I had expected a sick man, but here was a sturdy, broad-shouldered man, with a healthy color, a smile on his face, and a very resolute appearance; of all the self-portraits, the one before the easel is most like him at that period . . . Then Theo drew him into the room where our little boy's cradle was; he had been named after Vincent. Silently the two brothers looked at the quietly sleeping baby—both had tears in their eyes . . . He stayed with us three days and was cheerful and lively all the time . . . The first morning he was up very early and was . . . looking at his pictures, of which our apartment was full. The walls were covered with them . . . and there were more under the bed, under the sofa, under the cupboards . . . huge piles of unframed canvases; they were now spread out on the ground and studied with great attention" (van Gogh 1958, pp. L–LI).

18 May

Vincent and Theo visit Tanguy's shop, where Theo has rented a room to store their works of art, which include drawings and paintings by Vincent, as well as by other artists.

AUVERS

20 May

Vincent arrives in Auvers-sur-Oise, just north of Paris, where he stays at an inn, the Auberge Ravoux. Under the supervision of Dr. Gachet he continues to paint.

Early June

His first letter of June is to Theo and Jo:

165. *Houses at Auvers* (F 759, JH 1988), late May 1890
Oil on canvas, 60 x 73 cm
Ohio, Toledo Museum of Art

166. Ravoux's Inn, Auvers-sur-Oise, 1890
Amsterdam, Van Gogh Museum

"I am working at his [Dr. Gachet's] portrait, the head with a white cap, very fair, very light, the hands also a light flesh tint, a blue frock coat and a cobalt blue background, leaning on a red table, on which are a yellow book and a foxglove plant with purple flowers. It has the same sentiment as the self-portrait I did when I left for this place. Mr. Gachet is absolutely *fanatical* about this portrait, and wants me to do one for him, if I can, exactly like it . . . I shall most probably do the portrait of his daughter . . . Then I am looking forward to doing the portraits of all of you in the open air; yours, Jo's and the little one's" (L 638) (fig. 198).

Around 3 or 4 June, Vincent discusses his passion for portraiture in a letter to his sister Wil (see essay by Joseph Rishel in this volume for quote from LW 22).

Theo, Johanna, and the baby visit Vincent at Dr. Gachet's invitation on 8 June. Vincent is extremely productive in the early part of

the summer, averaging a painting per day. He paints scenes from the countryside, still-lifes, and portraits of the people he meets in Auvers.

24 June

Vincent describes his portrait of Adeline Ravoux (fig. 196): "Last week I did a portrait of a girl of about sixteen, in blue against a blue background, the daughter of the people with whom I am staying. I have given her this portrait, but I made a variant of it for you" (L 644) . In addition to Dr. Gachet, Vincent paints a portrait of his daughter Marguerite (fig. 194).

Theo writes to Vincent on 30 June that all is not well. The baby has been very ill, and Theo is having a difficult time at Boussod and Valadon and is considering becoming a private dealer (LT 39). Vincent responds immediately and arrives in Paris on 6 July. It is a difficult stay, however, as the baby is still not well, Theo is nervous about the future, and Vincent is not happy about how his pictures are being stored. Toulouse-Lautrec and Aurier come for lunch, but Vincent hurriedly returns to Auvers that afternoon, not waiting for an anticipated visit from Armand Guillaumin.

14 July

Theo accompanies his wife and recovering son to Leiden for a holiday with his mother, but he is only able to stay for two days. He leaves for Antwerp and then returns to Paris on 19 July, only to find that his request for a raise had been denied. On 20 July he writes to Johanna about Vincent: "I hope he is not getting melancholy or that a new attack is threatening again, everything has gone so well lately" (van Gogh 1958, p. LII).

23 July

Vincent writes Theo,

"Perhaps I'd rather write you about a lot of things, but to begin with, the desire to do so has completely left me, and then I feel it is

167. *Bank of the Oise at Auvers* (F 798, JH 2021), June 1890
Oil on canvas, 73.3 x 93.7 cm
The Detroit Institute of Arts

"Perhaps I'd rather write you about a lot of things, but to begin with, the desire to do so has completely left me, and then I feel it is useless . . . As far as I'm concerned, I apply myself to my canvases with all my mind, I am trying to do as well as certain painters whom I have greatly loved and admired . . . what I think is that the painters themselves are fighting more and more with their backs to the wall."

July 1890

useless . . . As far as I'm concerned, I apply myself to my canvases with all my mind, I am trying to do as well as certain painters whom I have greatly loved and admired . . . what I think is that the painters themselves are fighting more and more with their backs to the wall" (L 651).

In this last letter sent to Theo, Vincent sends a list of painting supplies he needs, indicating that he is planning future work.

25 July

In response to this letter, Theo writes to Johanna, "I have a letter from Vincent which seems quite incomprehensible; when will there come a happy time for him? He is so thoroughly good" (van Gogh 1958, p. LII).

27 July

In the wheat fields near Auvers, Vincent shoots himself in the chest with a revolver. He staggers back to the inn and Dr. Gachet is called. The doctor summons Theo, but he

sends the note to the gallery, and Theo does not receive it until the following day. He immediately leaves for Auvers. Upon arrival Theo writes to Johanna in Amsterdam, "We are all together . . . poor fellow, very little happiness fell to his share, and no illusions are left to him . . . he feels so alone. He often asks after you and the baby, and said that you could not imagine there was so much sorrow in life. Oh! If we could only give him some new courage to live" (van Gogh 1958, p. LII).

29 July

Vincent dies with his brother Theo at his side. Theo describes the end in a letter to his sister Elisabeth (Lies): "He himself desired to die. While I was sitting beside him, trying to persuade him that we would heal him, and that we hoped he would be saved from further attacks, he answered: 'La tristesse durera toujours.' I felt I understood what he wished to say. Shortly afterward he was seized with another attack, and the next minute closed his eyes" (Hulsker 1996, p. 480).

Theo writes to Johanna, "He had found the rest he could not find on earth . . . The next morning there came from Paris and elsewhere eight friends who decked the room where the coffin stood with his pictures . . . Dr. Gachet was the first to bring a large bunch of sunflowers, because Vincent was so fond of them . . ." (van Gogh 1958, p. LIII).

30 July

Vincent is buried in Auvers. The funeral is attended by many artists, including Bernard, Charles Laval, Lucien Pissarro, and the art dealer Tanguy. Bernard describes the scene in a letter to the art critic Albert Aurier on 1 August:

"All his most recent paintings had been hung on the walls of the room where the corpse was laid out, surrounding him as it were with a halo, and to the artists they made his death still more painful by the brilliance of the genius they revealed. A simple white sheet on the bier, and an abundance of flowers, the sunflowers he loved so much, dahlias, yellow flowers everywhere. It was, as you will remember, his favorite color, a symbol of the light he dreamed of, both in his heart and in his work" (Hulsker 1996, p. 480).

Theo writes to his mother,

"One cannot write how grieved one is nor find any comfort. It is a grief that will last and which I certainly shall never forget as long as I live; the only thing one might say is that he himself has the rest he was longing for . . . life was such a burden to him; but now, as often happens, everybody is full of praise for his talents . . . Oh Mother! He was my own, own brother" (van Gogh 1958, p. LIII).

September

With the help of Bernard, Theo holds a memorial exhibition of Vincent's paintings in his Paris apartment (22–24 September). Theo, whose health had long been precarious, begins to suffer from headaches and hallucinations.

October

Theo suffers a complete mental and physical breakdown in early October. He is admitted to a Paris clinic and diagnosed with *dementia paralytica*, the terminal stage of syphilis. A few weeks later he is taken to a clinic in Utrecht. He dies on 25 January 1891 and is buried in Utrecht.

1914

Theo's widow, Johanna van Gogh-Bonger, has her husband's remains exhumed and moved from Utrecht to Auvers, to be buried next to Vincent's grave. The two brothers remain side by side in the cemetery at Auvers.

168. The tombstones of Vincent and Theo van Gogh at Auvers
Amsterdam, Van Gogh Museum

169. *Self-Portrait* (F 626, JH 1770), 1 September 1889
Oil on canvas, 57.2 x 43.8 cm
Washington, D.C., National Gallery of Art

Famine to Feast

Portrait Making at St.-Rémy and Auvers

JUDY SUND

170. *Portrait of a Patient* (F 703, JH 1832), 20–22 October 1889
Oil on canvas, 32 x 23.5 cm
Amsterdam, Van Gogh Museum

Although the best-known works from van Gogh's sojourns at St.-Rémy and Auvers are evocative, unpeopled landscapes, including *Starry Night* and *Crows over Wheat Field,*[1] the artist himself much preferred to paint the figure—"the only thing that excites me to the depths of my soul."[2] His forays into other genres, however sustained and successful, were mainly undertaken by default,[3] for "what impassions me most," he declared, "much, much more than all the rest of my métier— is the portrait, the modern portrait."[4]

Van Gogh's notion of what comprised "modernity" in portraiture led him to approach his subjects from an eccentric angle and resulted in renderings that stood apart from both traditional portraiture and the sorts of likenesses his avant-garde peers were making. In an inversion of established practice, the subjects of van Gogh's portraits did not pay him to capture them on canvas but instead were asked by the artist to pose for him. Joanna Woodall links this procedure to a broader phenomenon, since "in the late nineteenth century, 'avant-garde' portraiture was markedly confined to uncommissioned images" of the artist's "friends and family."[5] But unlike his artist contemporaries who routinely undertook probing portraits of their intimates—Edgar Degas, Paul Gauguin, and Emile Bernard, for instance—van Gogh, in his uncommissioned portrayals, shied away from painting those he knew best,[6] preferring to paint acquaintances and virtual strangers (some of whom he paid to sit for him). The circumstances in which his figure pieces were produced eroded the usual obligations and concerns of the portraitist, whether traditional or in the vanguard.[7] And, though he claimed to value "the thoughts, the soul of the model"[8] above all else, van Gogh— rather than stressing his sitters' uniqueness—tended to slot them into a matrix of types he deemed recognizable.

Woodall asserts that "in van Gogh's portraiture . . . the images referred primarily to the identity of the artist, as opposed to that of the sitter,"[9] and certainly some of his depictions of others are scarcely veiled self-projections (for example, the images of Marie Ginoux and Paul Gachet made at St.-Rémy and Auvers respectively; figs. 184 and 198). In general, however, van Gogh's portraits do not so much reference his sense of self, as index his often-idealizing vision of the society he inhabited (or wished to inhabit), using pictorial language designed to make his imagery "comprehensible to the general public"[10] and to future generations.[11] The most important model for this portrait-based representation of an epoch was his Dutch antecedent Frans Hals,[12] an artist who, according to van Gogh, achieved the "simple great thing" that he himself was after: "the painting of humanity, or rather of a whole republic, by the simple means of portraiture"[13] (see essay by George Keyes in this volume).

The portrait practice van Gogh envisioned—figuration reflective of its time and place—may be seen philosophically to reflect the blurring of boundaries between portraiture and genre painting that characterized much impressionist production.[14] But whereas Degas, Edouard Manet, Auguste Renoir (and Claude Monet in the 1860s) posed family and friends in modern-life tableaux that, as Colin Bailey writes, "gave the illusion of being direct transcriptions of everyday life,"[15] van Gogh often did the opposite: plucking plebian individuals from their quotidian routines and surroundings, he removed them to the realm of formal portraiture and its frequently neutralized spaces. The portrait he made of Charles-Elzéard Trabuc in 1889 (fig. 171), for instance, gives no indication that the sitter was chief orderly at the asylum to which van Gogh was then confined. In something of a reversal of the process by which Manet, in *Le Déjeuner sur l'herbe,* or Renoir, in *La Loge,* ensconced their intimates in fictive situations with anecdotal dimensions,[16] van Gogh elided Trabuc's own "story," classing the unnamed sitter as a "type" (or, as Griselda Pollock would argue, thus un-classing him),[17] on the order of of the "Spanish grandee" etched by Alphonse Legros, whose "contemplative calm" recalled that of France's former premier, François-Pierre-Guillaume Guizot.[18] Thus was a physiognomy fitted to a category, Trabuc registering for van Gogh as a working-class variant on the elder statesman mode.

Trabuc was one of the handful of acquaintances van Gogh met at the asylum of St.-Paul-de-Mausole in St.-Rémy, the institution to which he voluntarily committed himself in May 1889 after suffering two nervous collapses at Arles. In the year he spent there, his keen desire "to make portraits, all kinds of portraits"[19] was thwarted by a dearth of suitable subjects; his fellow patients filled him with dread (see fig. 170),[20] and in his self-imposed isolation from them[21] he "despair[ed] of ever finding models"[22] for the sort of figural work he had found so fulfilling at Arles. Throughout his institutionalization he complained that "the impossibility of getting models,"[23] the thing which "I lack most here,"[24] kept him from making the sorts of pictures he most wanted to paint,[25] and though he initially felt "no desire to see my friends,"[26] his solitariness at St.-Rémy soon made him long for the company of Arlesien neighbors and further opportunities to portray his acquaintances there.[27]

Unwilling to pursue figuration without visual referents,[28] van Gogh spent his first months at St.-Rémy making garden

"What impassions me most—much, much more than all the rest of my métier—is the portrait, the modern portrait."
June 1890

171. *Portrait of Trabuc* (F 629, JH 1774), 5–6 September 1889
Oil on canvas, 61 x 46 cm
Solothurn, Switzerland, Kunstmuseum, Dübi-Müller Stiftung

172. *Self-Portrait with Dark Felt Hat in Front of the Easel* (F 181, JH 1090), spring 1886
Oil on canvas, 45.5 x 37.5 cm
Amsterdam, Van Gogh Museum

views and landscape vistas (*Starry Night* was begun in mid-June). His yen to paint people continued undiminished, but he made no attempt to do so until summer's end, as he recovered from a breakdown that had left him incapacitated from mid-July to late August. Van Gogh's realization, in the wake of this third collapse, that as "life passes . . . opportunities for working do not return"[29] and his fears that "a more violent attack may forever destroy my power to paint"[30] spurred him to act on his dearest ambitions rather than defer them any longer. In September, his desire to make portraits "terribly intense,"[31] he pursued three strategies for doing so: self-portraits, portraits, and copy-making.

Self-Portraits

Van Gogh first turned his sights on the most obvious of subjects and told Theo that "for want of another model"[32] he was making two self-portraits. Although this remark suggests that he took up his own image because he had no other option, his decision to paint himself in September 1889 surely had other dimensions. Artists' self-imaging gives tangibility to the split subjectivity that Christopher Bollas remarks as inherent to all self-experience (and which is particularly apparent in the act of dreaming): before the canvas, the painter enacts "the initiating subject who reflects upon the self"; upon it, she/he embodies the "experiencing self" that is being reflected upon.[33] Self-portraiture is a means of concretizing that divide, of stepping back from lived experience and taking stock. Feeling, in this era, like "a man who meant to commit suicide and, finding the water too cold, tries to regain the bank,"[34] van Gogh painted himself not only because his own form provided a ready figural subject but to ground himself in the aftermath of crisis.

Convinced that "working on my pictures is almost a necessity for my recovery,"[35] van Gogh not only picked up his brushes but also recorded his act of personal rehabilitation in a self-portrait with artist's implements (fig. 169). Begun "the day I got up,"[36] it shows him "thin and pale as a ghost,"[37] yet ready to resume his routine; palette and brushes in hand, artist's smock draped jauntily around him, eyes intent, he performs the role of the stereotypical artist, a role he generally eschewed[38] but had tried on twice before, in Paris. In 1886, as a fledgling painter in the world's art capital, van Gogh had assumed the established stance of the formally attired, palette-wielding artist at his easel (fig. 172). Slipping into the shoes of an illustrious and esteemed Dutch forebear, he took a self-portrait by Rembrandt as his model (fig. 29),[39] thereby

"I am now trying to recover like a man who meant to commit suicide and, finding the water too cold, tries to regain the bank."

September 1889

173. *Self-Portrait with Clean-Shaven Face* (F 525, JH 1665), 1889
Oil on canvas, 40 x 31 cm
Private Collection

174. *Self-Portrait* (F 627, JH 1772), 1889–90
Oil on canvas, 65 x 54 cm
Paris, Musée d'Orsay

proclaiming seriousness of purpose and firm grounding in the (still overshadowing) traditions of his chosen occupation. Revisiting this formulaic composition at the end of his two-year stay in Paris, van Gogh overlaid it with the vibrant hues and signature brush marks he had adopted in the interim (fig. 28). Bare-headed and in a "peasant's blouse,"[40] foursquare behind his easel, he assumed a workmanlike demeanor and stolid expression in an attempt to mask the feelings of hopeless malaise that his dissolute life in Paris had engendered.[41]

At St.-Rémy, engulfed by similar (now intensified) misgivings and struggling to "regain the bank," van Gogh again donned the mantle of professionalism to buck himself up. The first self-portrait made in the asylum (fig. 169) reasserted his vocational identity not only to himself and his brother (the audience of two to whom van Gogh most consistently played) but also to the hospital's director, Dr. Théophile Peyron, who had been reluctant to let him resume work.[42] Lacking the calibrated calm of the later Parisian self-portrait—wherein the rigid pose and faraway gaze create a sense of magisterial posturing—the St.-Rémy rendering reveals (by way of the artist's intense stare and lowered chin) the anxious scrutiny involved in its making. Its colors and strokes are not so interwoven as in the earlier work, making for a less rehearsed effect, and elimination of the artist's easel enhances its directness. In the Paris self-portrait, that studio prop distances the viewing subject from the portrayed one, not only by standing between them but by introducing the possibility of a fictive space (the surface of the turned-away canvas) to which the viewer has no access. In the St.-Rémy work, contact between artist and viewer seems less mediated, though a measure of concealment may be noted in van Gogh's presentation of the right side of his head, whereas his earlier depictions of himself before the easel (and the Rembrandt self-portrait to which they are linked) showed the left. He had disfigured his left ear at Arles in December 1888, and, though his process of recovery from that incident included making portraits of himself as a wounded man—with bandaged ear prominently displayed[43]—his self-images from the asylum emphasize wholeness by showing the side with ear intact.

Van Gogh's first St.-Rémy self-portrait was the last in which he insisted upon his professional status. An image of himself made shortly thereafter (fig. 173), though similar in expression and in the orientation of head and gaze, confirms his one-time assertion that "one and the same person may furnish motifs for very different portraits."[44] Van Gogh's initial description of this painting is minimal—"three-quarter length on a light background"[45]—and is widely assumed to refer to his well-known self-portrait on a swirling ground (fig. 174). The artist's subsequent assertion, however, that the picture in question showed him looking "vague and veiled,"[46] and "vaguer than before,"[47] makes that supposition questionable, as does his comment that "I have tried to make it simple."[48] Van Gogh looks intensely focused in the image on swirling ground (which may have been painted toward the end of his hospitalization[49]), and its backdrop of flamelike strokes is, arguably, elaborative rather than "simple." The latter term is more plausibly applied to the smaller and more modest depiction of the artist, clean-shaven, that was made in September 1889 for his mother (fig. 173) and which showed "that though I saw Paris and other big cities for many years, I keep looking more or less like a peasant . . . and sometimes I imagine I also feel and think like them."[50] Despite his assertion that "peasants are of more use in the world," van Gogh went on to compare his labors to theirs: "I am plowing on my canvases as they do on their fields."[51]

Long torn by the opposing pulls of the art world and an idealized rusticity,[52] the artist alternately envisioned himself as heir to Rembrandt and as a manual laborer drudging away. Self-imaging, as he told Theo, never came easily—linked as it was to the larger difficulty of knowing oneself[53]—but in September 1889 it provided a necessary forum for a reassuring reification of his working persona.

The Attendant and his Wife

Even as he worked at self-portrayal, van Gogh, intent on doing "a little figure work,"[54] revived a tactic he had used with varying degrees of success in the past: enlisting an obliging acquaintance to sit for him. He was soon at work on Trabuc's portrait and shortly thereafter painted Trabuc's wife (fig. 175), who, with her husband, lived just a few paces from the asylum.[55] Under other circumstances, this unremarkable couple might not have drawn van Gogh's attention, but their availability at this juncture must have seemed a godsend, and the artist's letters suggest his effort to validate them in his own mind as portrait subjects. Although "the attendant" (van Gogh never referred to him by name) was, according to the painter, "of the people and simpler," his visage sparked memories of illustrious men from history and past art;[56] van Gogh's stress on his resemblance to French premier Guizot and to Legros's nobleman seems to be both an attempt to aggrandize the sitter and an assertion of the artist's own erudition—the ability to discern such resemblances a demonstration of his mental alertness and visual acuity. Trabuc

175. *Portrait of Trabuc's Wife* (F 631, JH 1777), ca. 15 September 1889
Oil on canvas on panel, 64 x 49 cm
St. Petersburg, The State Hermitage Museum

176. *Three Novels* (F 335, JH 1226), spring 1887
Oil on panel, 31 x 48.5 cm
Amsterdam, Van Gogh Museum

"Though I saw Paris and other
big cities for many years, I keep
looking more or less like
a peasant . . . and sometimes
I imagine I also feel and think
like them."

October 1889

also appealed to him as a "Southern type;"[57] van Gogh at Arles
had set his sights on painting representative Provençals and
could now add the attendant to that category. Although the
artist emphasized Trabuc's "calm"[58] (despite his "quick black
eyes"),[59] the portrait the attendant sat for is a lively one, its
robust skin tones, vibrant black patches, and striations playing
off lighter tones in the sitter's hair, eyes, and especially his
clothing.

Since Trabuc's "faded" wife, a "creature of small account,"[60]
apparently could by no stretch of van Gogh's imagination be
endowed with verve, the artist claimed fascination with her
very "insignificance."[61] From the beginning of his career,
van Gogh had prided himself on his attention to society's
downtrodden—an engagement with the proletariat that he
saw paralleled in the work of Emile Zola and Edmond and Jules
de Goncourt, naturalist authors dedicated to hard-hitting but
empathic portrayals of men and especially women of the
working classes.[62] Although the naturalist school had, in the
1880s, ceded prominence to the symbolist movement in Paris,
van Gogh continued to see it as a literary pinnacle and to

believe—as he told his sister Wil—that "one can hardly be said to belong to one's time if one has paid no attention to it."[63] His penchant for naturalist novels is documented by a number of still lifes that include them (for example, fig. 176)—two of which he earmarked for his sister.[64] Unlike their brother Theo,[65] Vincent was convinced Wil should read naturalist literature, and he was miffed to learn, in September 1889, that she had not cared for *Germinie Lacerteux*, the Goncourts' fictionalization of the tragic course of events triggered by their long-time housemaid's nocturnal adventures. Even as he chided Wil for her failure to appreciate that "masterly book,"[66] van Gogh held up his portrait of the attendant's wife as an indication of his own capacity to appreciate subject matter in the naturalist vein: "The other day I finished the portrait of . . . an insignificant woman. The withered face is tired, pockmarked. A faded black dress . . . I often paint things like that—as insignificant and dramatic as a dusty blade of grass by the roadside—and it consequently seems only right to me that I should have a boundless admiration for de Goncourt, Zola, Flaubert, Maupassant, Huysmans."[67] His portrait of Madame Trabuc thus became a badge of honor, wielded as evidence of his ability to take interest in people often overlooked.[68]

Fanciful Projections

In addition to portraits and self-portraits, van Gogh took up a third sort of figuration in September 1889, when he decided to make an oil translation of a print after Eugène Delacroix's *Pietà* (fig. 177). Since he balked at inventing subject matter, had already painted such living models as the asylum seemed to offer,[69] and felt that "really I must do more figures,"[70] the artist decided to further his aims by making paintings after figural compositions he possessed in print form. Copying works by esteemed forebears was a time-honored student practice (and had guided van Gogh's first attempts at figuration), but since few artists continued to make literal copies in their maturity, van Gogh felt obliged to justify this pursuit at St.-Rémy. He stressed that his return to copy making had come about by chance,[71] when—during his recent illness—"that lithograph of Delacroix's 'Pietà' . . . fell into some oil paint and was ruined."[72] In his distress, van Gogh wrote, "I made myself sit down to paint it."[73] Presenting himself as virtually duty-bound to do so, he evaded further examination of his motives—which nonetheless are elucidated by his contemporaneous admission that, finding himself in "a fourth- or fifth-rate situation,"[74] he took "consolation"[75] in imaginatively allying himself with artists

177. Reproduction print after Eugène Delacroix's *Pietà* Amsterdam, Van Gogh Museum

178. *Pietà (after Delacroix)* (F 630, JH 1775), 6–7 September 1889
Oil on canvas, 73 x 60.5 cm
Amsterdam, Van Gogh Museum

he considered first-rate: "When I realize the worth and originality and superiority of Delacroix and Millet, for instance, then I am bold enough to say . . . I can do something. But I must have a foundation in those artists and then produce the little I am capable of in the same direction."[76]

Van Gogh's copies were another means of grounding himself, and—citing illness and lack of models as factors in his decision to continue making them[77]—he argued against those who might see such work as merely imitative by comparing the act of pictorial *re*-presentation to instrumentalists' renderings of composers' music. "If some person or other plays Beethoven, he adds his personal interpretation," van Gogh remarked as a preamble to his assertion that the creative dimension of his practice resided in the color choices he made for works that "posed" for him in black and white.[78] In infusing them with color—a process he compared to musical improvisation—he not only reflected his own sensibility but also his memories of "feelings" generated by the original artists' larger oeuvres and their palettes.[79] In the case of the *Pietà,* the last was especially important, since—as Cornelia Homburg notes—van Gogh's colorism owed so much to Delacroix's.[80] Rather than constituting a substantive twist on Delacroix's original, van Gogh's variant (fig. 178) coloristically circled back to the older artist's work; he had first explored the sorts of complementary color plays that enliven it[81] under the influence of written accounts of Delacroix's theory and practice.[82] His work on the *Pietà* also afforded van Gogh the opportunity to work on an image of Christ—something he had found as impossible as it was alluring.[83]

In letters discussing his copy, van Gogh made no mention of what some viewers consider his most striking imposition of self upon Delacroix's *Pietà*: the van Gogh-like features—especially the red hair and beard—that suggest the painter's resemblance to (hence, identification with) the martyred Savior.[84] If accepted as such, this unorthodox self-image reads as the result of a co-optive act whereby van Gogh figuratively "defaced" Delacroix's Christ—an image that already had suffered literal defacement by its "accidental" immersion in his paints. The artist's failure to acknowledge this self-projection may mean the resemblances between his self-portraits and his portrayal of Christ were unintended; it might also indicate, however, that van Gogh feared his own hubris as he maneuvered himself into both Christ's place within the drama and Delacroix's before the easel.[85]

As self-reflection, van Gogh's *Pietà* not only suggests his sense of victimization but also his longing for feminine

> "If I had had the strength to continue, I should have made portraits of saints and holy women from life who would have seemed to belong to another age."
>
> September 1889

solace—possibly in the form of his own far-off mother,[86] but more probably in that of mother substitutes he had found among his working-class neighbors at Arles—Augustine Roulin (*La Berceuse*; fig. 125) and Marie Ginoux (*L'Arlésienne*; fig. 181)— women who offered comfort during his convalescence there. Van Gogh's description of the Virgin's hands—"the good sturdy hands of a working woman"[87]—applies equally well to those that rock the cradle in *La Berceuse,* though her face, rather than resembling either Arlésienne, recalled that of a fictional Parisienne: "the grayish white countenance" and "lost vague look of a person exhausted by anxiety and weeping and waking" were, van Gogh thought, "rather in the manner of Germinie Lacerteux."[88] It is nonetheless likely that fond memories of those who were "kind and gentle with me" during previous bouts of illness[89] informed van Gogh's painted response to the lithographic image of a tortured male form supported by a feminine stalwart. *La Berceuse* was on his mind at the time, and van Gogh remarked that "however feeble that attempt may be, if I had had the strength to continue, I should have made portraits of saints and holy women from life who would have seemed to belong to another age, and . . . [yet] would be middle-class women of the present day . . . [who] would have had something in common with the very primitive Christians."[90]

Van Gogh's desire to use middle-class contemporaries as models for "saints and holy women" of an earlier era was encouraged by what he described as Delacroix's incorporation of "firsthand" experience in his biblical scenes, to show that "people whom history tells us about . . . apostles, holy women, were of the same character and lived in a manner analogous to their present descendants."[91] Van Gogh's sense of the "primitive" faith guiding those who followed Christ in his lifetime, however, owed more to a literary source than any pictorial one, having been shaped some years earlier by Ernest Renan's *Vie de Jésus* (1863), a controversial biography in which the author refuted Christianity's most cherished claim—that Christ was God made man—and held instead that the faith's founder was only human.[92] Van Gogh had long admired Renan's earthbound Jesus[93] and clearly was intrigued by his descriptions of the "simple folk" who formed Christ's entourage: country bumpkins whose naïveté and provincial slang made them laughingstocks among the urbane inhabitants of Jerusalem, but who, according to Renan, "triumphed by their very humanity."[94] Van Gogh's appreciation of Renan paralleled (and perhaps fostered) his painter's interest in the "utterly human" aspects of saintliness— the rendering of which helped modern viewers feel the actuality of people long dead.[95]

His interest in doing "saints and holy women from life"—
explored in *La Berceuse* and revisited as van Gogh copied the
Pietà—shaped another of the reworkings he made at St.-Rémy,
this one based upon a Rembrandt etching of *The Raising of
Lazarus,* a reproduction of which Theo sent as a get-well
offering (fig. 179). Van Gogh's "translation"[96] of this Rembrandt
print (fig. 180) differs much more significantly from the image
that inspired it than does his *Pietà*: its hues and lighting are
decidedly un-Rembrandtesque, and van Gogh's derivative
focuses on a small portion of the multifigured original. While
all these changes contribute to the altered tenor of van Gogh's
Lazarus, his drastic pruning of its figural component was the
most transformative.[97] Eliminating Rembrandt's commanding
Christ and deleting two clutches of awestruck onlookers,
van Gogh focused on the recumbent figure of Lazarus and his
hovering sisters, Martha and Mary; in so doing, he gleaned
aspects of familial intimacy and human fragility from a public
demonstration of superhuman power. In the absence of the
divine miracle worker,[98] Lazarus seems both saddled and
credited with his own revival, which may yet hang in the
balance. Mining the metaphoric potential of the biblical
narrative, van Gogh actualized it in emphatically familiar
terms, giving the protagonist his own face and beard and
casting Mesdames Roulin and Ginoux as the concerned
kinswomen who seem to implore his recovery.

Made in the aftermath of yet another long episode of
illness—which began on a hospital-sanctioned day trip to Arles
in February 1890—van Gogh's fanciful group portrait of
himself with former neighbors was made as he fought once
more to "regain the bank," having resolved to leave the asylum
and Provence.[99] A scene of mythic regeneration, van Gogh's
Lazarus is dreamlike in its dramatization of wishfulness,[100] as
well as in its conflations of past and present, the literary and the
lived; the artist himself affirmed that its "personalities are the
characters of my dreams."[101] The picture clearly reflects his
intention to recover and more obliquely hints at van Gogh's
suspicion that he, like the Lazarus he envisioned, had been left
to his own devices—by both the Almighty and the hospital
administration. In van Gogh's case, the most effectual of those
devices was picture making (and, notably, picture remaking).
At St.-Rémy, painting became his main recuperative strategy.

Van Gogh's *Lazarus* also indicates the painter's need to have
his efforts to rebound noticed, even lauded, by those closest to
him; the biblical Lazarus's triumph over death was witnessed
by caring siblings, and the secondary figures of van Gogh's
painting probably should be seen not only as "primitive

179. Reproduction print after Rembrandt van Rijn's etching *The Raising of Lazarus*
Amsterdam, Van Gogh Museum

180. *The Raising of Lazarus (after a detail from an etching by Rembrandt)*
(F 677, JH 1972), 3 May 1890
Oil on canvas, 48.5 x 63 cm
Amsterdam, Van Gogh Museum

Christians" enacted by "middle-class women of the present" but also as allusions to Theo and Wil, the blood relations whose perceived psychic closeness sustained him day to day.[102] In the conjured presence of these most significant others, Lazarus/ van Gogh (the "experiencing self") usurps Christ's role by pulling himself from death's door, even as van Gogh the painter (the "reflecting self") usurps Rembrandt's role by an act of artistic revivification, giving a pre-existent (if not exactly "dead") vessel a second life.[103] As a narrative of reinvigoration, the Lazarus story seems pertinent not only to van Gogh's overwhelming desire to resume his life (that is, his existence outside the asylum) but also to his contemporaneous compulsion to revive and enliven his predecessors' figuration.

L'Arlésienne Revisited

Retrospectively, van Gogh attributed his breakdown of February 1890 to his work that month on a series of new portraits of the Arlésienne, Marie Ginoux,[104] in which the artist reconsidered a favorite model[105] and recalled a less isolated existence.[106] Ginoux's husband owned the café van Gogh had frequented at Arles (and immortalized in *The Night Café*), and she had posed for him and Gauguin there more than a year before, in November 1888. On the basis of that sitting, each artist made both a sketch and a more finished portrait of Ginoux. Van Gogh's first impression (fig. 148) shows her seated in three-quarters view at a café table that holds a parasol and gloves; in a subsequent, more carefully worked picture (fig. 181), Ginoux retains her distracted air, but the artist has subtly converted her expression to one of thoughtful reverie by substituting three well-thumbed paperbacks for the accessories of a woman about town. Gauguin's initial depiction of the same model—rendered in crayon and charcoal—was done from her other side and presents her almost frontally (fig. 182); a subsequent elaboration—Gauguin's own painting of *The Night Café* (fig. 183)—presents her as a bemused denizen of that low-brow haunt.

Gauguin later gave van Gogh the crayon likeness he made of Ginoux (or inadvertently left it behind when he hastily departed Arles in December). The drawing ended up at St.-Rémy, where it betokened those who sat for and made it, during a period of camaraderie and collegiality that van Gogh recalled with nostalgia. It also inspired yet another portrait of the sitter when, in February 1890,[107] van Gogh made a painted translation of Gauguin's drawing (fig. 184).[108] As a colorized variant upon a black and white figural composition by an artist

181. *L'Arlésienne (Madame Ginoux) with Books* (F 488, JH 1624), November 1888?
Oil on canvas, 91.4 x 73.7 cm
New York, The Metropolitan Museum of Art

he admired, van Gogh's St.-Rémy portrait of Ginoux is related
to the improvisations he had begun making in September 1889
(with the *Pietà*) and continued producing throughout his stay
(*The Raising of Lazarus* being the last such work van Gogh
produced). The Ginoux portrait stands apart, however, as an
elaboration of a preliminary drawing (rather than the revision
of a finished work) made by a living artist with whom van Gogh
had worked and depicting a living model he knew and had
painted. Van Gogh himself was inclined to see *L'Arlésienne* of
1890 as a collaboration rather than a copy—a "synthesis," he
told Gauguin, "belonging to you and me as a summary of our
months of work together."[109] As such, it was a substitute for the
in-person interaction that van Gogh craved.

In the fall of 1889, van Gogh had written of "the aching
void" he felt in his distance from Gauguin[110] and at the same
time expressed his hope and expectation that they would
"work together again."[111] Generalized longing for renewed
collegiality surely informed his decision to make a Gauguin-
based improvisation, which was more specifically activated by
a confluence of significant events. In mid-January 1890,
van Gogh traveled to Arles for the first time in several months
and there saw Madame Ginoux, whom he found ill and "much
changed" by a difficult menopause that caused "nervous
attacks" and made her seem "like an old grandfather."[112] He was
struck by the fact that the onset of her illness had coincided
with his own first breakdown, and in a letter he posted to her
upon his return from Arles in January 1890, he remarked, "We
suffer together."[113] That comment proved prophetic when, two
days later, van Gogh fell ill for a week; his collapse may have
been precipitated by his visit to Arles, and this relapse surely
reinforced the empathy he felt with his sick friend there. As he
recuperated, a letter from Gauguin arrived. Dated 28 January,
it contained a suggestion that the two artists consider living
together again.[114] Given these stimuli—and his concurrent
preoccupation with copying—it is hardly surprising that
van Gogh commenced a painting based on Gauguin's drawing
in early February. The resultant "synthesis" is at once the
revised image of a changed friend, a reflection of the artist's
own illness and his attempts to cope with it, and a co-operative
gesture toward an erstwhile colleague who hinted at reunion.

As portrayed by van Gogh in 1890, the Arlésienne seems
a different person from the woman depicted some fifteen
months before (compare figs. 181 and 184), and while the gap
between his images of her surely reflects illness-induced
changes in the model's appearance, it likewise indicates the
artist's altered state. As before, he bent Ginoux's expression

182. Paul Gauguin, *L'Arlésienne, Madame Ginoux,* 1888
Chalk and charcoal, 56.1 x 49.2 cm
Fine Arts Museums of San Francisco

183. Paul Gauguin, *The Night Café*, 1888
Moscow, Pushkin State Museum of Fine Arts

and demeanor to a mental construct: that of an ideal female companion and counterpart. Before the onset of his illness, the desired entity was a reflective intellectual with a taste for modern literature (a far cry, no doubt, from the person Ginoux actually was),[115] but in the aftermath of his breakdown (as he experienced "a tempest of desire to embrace . . . a woman of the domestic hen type"),[116] the feminine touchstone of his mind's eye became softer and more maternal (compare *La Berceuse* of January 1889; fig. 125) and by early 1890 took on aspects of the fellow sufferer van Gogh perceived Ginoux to be. Thus were the crisp angularities and vibrant hues of his earlier *L'Arlésienne* jettisoned for rounded forms and silvery pastels that make the sitter seem older and more sedate.[117]

184. *L'Arlésienne (Madame Ginoux) with Pink Background* (F 542, JH 1894), early February–20 February 1890
Oil on canvas, 65 x 54 cm
Museu de arte de São Paulo Assis Chateaubriand

185. *L'Arlésienne (Madame Ginoux) with Light Pink Background* (F 541, JH 1893), early February–20 February 1890
Oil on canvas, 65 x 49 cm
Otterlo, Collection Kröller-Müller Museum

Sensitive colorism was, to van Gogh's mind, crucial to evocative portraiture, and for that reason (among others) he disdained photographic portrayals: "I should like to paint portraits which would appear after a century to the people living then as apparitions . . . I do not endeavor to achieve this by a photographic resemblance, but by . . . using our knowledge of and our modern taste for color as a means of arriving at the expression and the intensification of the character."[118] Having noted, in 1888, that "unless we are painted in color, the result is nowhere near a speaking likeness," van Gogh posed a rhetorical question: "Would Germinie Lacerteux be Germinie Lacerteux without her color? Obviously not."[119] The Goncourts describe that unfortunate character as "lymphatically" pale, and van Gogh compared the "grayish white countenance" he gave the Virgin of his *Pietà* to Germinie's.[120] Now, in rendering the ailing Ginoux, he opted for "drab and lustreless"[121] flesh tones, and in her clothing and surroundings employed the grayed colors he associated with adversity and illness. In November 1889, recounting his decision to add a "dull, dirty white" to the "pure and brilliant hues" of a painting underway, van Gogh remarked that the practice "softens the tones, whereas one would think that one would spoil and besmirch the painting," and added, "Don't misfortune and disease do the same thing to us?"[122] Van Gogh considered the sorts of pink and green tonalities that mark his late portrayals of Ginoux both "mild"[123] and "sickly,"[124] and in remarks to Gauguin about his reinterpretation of the Arlésienne, he noted that its color scheme was intended to connote sobriety.[125]

The changes in Ginoux (and himself) that van Gogh expressed in the softened line and color of his later portraits of her are likewise indicated by the books that adjoin the figure. Unlike the casually rendered, unspecified books of the second Arles portrait, those of the St.-Rémy series are stacked with spines turned toward the viewer and clearly labeled: Harriet Beecher Stowe's *La cas de l'Oncle Tom* (*Uncle Tom's Cabin*) and Charles Dickens's *Contes de Noël* (*Christmas Stories*). While the bright bindings of the dog-eared paperbacks painted at Arles mark them as recent offerings from van Gogh's favorite Parisian publishers,[126] those included in *L'Arlésienne* of 1890 are French translations[127] of English-language books from another era; Beecher Stowe's unabashedly Christian treatment of the slavery issue was published in 1852, and *Christmas Stories* is a compilation of magazine pieces written in the 1850s and 1860s. Both books were sentimental favorites from van Gogh's younger years,[128] and he had returned to them

"I should like to paint portraits which would appear after a century to people living then as apparitions."

June 1890

while hospitalized at Arles (the period in which Madame Ginoux had been most attentive to him) in the hope of "putting a few sound ideas in my head."[129] As he told his sister, "I have reread 'Uncle Tom's Cabin' . . . with *extreme attention,* for the very reason that it was written, as she tells us, while she was making soup for the children—and after that, also with extreme attention, Charles Dickens's 'Christmas Stories.'"[130] He went on to note, "Every day I take the remedy which the incomparable Dickens prescribes against suicide . . . a glass of wine, a piece of bread with cheese and a pipe of tobacco."[131] Some months later—after his first collapse at St.-Rémy— van Gogh claimed that "reading a fine book, like one by Beecher Stowe or Dickens," "braced" him,[132] and his belief in the curative effects of such volumes doubtless inspired their inclusion in a portrait alluding to illness. These books evoked thoughts of Beecher Stowe's maternal ministrations and of Dickens's common-sense antidotes to despondency, and the artist would seem to proffer them as textual equivalents of homespun remedies like hot soup or a good smoke.

It seems likely, too, that the artist considered the volumes included in his 1890 portrayal of Ginoux—though they were his books rather than hers[133]—well-suited to traditional feminine sensibilities. In 1889 he had come to suspect that the sorts of French books he had so often urged upon his sister (and alluded to in his previous portrait of Ginoux) were in fact "books written by men for men, and I don't know whether women can understand them."[134] Wil's apparent dissatisfaction with *Germinie Lacerteux* (and her concurrent enthusiasm for Edouard Rod's *Le sense de la vie*[135]) strengthened van Gogh's conviction that female readers preferred more reassuring narratives,[136] and rather than include hard-hitting "Parisian novels" of the sort he had frequently depicted in the past (fig. 176), he used old-fashioned tomes of edifying content to round out his newly "mild" vision of the matronly Ginoux.

Although he had previously included titled books in still lifes (and untitled books in his prior treatment of Ginoux), the St.-Rémy *L'Arlésienne* is the first of van Gogh's figural works to include labeled volumes—which connote personality as surely as do the costuming, accessories, and settings of more traditional portraits. Given the context of this picture's production, it seems possible that van Gogh's decision to elaborate on Ginoux's character by means of literary allusion was inspired by Gauguin's inclusion of titled books in his *Portrait of Meyer de Haan* (fig. 186), where copies of Thomas Carlyle's *Sartor Resartus* and John Milton's *Paradise Lost* adjoin the sitter.[137] He never saw Gauguin's painting (a panel piece that was part of a collaborative decor for a Breton inn), but van Gogh may have known it through a sketch of the ensemble that Gauguin sent some weeks before *L'Arlésienne* of 1890 was conceived.[138] Like Gauguin's portrait of de Haan, van Gogh's late rendering of Ginoux does not present the sitter as an active reader; the books in each are displayed as emphatically connotative artifacts rather than texts in the process of being consumed, and they clearly are intended to "speak volumes" to viewers in the know.[139] Indeed, while the splayed paperback of van Gogh's earlier portrait of Ginoux helps establish the model's remove from the viewer (her musing on its contents apparently taking her to a realm beyond our ken), the closed volumes of the St.-Rémy portraits—calculated clues to Ginoux's nature—seek to make an open book of the sitter herself. Ironically, the portrait van Gogh painted at the greatest geographic and temporal distance from his model is the one in which she seems most engaged with the artist/spectator— perhaps because the synthetic rendering that Gauguin's drawing inspired is as much about van Gogh as his ostensible sitter.

The satisfaction van Gogh derived from making this multivalent portrait is made evident by his multiple reprises of it (see, for example, fig. 185); within three weeks, he reproduced the composition four times, with only minor variations— much as he had made multiple versions of *La Berceuse* the year before. The two series almost certainly were as allied in van Gogh's mind as the solacing women they represented; the mental linkage of Ginoux and Roulin expressed in several letters[140] is made most strikingly manifest in van Gogh's translation of Rembrandt's *Raising of Lazarus*, and the singular images of these women that he remade almost obsessively in 1889 (*La Berceuse*) and 1890 (*L'Arlésienne*) are icons of stability and calm designed to comfort their maker in periods of recovery and reflection.[141] "Portraits," van Gogh asserted in January 1890, "are something almost useful . . . Like furniture one knows, they remind us of things long gone by."[142]

His first reworking of *L'Arlésienne* (fig. 184) presumably was the one that went with him to Auvers when he left the asylum in May 1890. Three versions of the portrait were sent to Paris (one for Theo to keep, the others to be given to Gauguin and the critic Albert Aurier); another, intended for Ginoux, was lost when van Gogh suffered yet another breakdown on a visit to Arles in late February. His recuperation from this Arles-induced collapse was slow, and he did not feel fully himself again until late April or early May. It was during this last period of extended illness that he attempted small-scale figuration based on memory and imagination[143]—a practice Gauguin

186. Paul Gauguin, *Portrait of Meyer de Haan*, 1889
Oil on wood, 80 x 52 cm
New York, Private Collection

advocated but van Gogh generally steered clear of, fearing that such "abstractions . . . would make me soft."[144] Writing from St.-Rémy, van Gogh acknowledged that "once or twice, while Gauguin was in Arles, I gave myself free rein with abstractions" and noted that while "abstraction seemed to me a charming path . . . it is enchanted ground . . . and one soon finds oneself up against a stone wall."[145] In the spring of 1890—finding himself up against the figurative wall of his illness and the actual walls of St.-Paul-de-Mausole—he perhaps felt he had little to lose, for despite his inkling of its inherent dangers he returned to imaginative figuration based on memories of things seen and (in some cases) previously painted. The first of his memory pieces of 1890 were reminiscences of rural Holland, and then—as he prepared to leave Provence—he produced two compelling souvenirs of the region he had more recently inhabited: *Road with Cypress and Star* (fig. 187)[146] and *Evening Promenade* (fig. 188), the latter featuring a wishful double portrait of the red-bearded and blue-suited artist strolling through an olive grove at twilight with an invigorated Madame Ginoux (recognizable by her dark hair and trademark coiffure).[147] Unfettered by illness, the two traverse "enchanted ground" that—though dimly lit by a waning crescent moon— is intensely hued, the pastel tones of illness overridden by vibrant blue, green, yellow, and orange. The scene incorporates beloved aspects of van Gogh's Provençal experience: the cypress and olive trees, the rolling foothills of the Alpilles, the luminous night sky, the fellowship of caring friends. It is a picture that is at once playful and poignant, a wistful envisioning of the way his southern sojourn might have been: absent the burdens of mental and physical fragility.

Panoramic Vistas and a Panorama of Visages

Van Gogh left Provence in mid-May 1890. After a three-day stopover in Paris—where he visited Theo and met both his sister-in-law, Jo, and his four-month-old namesake nephew— the artist traveled on to Auvers-sur-Oise, which, though just twenty miles northwest of Paris, offered the experience of "real country."[148] Picturesque and conveniently close to the capital, Auvers had long attracted artists: Charles-François Daubigny, Camille Corot, Honoré Daumier, Camille Pissarro, and Paul Cézanne were among those who had painted there.[149] It was also home to two collectors of impressionist art: novelist Eugène Murer and Dr. Paul Gachet, the homeopath and sometime artist whose presence inspired van Gogh's relocation.[150] Pissarro had recommended Dr. Gachet to

187. *Road with Cypress and Star* (F 683, JH 1982), 12–15 May 1890
Oil on canvas, 92 x 73 cm
Otterlo, Collection Kröller-Müller Museum

188. *Evening Promenade* (F 704, JH 1981), 12–15 May 1890
Oil on canvas, 49.5 x 45.5 cm
Museu de arte de São Paulo Assis Chateaubriand

Theo,[151] and both van Gogh brothers took comfort in Vincent's proximity to an art-loving physician who took a particular interest in melancholy.[152]

Stimulated by his new environment, van Gogh was incredibly productive at Auvers; Carol Zemel notes that in the nine weeks he spent there he produced more than one hundred finished works,[153] many of which were figural pieces. After the isolation endured at St.-Rémy, he reveled in renewed opportunities for the sort of work he liked best and delighted in the look of the locals, who struck him as hearty souls —an impression doubtless heightened by his year-long exposure to the clients of St.-Paul-de-Mausole and by his recent visit to Paris, where he became convinced that the urban lifestyle of Theo's family was undermining their health. The chubby children and red-cheeked women van Gogh painted *en plein air* at Auvers may be seen as visual accompaniments to his relentless verbal campaign to move Theo, Jo, and "the little one" to an environment that promoted physical well-being.[154] He noticed that "children here in the healthy open air look well," and as he painted them—against backdrops of thatch-roofed cottages (fig. 189) and flowering meadows (fig. 190)[155] —van Gogh reported to his brother and sister-in-law that the children of Auvers (even "youngsters who were born in Paris and really sickly") thrived.[156] He evoked "the health and restorative forces that I see in the country"[157] not only in lustrous and expansive landscapes but in images of robust townspeople ranging from grinning tykes to a mop-haired youth chewing a flower stem (fig. 191) to colorfully clad women traipsing along a country road (JH 2112), their faces "browned by fresh air, burned by the sun."[158]

In late June, van Gogh wrote that "if you could make the people you see walking past pose [for] portraits, it would be as pretty as any period whatever in the past,"[159] and his next letter included a sketch and description of "a peasant woman [in a] big yellow hat" that together suggest his success in inducing such a passerby to model for him.[160] This unidentified woman, painted in early July, can plausibly be construed as someone who agreed to pose amid swaying wheat after being detained en route (fig. 192). Broad, blunt strokes model her "very red face [and] rich blue blouse with orange spots," and the canvas "is really a bit coarse."[161] Although perhaps not planned as such, this painting might be seen as a feminine counterpart to his Arlesien portrait of Patience Escalier (fig. 193), whom van Gogh likewise labeled a "peasant" and rendered with deliberate "crudeness" intended to reflect the model's class affiliation and rusticity.[162] Convinced, at that time, that some would see his

"I almost think that these canvases will tell you what I cannot say in words, the health and restorative forces that I see in the country."

June 1890

189. *Two Children* (F 784, JH 2052), June–July 1890
Oil on canvas, 51.5 x 46.5 cm
Private Collection

190. *Child Sitting in the Grass with an Orange or a Ball*
(F 785, JH 2057), late June 1890
Oil on canvas, 50 x 51 cm
Private Collection

191. *Head of a Boy with a Carnation between His Teeth*
(F 787, JH 2050), June–July 1890
Oil on canvas, 39 x 30.5 cm
Private Collection

"exaggeration" as mere "caricature," van Gogh brandished his
naturalist credentials, declaring, "We've read [Zola's] 'La Terre'
and 'Germinal,' and if we are painting a peasant, we want to
show that . . . what we have read has come very near to being
a part of us."[163] He noted, in 1888, that his image of Escalier
would make an interesting pendant to a Toulouse-Lautrec
portrait Theo owned: "That sun-steeped, sunburned quality,
tanned and air-swept, would show up still more effectively
beside all that face powder and elegance."[164]

Van Gogh's interest in the opposition of rustic simplicity
and cultivated urbanity reawakened at Auvers—where the
indigenous population of the "real country" rubbed elbows
with modern and artistic types—and he seems to have
conceived his *Peasant Woman in Wheat Field* to complement and
contrast with *Mademoiselle Gachet at the Piano* (fig. 194)
—a painting that in fact bears a remarkable resemblance to
a Toulouse-Lautrec figural piece Theo had admired that spring,
Mademoiselle Dihau at the Piano (fig. 195).[165] Van Gogh's
portrayal of Dr. Gachet's twenty-one-year-old daughter,
Marguerite, presents a paradigm of bourgeois femininity
inculcated by the artist's middle-class upbringing:[166] pale, and
of unassuming demeanor,[167] Mademoiselle Gachet is attired in
clothing of "mild" hue[168] and acts out her enculturation, making
music in the confines of her family's dim parlor.[169] Thus
rendered, she appears in many ways the antithesis of the
unnamed woman of high color van Gogh painted in full
sunlight on a backdrop of wheat just days later. Indeed, before
he had even begun Marguerite's portrait, van Gogh had a
"natural" counterpart in mind: "I hope to do the portrait of
Mlle. Gachet next week," he wrote in late June, "and perhaps I
shall have a county girl pose too."[170] At Auvers, the artist surely
recalled the portrait project that had absorbed him at Arles—
the capture of characteristic types within a small-town
population—and as one local woman emerged on canvas as the
quintessential "country girl," another (named, rather than
anonymous) embodied the more citified sophistication of
middle-class womanhood.[171] If his straightforward rendering
of the former encapsulated rural vigor, van Gogh's rather
studied portrait of Mademoiselle Gachet might be read as
something more than a bow to bourgeois propriety and
accomplishment. Given the performative act it depicts,
Marguerite Gachet's image may be seen to celebrate the
artistic persona (while acknowledging its overbred, almost
sickly aspects); van Gogh—a self-proclaimed "musician in
colors"[172] who recently had compared his "translations" of
others' pictures to a pianist's interpretation of Beethoven—

192. *Peasant Woman in Wheat Field* (F 774, JH 2053), late June 1890
Oil on canvas, 92 x 73 cm
Las Vegas, Bellagio Gallery of Fine Art

193. *The Old Peasant Patience Escalier* (F 443, JH 1548), 8–10 August 1888
Oil on canvas, 64 x 54 cm
Pasadena, California, Norton Simon Art Foundation

may well have drawn a parallel between his painter's procedures and the rapt musician's keyboard maneuvers. He rarely showed his portrait subjects "in action," and his depiction of Mademoiselle Gachet's engagement in a characterizing pursuit presumably owes something to realist and impressionist paintings in which portraiture and genre merge.[173]

The portrait of another young woman of Auvers, Adeline Ravoux, is more typical of its maker in both its stasis and its minimal background (JH 2035; see also figs. 196 and 197). The thirteen-year-old daughter of van Gogh's landlord, she was barely acquainted with the painter when he asked her to pose.[174] Her wide-eyed look, pursed mouth, and flexed fingers hint at restiveness (though van Gogh reportedly complimented her on her deportment),[175] and the painter's decision to render Ravoux in the pure profile view (long used to suggest a female sitter's modest refusal to meet a stranger's gaze) adds to the viewer's sense of the girl's uneasiness under van Gogh's scrutiny. Although a three-quarters view of a subject's head is generally held to be more revealing of mood and personality than a profile,[176] Ravoux's sidelong pose conveys youthful shyness and thus seems to enhance rather than undermine her portrait's psychological resonance. Moreover, the lateral vantage point offers up the most physically distinctive aspect of the subject's face—the sharp silhouette of brow, nose, and chin—and renders physical likeness more clearly than would an oblique view.[177]

While clearly denoting a particularized individual, Ravoux's portrait also seems connotative of a more general type that van Gogh had treated before, corresponding in this regard to the image of an Arlésienne model the artist labeled a *mousmé* (borrowing a term novelist Pierre Loti used to describe " a young girl or very young woman").[178] Roughly the age of Adeline Ravoux, the model who posed for *La Mousmé* (fig. 143) wears a dress and hairdo of similar style, and though she faces and makes eye contact with the artist/viewer, she does so with a touch of stiffness that betrays ingenuous adolescence. The sprig of blossoming oleander held by *la mousmé* would seem to emblematize the unfurling of mature beauty,[179] and the painting's vibrant hues lend an aura of boldness that counteracts its subject's restrained demeanor. By contrast, the emphatic coolness of the palette van Gogh chose in depicting Adeline Ravoux, a young girl of Auvers, underscores the diffidence conveyed by her pose and expression and perhaps reflects a darkening of the painter's outlook.

Paul Gachet: Melancholic Modernity

Although his portraits of Mesdemoiselles Gachet and Ravoux may represent attempts to communicate "the thoughts, the soul of the model," that aim was most successfully realized at Auvers in the sole adult male portrait that van Gogh made there, that of Paul Gachet, whom the artist deemed "rather eccentric" and victim to "nervous trouble from which he certainly seems to me to be suffering at least as seriously as I."[180] He admired the doctor's collection of contemporary art[181] and enjoyed his reflections on both "artists of the new school"[182] and "the days of the old painters."[183] Having no prior knowledge of van Gogh's work, Gachet seems to have found it immediately compelling; according to van Gogh, Gachet was "absolutely fanatical about" the self-portrait on swirling ground (fig. 174) and "wants me to do one for him, if I can, exactly like it. I should like to myself."[184] By early June, van Gogh reported not only that he and Gachet were "great friends already"[185] but also that he was at work on the doctor's portrait.

Probably because he perceived Gachet as a soul mate of sorts who could truly understand and appreciate it, van Gogh's portrait of the doctor (fig. 198) is much more complex than most of the portraits he made, a tour de force with multiple references that seem to be both geared to the sitter and self-referential—a dualism elucidated by van Gogh's conviction that Gachet was "something like another brother, so much do we resemble each other physically and also mentally."[186] The doctor's enthusiasm for van Gogh's self-portrait made it a point of reference;[187] there, the artist presented his own head (seat of reason and reflection) as an island of steadfastness at the center of an unremarked (even pointedly ignored) maelstrom, and in his portrait of Gachet van Gogh shows the doctor slumped but steadily moored within a surround of quavering strokes and pervasive blueness.[188] In combination with the line and color he used to suggest disequilibrium and mournfulness, van Gogh employed more specific markers of despondency: the slouching posture and head supported by a balled fist are timeworn markers of the melancholic,[189] and Gachet's drooping features and vacant stare create an expression that verges on a "grimace."[190] Interestingly, in light of his own identification with the Christ of Delacroix's *Pietà*, van Gogh recalled Gauguin's description of his own *Christ in the Garden of Olives*[191] as he considered Gachet's martyred look.[192] Two years earlier, at Arles, van Gogh had attempted to paint Christ in the Garden himself, but—convinced that "I must not do figures of that importance without models" —he destroyed his studies,[193] and in the fall of 1889

196. *Adeline Ravoux* (F 769, JH 2037), ca. 24 June 1890
Oil on canvas, 71.5 x 53 cm
Private Collection

197. *Adeline Ravoux* (F 786, JH 2036), ca. 24 June 1890
Oil on canvas, 52 x 52 cm
Cleveland Museum of Art

(as Gauguin and Emile Bernard worked on images of Christ betrayed) he expressed his belief that "one can try to give an impression of anguish without aiming straight at the historic Garden of Gethsemane."[194] The portrait of Gachet apparently struck van Gogh as an attempt in that direction, for the doctor's "heart-broken expression," he wrote, if very much "of our time," was also "*if you like,* something like . . . 'Christ in the Garden of Olives.'"[195]

Despite its potential for historical resonance, Gachet's portrait was conceived as a decidedly "modern head," one that looked both "clear and intelligent."[196] A probable model in this regard was Puvis de Chavannes's portrait of Eugène Benon, which, to van Gogh's mind, presented "modern life as something bright, in spite of its inevitable griefs."[197] The brightness (both coloristic and iconographic) in Benon's portrait is found in the yellow book he reads and the still life of paint brush and cut flowers—hints of the consolation to be found in modern literature, art making, and nature's incursions into "culture." The red-topped garden table that anchors van Gogh's image of Gachet[198] holds similar bright notes: two stems of foxglove in a glass and two yellow books. Foxglove is a member of the genus *Digitalis,* and its dried leaves can be used as a heart stimulant; thus, the floral motif in Gachet's portrait not only provides visual punctuation (the buds echoing the color and disposition of the jacket's buttons) but also alludes to the homeopath's art.[199] The model's hands—which van Gogh described, somewhat oddly, as those of "an obstetrician"—were likewise included as tools of his trade;[200] Gachet's portrait, like van Gogh's self-portrait in a painter's smock (fig. 169), can be seen to ground the subject in his profession. The books included in the doctor's portrait are generally suggestive of his modernity—van Gogh thought that images of men with books (he specifically mentions a portrait by Ernest Meissonier[201] and Albert Besnard's *Modern Man,*[202] in addition to Puvis's *Benon*) struck a "nineteenth century note"[203]—and, being titled (*Germinie Lacerteux, Manette Salomon*), they seem more explicitly significant as well. Owned by the artist rather than his sitter,[204] the books nonetheless are bound up with van Gogh's impressions of Gachet. Both were written by the Goncourt brothers, a fraternal team van Gogh admired,[205] and "brotherhood" of a figurative sort seems to be a leitmotif of van Gogh's characterization of the doctor, who, as he told Theo, "is very, yes very, like you and me."[206] Van Gogh often recalled the Goncourts' evocative description of Germinie Lacerteux in connection with despair, and thought of that pallid character, "exhausted by waking and weeping," when he rendered the

"I have a portrait of Doctor Gachet with the heart-broken expression of our time."

June 1890

198. *Doctor Gachet* (F 753, JH 2007), 3 June 1890
Oil on canvas, 66 x 57 cm
Private Collection

careworn Virgin of his *Pietà*. The other book at Gachet's elbow, *Manette Salomon,* is a novel of the art world of the 1840s that recalls—as did Gachet—"the days of the old painters." Its male protagonist, Coriolis (the artist husband of Manette) is described by the Goncourts as a "nervous" and "sensitive" soul;[207] burdened by familial obligations that thwart his aspirations,[208] he experiences the "heartbreak" that "seems to crown the careers and lives of this century's great painters of modern life."[209] As in *Germinie Lacerteux, Manette Salomon* details a downward spiral, and both were novels of the sort that van Gogh characterized as offering "life as it is," thus "satisfy[ing] the need we all feel of being told the truth."[210] Gachet's portrait seems to have been conceived in much the same spirit—pulling no punches and offering scant consolation—perhaps because van Gogh believed that the physician, armored by his science, needed none. On meeting Gachet, the artist had noted that "his experience as a doctor must keep him balanced enough to combat the nervous trouble from which he seems to be suffering,"[211] and the misery and frustration signaled by the books placed beside him are counterbalanced by indications of the physician's capacity to heal himself (or at least maintain calm): the medicinal plant, and pale, worn, but sturdy hands that buttress his sagging form.

A display of closed and titled books links the portrait of Gachet to Gauguin's image of Meyer de Haan (fig. 186), which it formally resembles, and ties the doctor's image to that of Marie Ginoux (fig. 184), which, according to van Gogh, Gachet admired and "understands . . . exactly."[212] Joined in the artist's mind by his empathy with their sufferings, Ginoux and Gachet, who never met, are forever coupled by the portraits made of them, which are of the same size and show their heads inclined on closed hands. Resembling each other enough to ensure their reading as pendants, the portraits of Ginoux and Gachet also make for a study in contrasts (many of them doubtless gender-based).[213] The pink ground of long parallel strokes on which Ginoux is shown indicates the wall of a room, whereas the deep blue bands behind Gachet—animated by choppy vertical and diagonal brush marks of lighter hue—place him outdoors, against a vista of hills, perhaps suggesting his broader experience of the world. While Gachet's face is, as van Gogh described it, "grief-hardened,"[214] Ginoux wears "her habitual smile"[215] and sits more or less erect—especially compared to Gachet, whose cares lay him low. Ginoux manifests a capacity for cheerfulness, and the books displayed before her are not only of milder hue than those beside Gachet but also of milder tone: uplifting sentiments of the sorts expressed by Beecher

Stowe and Dickens are anathema to the Goncourts' hard-boiled tales of modern travails and ignoble death. The latter are, arguably, "books written by men for men,"[216] but the books in Ginoux's portrait were volumes that van Gogh could comfortably recommend to his sister.[217]

In addition to setting down likenesses of his friends, in his portrayals of Ginoux and Gachet van Gogh rendered types he considered all too typical: beleaguered individuals "subject to the circumstances and maladies of our times."[218] Theirs were the sorts of "modern heads which people will go on looking at for a long time to come, and which perhaps they will mourn over after a hundred years,"[219] and the portraits Ginoux and Gachet inspired (which van Gogh clearly came to pair while conceiving the doctor's image) may be seen, in juxtaposition, as alternative modes of coping with affliction. Ginoux personifies resolute optimism—a mood amplified by the books, which evoke Dickensian common sense and Beecher Stowe's abiding faith in a better world to come. In light of the books used to inscribe it (favorites from the artist's youth), Ginoux's attitude might be seen as something of an anachronism, untenable to the sort of reflective contemporary soul (and masculine sensibility) that Gachet embodies. Gachet—in assuming the posture of the "broken man" van Gogh saw him to be[220]—conveys an attitude of resignation to "life as it is," the harsh modern reality the Goncourts insistently detailed. The doctor unabashedly wears what van Gogh called "the heart-broken expression of our time"[221] and seems but marginally buoyed by the curatives modern medicine proposed.

Clearly, these portrayals of people with whom he so closely identified should also be seen to reflect the artist's attitudes toward his own illness and his assessment of his ability to live with it. Van Gogh's personal malaise is a subtext of both Ginoux's and Gachet's portraits, and—as the doctor's image may be taken to indicate—pessimism about its long-term ramifications for his life and work ultimately trumped the artist's attempts at hopefulness in the summer of 1890. Within weeks of painting Gachet, van Gogh was dead, of a self-inflicted gunshot wound. Throughout his career, he had aimed for portraits that went beyond mere appearance to become what one might well call "speaking likenesses." Had he lived longer, he would certainly have continued in this vein—and perhaps even tackled portrayals of those he loved best. As he remarked apropos his "modern heads" in a final letter to Wil: "Knowing what I know now, if I were ten years younger, with what ambition I should work at this! . . . I sincerely hope to be able to paint your portrait someday."[222]

199. Henri Matisse, *Portrait of Madame Matisse: The Green Line*, 1905
Oil on canvas, 40.5 x 32.5 cm
Copenhagen, Statens Museum for Kunst

The Modern Legacy of Van Gogh's Portraits

JOSEPH J. RISHEL

with KATHERINE SACHS

200. *The Old Peasant Patience Escalier with Walking Stick*
(F 1461, JH 1564), ca. 29 August 1888
Ink, 14 x 13 cm
Private Collection

The modern portrait begins with van Gogh. He would have had it so:

> That which excites me the most, much, much more than the others things in my work—is the portrait, the modern portrait . . . I would like, you see, I'm far from saying that I can do all that but finally I'm getting there, I would like to make portraits that, a century later, might appear to people of the time like apparitions. Accordingly, I don't try to do that by the way of photographic resemblance, but by way of our impassioned expressions. Using as means of expression and exaltation of character our science and modern taste for color . . . [1]

Van Gogh made this statement in a letter to his sister in 1890. Since then portraiture has been a complex and in many ways a marginalized element in the history of modern art and only recently has undergone a reconsideration.[2] However, van Gogh's hope for the future effect of his own portrait images seems to have been completely fulfilled and one can safely assume that their power is a central element in his vast appeal. But can portraits be isolated as a factor in the overall critical fortunes of van Gogh? And how, in fact, are van Gogh's portraits linked with what was created afterward? And what, if anything, can be learned about van Gogh and the grandeur of his declaration from comparisons with later works?

For the first two decades following van Gogh's suicide in 1890, the patterns of influence are quite clear and, recently, have been explored in two major books and one exhibition.[3] His importance in France for those painters associated with the Fauves and, simultaneously, with the German expressionists, is vivid and profoundly moving, with portraiture playing a central role in these artistic movements. Thereafter— essentially after 1914—even while van Gogh's fame built toward the nearly mythic level it holds today, the concrete evidence of his influence is limited and seems best explained outside the conventional categories of modernist art history. At its most revealing, the evidence points to the deeply felt, completely ahistorical response of one artist to another, led by expressive intention as much as by formal solutions (just as Vincent would have had it, perhaps).

The link between the work of van Gogh and that of Henri Matisse can serve as a good early example of the rather oblique, yet penetrating, nature of van Gogh's influence on subsequent portrait making. Matisse is known to have owned three van Gogh drawings. Two of these were landscapes. The third, purchased from Ambrose Vollard in 1899, was a little square drawing of Patience Escalier, the Arles cowherd turned gardener (fig. 200). The person seen here is a far cry from the stern and passive survivor who sat for two paintings[4] (see fig. 193) and whom van Gogh felt had the earthy, persevering quality of Jean-François Millet's *Man with a Hoe*. What attraction could this droll and fond image have held for Matisse? The sparsity of the drawing, in sharp and long strokes, certainly has some parallels with Matisse's own ink drawings of the period. Oneis on safer ground, however, searching for a link in a work which Matisse did not buy (for financial reasons, although he seriously considered it) from Vollard at the same time: one of the portraits of the Arlésienne,[5] painted after a Gauguin drawing which van Gogh took with him to the asylum at St.-Rémy. That kinship between Matisse and van Gogh which Hilary Spurling has recently explained in terms of Matisse's deep sense of his own "northernness" begins to emerge: the identification by Matisse, born near the Belgian border, with the famous Dutchman, whom he saw as an example of radical independence from Parisian centrality.[6]

Van Gogh's influence is more easily demonstrated some five or six years later in such works as the 1905 *Portrait of Madame Matisse: The Green Line* (fig. 199). Here the blunt separation of fields of color and their mutual aggression—quite apart from any local reference—is further exaggerated by the varied textures and the direction of the coarse brushstrokes, which pitch this image to a level of high exaltation, a quality very like that of the "apparitions" which Vincent hoped the future would find in his own portraits. Four years earlier, in March 1901, André Derain had introduced his friend Maurice de Vlaminck to Matisse at the van Gogh show held at the Bernheim-Jeune gallery in Paris, where they could have seen some seventy-one works. However, it was only with the 1905 van Gogh retrospective of forty-five paintings, as well as drawings (including a loan from Matisse), at the Salon des Artistes Indépendants that the full intensity of van Gogh's work seems to have hit these young artists. At their own strong showing later that year at the Salon d'Automne, their work was declared by the critic Louis Vauxcelle to be "orgies of pure color," the products of "wild beasts [*les fauves*]."[7] A quick survey of some of the portraits produced that year by the central figures of the Fauve group (figs. 201–3) gives abundant evidence of their direct dependency on van Gogh, not only as a point of liberation in the use of color but also, in terms of the sense of urgency to be gained by moving in closely to the subject, in setting just the head and shoulders against an elaborately worked and patterned background. As John Rewald says of Vlaminck:

Above
201. André Derain, *Self-Portrait*, ca. 1905–6
Oil on canvas, 33 x 25.5 cm
Private Collection

Opposite above
202. Maurice de Vlaminck, *Portrait of Derain*, 1905
Oil on canvas, 27.3 x 22.2 cm
The Jacques and Natasha Gelman Collection

Right
203. André Derain, *Portrait of Maurice de Vlaminck*, 1905
Oil on canvas, 41.3 x 33 cm
Chartres, Musée des Beaux-Arts

Vlaminck had received a profound shock from the work of van Gogh, which was for him an almost dolorous revelation. For, in spite of all the admiration which seized him in front of van Gogh's canvases he immediately recognized in him a formidable adversary. Here was a man who had had the same aspirations which he felt, who had translated in his work the same torments and exaltation, the same visions and impressions with which he struggled himself. And he had translated them with pure colors and brush strokes so vibrant that all his emotions seemed to lie bare on his canvases.[8]

Once, Vlaminck even went so far as to declare: "I loved van Gogh better than my father."[9] The others in the group were less abandoned in their enthusiasms, especially Matisse, who consciously steered his own development between excess and order. Matisse's own memory of the meeting is telling:

> Looking in at the Van Gogh exhibition one day at Bernheim's, in the Rue Laffitte, I saw Derain accompanied by a young giant who was voicing his enthusiasms in dictatorial tones and declaring that one must paint with pure cobalt blue, pure vermilion and pure Veronese green. Derain, I think, was a little afraid of him, but admired his ardor and eagerness. He came up to me and introduced me to Vlaminck . . . To tell the truth, the painting of Derain and Vlaminck did not surprise me, for it was closely related to my own line of research. But I was moved to find that there were young men who had convictions similar to mine.[10]

For Matisse, the urgency prompted by van Gogh would subside very quickly after 1905. However, his deep regard for van Gogh and balanced view of his contribution is nowhere better witnessed than in his general statement: "From Delacroix to Van Gogh and chiefly to Gauguin by way of the Impressionists, who cleared the ground, and Cézanne, who gave the final impulse and introduced colored volumes, we can follow this rehabilitation of color's function, this restoration of its emotive power."[11] In France, this less-heated view would prevail, with awareness of van Gogh's work, particularly as a portraitist, shining through numerous creations. Such awareness was always being tempered and restrained and was more reflective of profound formal and compositional inventions, less concerned with that quality of "apparition" which the Dutch artist hoped would be his strongest legacy.

A different line would be followed by the Rotterdam-born Kees van Dongen, who exhibited with the Fauves in 1905 and who, of all this group, was most directly involved with the works of van Gogh, having been asked by Bernheim-Jeune to organize another ambitious van Gogh exhibition in that gallery

204. Gabriele Münter, *Marianne von Werefkin*, 1909
Oil on cardboard, 81 x 55 cm
Munich, Städtische Galerie in Lenbachhaus

Below
205. Kees van Dongen, *Portrait of Augusta Preitinger*, 1910
Oil on canvas, 146.9 x 114.9 cm
Amsterdam, Van Gogh Museum

Right
206. Ernst Ludwig Kirchner, *Self-Portrait*, 1907
Location unknown

in 1907. Always alert to the coloristic intensity of van Gogh's palette and the energy of his brushstrokes, van Dongen experimented at this point with a very high-pitched palette, while stylizing and simplifying the outlines of his figures in a cloisonnist fashion that was as much indebted to Gauguin as it was to van Gogh (fig. 205). Noted for his Dutchness even by his contemporaries (although he rarely left France after his move to Paris in 1899), van Dongen is the bridge between Paris and northern Europe and, as such, reopens that question of Vincent's northernness which so engaged Matisse and has become a major focus of investigation in van Gogh scholarship. [12]

The reception of van Gogh's work in northern Europe has been a particularly rich field of investigation. In 1972 Robert Rosenblum in his Slade Lectures[13] proposed a new consideration of historical influences contrary to the canonical Parisian reading, thus launching new inquiries. Much new evidence has come to light documenting the number of important works by van Gogh that moved across Europe, particularly in German-speaking countries, during the first two decades of the twentieth century[14] and proving that Berlin served as a much more active conduit in making van Gogh's works available than did Paris at this time. The works on exhibition in Berlin, both in commercial galleries and in independent shows, far exceeds in number those seen in Paris.

Van Gogh's influence had deep and provocative ramifications for the development of painting throughout northern Europe. The story of how his influence spread begins almost simultaneously with the sensation caused by the Fauves in Paris in 1905 and the showing that same year of some fifty-four of van Gogh's works (all from the family collection) in several German cities.[15] The exhibition had its greatest impact on a group of young Dresden artists who in June of 1905 had founded a union they called Die Brücke.[16]

The making of portraits claimed a particularly large proportion of artistic concentration in Germany at the beginning of the twentieth century, following a very strong tradition reaching back to Dürer and Cranach but also, it has been argued, gaining new focus from the opening of new means for exploring the psychology and inner life of individuals launched by Freud and his circle.[17]

Van Gogh's portraits had a very strong impact on the next generation of German artists in a more pervasive and sustained way than is visible in any other pattern of influence in France or other areas of Europe at that time. As Magdalena Moeller has outlined so clearly, this permeation of Europe by van Gogh's influence followed a specific geographical pattern, moving from east to west, being felt first in Dresden and culminating in the response to the showing of 125 works by van Gogh at the Sonderbund exhibition in Munich in 1912.[18]

Examples abound: already by 1907, in a youthful self-portrait (fig. 206), Ernst Ludwig Kirchner, one of the four principal figures in Die Brücke, seems to have placed himself and his swiftly recorded features into a flattened, broadly stroked landscape, strongly reminiscent of the van Gogh portrait he might already have seen at Cassirer's in Berlin. He and his fellow students had given a rapturous reception to the first serious monograph ever devoted to Vincent, a lengthy section in Julius Meier-Graefe's abundantly illustrated book on modern art, which appeared in its first (German) edition in 1904. As a contemporary stated, "they went wild for Van Gogh,"[19] although this enthusiasm was moderated by a strong residue of influence from a form of Manet-like impressionism specific to Berlin and practiced there by Max Lieberman. Much the same may be noted in the 1906 *Self-Portrait* by Kirchner's comrade-at-arms, Erich Heckel (fig. 207). Another member of this bohemian group residing in the heart of deeply bourgeois Dresden, Karl Schmidt-Rottluff, seems to have been the first to fully employ high color, flattened spaces, and abrupt strokes

207. Erich Heckel, *Self-Portrait*, 1906
Oil on board, 47.5 x 36 cm
Berlin, Brücke Museum

Opposite above
208. Karl Schmidt-Rottluff, *Self-Portrait*, 1906
Oil on canvas, 44 x 32 cm
Seebüll Foundation Ada and Emile Nolde

Below
209. Alexej Jawlensky, *Self-Portrait*, 1912
Oil on board on wood, 53 x 49 cm
Private Collection

of the brush to achieve expressive power, as is evident in his highly charged 1906 *Self-Portrait* (fig. 208).

Van Gogh's influence took hold more slowly, but perhaps more absolutely—certainly as far as portraits are concerned—farther west. Alexej Jawlensky's 1912 *Self-Portrait* (fig. 209) is the most directly linked correspondence one can make to any German work created in this decade by those with their heads full of van Gogh. Although here again, in retrospect, and particularly as regards the past and future development of Jawlensky as an expressionist artist, the equally pervasive influence of the Norwegian Edvard Munch as a portraitist is also very strongly in play. Part of the dichotomy established by these two forces—the thinly worked, emotionally stretched quality of Munch's works versus the high energy and depth of human perception found in all emanations of van Gogh—is reflected in the early work of Gabriele Münter (fig. 204), who possessed perhaps the most sophisticated historical sensibility of all her colleagues in Munich, including her close friend Jawlensky and her lover at the time, Wassily Kandinsky.

This mining of van Gogh's works, particularly the portraits, for their subjective intensity, their "expressiveness" (the characteristic that gave its name to the very diverse German responses) lasted just over a decade in the years preceding World War I. The radical use of color in a combination of expressive and formal ways, best understood among the Fauves by Matisse, began to diminish. Thereafter, one cannot find any pattern of group response, in part because the works had become more widely known through exhibitions, publications, and the very wide distribution of the paintings themselves, but also because the impact of the new was simply past. One can best search for links through the individual responses of artists, quite detached from any general movement.

One such response can be seen in the work of Pablo Picasso. Already by 1901, the young Picasso, just arrived in Paris from Barcelona for the first time, painted a *Mother and Child* (fig. 211), which must depend on a direct knowledge of *Augustine Roulin with Her Baby* (fig. 149). He arrived too late to see the large Bernheim-Jeune show in that same year; however, the dealer Ambroise Vollard (who would become one of Picasso's strongest supporters) had in fact had this picture in his possession since at least 1894. As has recently been noted,[20] Picasso's placement of the two figures in the space, his use of the yellow backdrop, and particularly the mother's large and somewhat spectral hand supporting the child's chest are derived from van Gogh. Picasso's expressive intentions are, of course, quite different and, in comparison to those of van Gogh,

slightly conventional. The child's attention is caught by something offstage to the left, while the mother gazes at her fondly; whereas Madame Roulin holds up her child like an almost sacred trophy for our consideration, her own features are as mute and neutral as those of a Raphael Madonna. The iconic quality of van Gogh's work—its apparitional aspect and its "exaltation" in this case?—seems to have been of little interest to the young Picasso, whose own picture is still charmingly within a purely genre tradition.

The power of van Gogh's vision seems to have been released in waves of building intensity in Picasso's comprehension, and it is especially evident in the self-portraits, climaxing in the bluntly authoritative Prague portrait of 1907 (fig. 210), which, as John Richardson notes, seems to be a combination of Picasso's memory of van Gogh's self-examinations and his own love of the new development of the film close-up. The hold on him was certainly, in part, that quality which he admired in his own work of being "painted all at once, like a van Gogh."[21] But it is as much the life and character of van Gogh as it is the paintings that held Picasso. In painting the portrait of Casagemas on his deathbed—the victim of his own gunshot—Picasso's feelings are full of

Above left
210. Pablo Picasso, *Self-Portrait*, 1907
Oil on canvas, 56 x 46 cm
Prague, Národní Galerie

Above right
211. Pablo Picasso, *Mother and Child*, 1901
67.5 x 52 cm
Bern, Kunstmuseum

Opposite above
212. Chaïm Soutine, *Portrait of Moïse Kisling*, ca. 1919–20
Oil on board, 99.1 x 69.2 cm
Philadelphia Museum of Art

Below
213. Oskar Kokoschka, *Hirsch as an Old Man*, 1907
Oil on canvas, 70.5 x 62.5 cm
Neue Galerie der Stadt Linz

van Gogh, the victim/hero, and certainly, as Richardson notes so eloquently: "Picasso could not escape his [van Gogh's] violent wake. Van Gogh helped him to unlearn all accepted notions of artistic decorum and pour his heart and guts, spleen and libido onto canvas—not just at this moment but at other times, especially toward the end of his life, when he set out to make angst palpable in paint."[22]

Chaïm Soutine "hates Van Gogh," said his dealer Paul Guillaume.[23] It seems more likely, and there are many to testify to this, that he really hated the simplified comparison between himself and van Gogh, which must have insulted his bohemian sense of radical independence and innovation. Dr. Albert Barnes, who bought fifty-two canvases by Soutine in one evening in 1922, astutely called him an amalgamation of van Gogh, African sculpture, and Cézanne.[24] Arriving in Paris via Lithuania in 1913, Soutine had abundant access to paintings by van Gogh. He quickly established himself as independent from the Fauves, although his use of encrusted paint and a highly keyed palette certainly may reflect his knowledge of them. But it is his exaggeration of features and the almost abstract use of color that make the comparisons so telling. It is extremely difficult to doubt that some memory of *The Postman: Joseph Roulin* (fig. 145) lies behind Soutine's *Portrait of Moïse Kisling* (fig. 212). Most importantly, there is a poetic quality about these images that suggests a profound understanding—the "impassioned expressions" once again—of van Gogh as a portraitist. And unlike the other encounters we have discussed, the ghost of van Gogh seems to be omnipresent throughout Soutine's entire career.

In this sense—in the very general category of the expressionist portrait—another masterful and prolific figure who drew deeply upon van Gogh must be considered: Oskar Kokoschka. As early as 1910, a critic in *Der Sturm* questioned whether one should judge the young painter by the "iron standard of Van Gogh."[25] Julius Meier-Graefe noted (in 1922) that, for a time, "Kokoschka could be regarded virtually as the Dutch artist's successor," who needed van Gogh as "the brutal field surgeon" to free him from the "fatal sweetness of the Viennese orient,"[26] the reference being, of course, to the highly eroticized symbolism of Gustav Klimt and Egon Schiele. Kokoschka's portrait *Hirsch as an Old Man* (fig. 213) is a tentative beginning, with color still playing a very minor role in an image full of exaggeration and intensity. Kokoschka in his later work would explore the high-pitched and varied palette of van Gogh to a degree unprecedented in the twentieth century (becoming one of its most practiced and serious portrait painters).

It is provocative in this context to look back a generation. When Ferdinand Hodler did a portrait of his friend, the Geneva-based sculptor James Vibert, in 1907 (fig. 214), the painter was fifty-five years old and firmly established (at least in advanced circles) as the pre-eminent modernist Swiss painter of his day. Hodler was deeply steeped in a symbolist tradition not unrelated to Klimt and Schiele (he participated in the Vienna Secession show in 1904, as a part of that very generation and style from which, according to Meier-Graefe, Kokoschka had needed to be forcibly liberated). And yet, faced with a portrait such as this, it is impossible to think he was not responding, like so many in the succeeding generation, to an encounter with van Gogh's images (the isolated heads of the Postman Roulin come to mind; see figs. 215 and 153), works which he might have seen at the Vienna Secessionist exhibition in 1904. Is the comparison too easy, too superficial? The flattened silhouette and sharp outline of the figure follow ideals that Hodler had already outlined in his notion of parallelism in the 1870s, a theory quite in the spirit of Swiss and German Renaissance portraiture, which he so admired. But by placing his image so emphatically against the brilliant yellow background—raising this carefully rendered likeness of a friend to the level of an iconic image—Hodler has created a work close in spirit to van Gogh's "apparitions." It seems too close to be accidental and is, perhaps, a provocative example of the power of van Gogh's images to influence even a mature artist whose style and aesthetic attitudes were already well established.[27]

One of the most disarming uses of van Gogh's portraits, simply in terms of the quickness of mind and nimble assurance with which the deed is done, is seen in the work of the young Joan Miró. In 1917 and 1918, just at the time he was having his first one-man show in Barcelona, he painted a group of half-length portraits in which the reference to specific works by van Gogh must be taken as a deeply human, and very witty, play on and against the by-then famous images. "Miró's earliest work was a typical advanced art-school product of the period. This character gradually gave way . . . to a clearly fauve approach, or more exactly a personal derivation from the manner of the fauves' own predecessor, van Gogh."[28] Miró was twenty-five at the time and would not go to Paris until the following year. Yet much was available to him in Spain, as he noted himself: "In Barcelona I had already received a blow with Picabia and Apollinaire. They confirmed for me that painting did not only consist of plastic problems. For this reason, for example, I was much more interested in Van Gogh than in Cézanne. For a long time I distrusted Cézanne . . ."[29]

214. Ferdinand Hodler, *James Vibert, Sculptor*, 1907
Oil on canvas, 65.4 x 66.4 cm
Art Institute of Chicago

215. *The Postman: Joseph Roulin*, (F 433, JH 1524), 31 July–3 August 1888
Oil on canvas, 64.1 x 47.9 cm
The Detroit Institute of Arts

Opposite
216. *Portrait of Père Tanguy* (F 364, JH 1352),
detail, winter 1887–88
Oil on canvas, 65 x 51 cm
Private Collection

Above
217. Joan Miró, *Portrait of E.C. Ricart
(The Man in Pajamas)*, 1917
Oil and print glued on canvas, 81 x 65.1 cm
New York, The Museum of Modern Art

Right
218. Joan Miró, *Portrait of Heriberto Casany
(The Chauffeur)*, 1918
Oil on canvas, 70.2 x 62.5 cm
Fort Worth, Texas, Kimbell Art Museum

One of the versions of *La Berceuse* (see fig. 125) must have informed Miró's *The Chauffeur* (fig. 218), although in lieu of wallpaper a framed automobile forms the background. His *Portrait of E.C. Ricart* (fig. 217) is certainly an updated *Père Tanguy* (it initially had a Japanese print glued to the canvas fig. 98; also figs. 99 and 216). Miró's engagement with van Gogh, which has all the appearance of a game with the recent past, seems to play itself out by 1919, when Miró's *Self-Portrait* (which would eventually be owned by Picasso), for all of its blunt frontality and rather brutal authority in the manner of one of the half-length versions of the Postman Roulin, is now pervaded with an animation and poetic restlessness of touch and surface, which is his own amalgamation of cubism with the splinteringly intelligent wit and rhythmic complexity that would come to dominate his work in the 1920s.

Although Soutine, in his unique fashion, and Kokoschka continued to renew the van Gogh legacy, nothing in the portrait making of the 1920s and 1930s even vaguely resembled the wave of influence that surged through Paris, Dresden, Berlin, Munich, and, for a moment, Barcelona, in the twenty years after the artist's death.

In 1935 the Museum of Modern Art in New York opened the first large van Gogh retrospective held in the United States, which then toured throughout the country.[30] In his review, Walter Pach worried that it may have been an event delayed too long, that the moment might have essentially passed for van Gogh's work as a vital and renewing force:

> When the exhibition was first proposed to the committee in charge at the museum, a number of persons objected to it as not sufficiently modern. And there was much reason on their side. The painter had been dead for forty-five years, his work had influenced at least two generations of later artists: surely such a man came more within the province of the museums that occupy themselves with the older arts—the modern museum exists to deal with matters of our own day.[31]

Ironically, in terms of the shifting fortunes of van Gogh, in that same year, Irving Stone published *Lust for Life,* the first popular biography of van Gogh in English. The book was an immense success, going through multiple editions until it was made into an even more popular movie in 1956. From this moment onward the person of Vincent—the vivid and tragic details of his life and death, his words in the letters—took over from the art or rather merged with it into an immensely potent amalgamation whose ramifications are as much felt through theater, film, and the making of mass culture as through the examination (and influence) of any individual painting. And when, thereafter, artists made direct responses to the paintings—and particularly the portraits—the "myth" of Vincent inevitably becomes an essential element.

The most poignant and direct post-World War II example of the power of van Gogh's portrait images to attract and to serve as elements of re-creation is the series of eight works by Francis Bacon which explore, by theme and variation, van Gogh's *The Artist on the Road to Tarascon* (fig. 221). This work was moved with other art treasures from the Kaiser Friedrich Museum in Magdeburg to the salt mines at Neustassfurt in 1942, where it was destroyed by a fire bomb in 1945. A color photograph is all that survives. Bacon's paintings were first shown at the Waddeston Gallery in London in March 1957. In each series a man in a straw hat passes through a landscape, of horrific agitation in three cases (see fig. 219), and in one case through a still worse banded emptiness (fig. 220). The man sometimes pauses, lost and certainly doomed. Sometimes he plods blindly on. As John Russell noted in his review of the show, Bacon's figure is van Gogh as understood by the actor, poet, and painter Antonin Artaud:[32] "he preferred to become

219. Francis Bacon, *Study for Portrait of van Gogh III*, 1957
Oil on canvas, 198.4 x 142.6 cm
Washington, D.C., Hirshhorn Museum and Sculpture Garden

220. Francis Bacon, *Study for Portrait of van Gogh V*
Oil on canvas, 198.1 x 137.2 cm
Washington, D.C., Hirshhorn Museum and Sculpture Garden

221. *The Artist on the Road to Tarascon* (F 448, JH 1491), July 1888
Oil on canvas, 48 x 44 cm
destroyed during World War II, formerly Magdeburg, Kaiser Friedrich Museum

what society calls 'mad' rather than forfeit a certain, superior idea of human honour."[33]

The van Gogh of the letters and of literary creation has now completely taken over. The man who moves through the brightly lit landscape outside Arles in the original painting does so rather jauntily and plays the role, as figures often do in van Gogh landscapes, of a kind of neutral staffage (although in this case the figure embodies a rather charming degree of self-reflection as the artist sees himself setting out with his shadow for a day's work). Bacon has turned all of this into a very different encounter—which is no less true, certainly in that it captures his own sense of suffering and its costs. In their "terrible beauty,"[34] the works of Bacon's Tarascon series are on a par with van Gogh's work, yet very far from it in intention.

Three years later, in another work, Bacon seems to draw much closer to van Gogh's expressive intent. *The Head of a Man—Study of Drawing by Van Gogh* (fig. 222) is probably a reference to a little *Self-Portrait* now in the Van Gogh Museum in Amsterdam (fig. 223). In this work (unlike in the Tarascon series in which the notion of the artist as a human totality, and the horrible circumstances surrounding the Magdeburg self-portrait, seem to compel its creation), Bacon reveals a more modest response to van Gogh as a maker of self-portraits. In so doing, he closely approached that quality of "apparation" in the sense of spectral terror that Van Gogh anticipated.

The postwar revival of painting, on both sides of the Atlantic, as a highly charged, extremely expressive act, inevitably brought van Gogh's ghost back into play. It is tempting to see the Dutch-American Willem de Kooning (who came to the United States at age twenty-two) as in some way inheritor of the national mantle. This is particularly apparent in such "portraits" as those in the *Woman* series (see fig. 224). While these works may be fraught and extremely energized like a van Gogh portrait, de Kooning's portraits proper, from an earlier date, suggest no reference to van Gogh. In actuality, the desire to see an "expressionist" character as somehow a central element in van Gogh's portraits is essentially to miss their point. They certainly are deeply felt and universal in their reference, but to see them through the lens of de Kooning, and of Bacon in the Tarascon series, is to miss their profound, deeply still authority, much closer to an icon than to a Munch *Scream*.

The best reflection of what van Gogh meant to an immediately postwar world can be found not in a painting but in a beautiful statement by a great painter who, as we have noted, dipped deeply into van Gogh's work and who saw much in the life and meaning of van Gogh to be celebrated. In

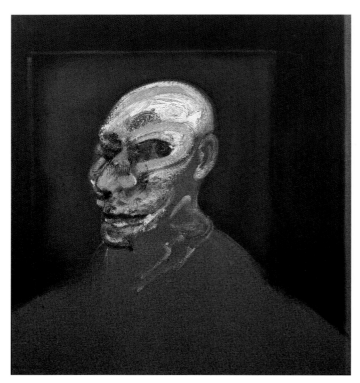

222. Francis Bacon, *The Head of a Man—Study of Drawing by Van Gogh*, 1959
Oil on canvas, 66 x 61 cm
Private Collection

223. *Self-Portrait* (F 1379, JH 1196), summer 1887
Graphite, 19 x 21 cm
Amsterdam, Van Gogh Museum

224. Willem de Kooning, *Woman V*, 1952–53
Oil and charcoal on canvas, 154.5 x 114.5 cm
Canberra, National Gallery of Australia

225. Chuck Close, *Lucas, II,* 1987
Oil on canvas, 91.4 x 76.2 cm
Private Collection

response to a request for his thoughts on van Gogh's influence on modern art, on the occasion of his centenary in 1953, Oskar Kokoschka wrote,

> It has always been the practice of artists to build their edifice with some bricks of the past. But Van Gogh's effect on contemporary art I should like to compare to that of delayed action because modern painters, under his influence, seem to feel that something is changing, something new is coming, but they do not know how and why . . . No visitor could ignore evidence of the disruption in the traditional approach to art in any exhibition of van Gogh's works which included the Fauves, Cubists, Surrealists or Non-objective artists. Society's general uneasiness about how to give a verdict on art lends a sombre significance to all art, that of the past and that which is to come.[35]

This ability to introduce a sense of the new—that quality of revelation/apparition that van Gogh hoped would endure—is, of course, at the root of his immense popularity. His universal appeal lies in the power of his works to transcend time for the viewer, albeit in an encounter that is likely to be tangled with other associations unrelated to art. But is van Gogh still alive as an "active ingredient" in the making of art and particularly of portraits?

In 1959 the young Chuck Close journeyed from Everett, Washington, to Seattle to visit a traveling exhibition of van Gogh's works. Close would become what is, for his generation, a revived species, a portrait painter—or, at least, an artist who makes the human presence his primary subject.[36] In his portraits (fig. 225)—the placement of the figure in the space, the "touch"—there is much to remind one of van Gogh. Beyond this, both artists share to a remarkable degree an ability to give the images a deeply human, unblinking presence and authority. In 1991 Close was asked to put on an exhibition from the collections of the Museum of Modern Art in New York. He decided to do a portraiture show because, as he recalled, "I realised that I spent most of my time in front of the portraits from van Gogh to Velázquez. I chose the painters I liked and juxtaposed them on shelves, like at a supermarket, to celebrate the similar mark-making and pictorial syntax."[37] As in the works of Matisse or Jawlensky, many elements are at work in the making of the image, and Close does not allow one "influence" to predominate. Yet it is satisfying to see—and the artist himself is bemused by such speculation—that when dealing with the most current portrait makers, notions of van Gogh can still be brought into play.

226. *Self-portrait with Felt Hat* (F 344, JH 1353), detail, winter 1887–88
Oil on canvas, 44 x 37.5 cm
Amsterdam, Van Gogh Museum

227. *Peasant Woman* (F 1184, JH 597), December 1884–January 1885
Graphite and chalk, 53.6 x 20.9 cm
Amsterdam, Van Gogh Museum

Notes

The Dutch Roots of Vincent van Gogh

1. L471.

2. Van Uitert 1981–82, p. 228, points out that van Gogh's signature conformed to the fashion of the 1870s in emulation of many successful salon painters.

3. Vincent signed the visitors' register book of the Department of Prints and Drawings of the British Museum in 1874 and in September 1887 also studied the Rembrandt print collection at the Trippenhuis, the previous quarters of the Rijksmuseum before it moved to the Cuypers building that now houses this institution. See Pollock 1980, pp. 532, 602, n. 32. The contents of the first four chapters of Pollock's dissertation are recapitulated in modified form in Amsterdam 1980. While at the Trippenhuis, van Gogh learned about the Rembrandt drawings in the Fodor collection in Amsterdam; see R. Pickvance, "An Insatiable Appetite for Pictures— Vincent the Museum-goer," in Amsterdam 1987, p. 62.

4. L 30 (6 July 1875). In this selection he also cites prints after French realist artists, including Camille Corot, Jules Dupré, Jean-François Millet, and Charles-François Daubigny, as well as the Dutch artist Jacob Maris.

5. Mentioned in a letter of 6 October 1875 (which is not in the English edition of the *Letters,* Van Gogh 1958). Cited by D. Silverman in London 1992, p. 131.

6. LW 14.

7. Pollock 1980, p. 38.

8. Pollock stresses the fact that initially van Gogh "apprenticed himself" to art instruction manuals and reproductions. Thus he became a self-appointed apprentice to a wide range of artists he never knew personally—Millet, Théodore Rousseau, and Daubigny, as well as the Dutch old masters. Pollock 1980, p. 52.

9. D. Silverman, "Pilgrim's Progress and Vincent van Gogh's Metier," in London 1992, p. 100.

10. Ibid., pp. 101–2.

11. Mauve was an obvious contact because he had married Ariëtte Carbentus, a cousin of van Gogh on his mother's side, in 1874.

12. Of all the Hague School artists, van Gogh admired Jozef Israëls and Anton Mauve the most. Mauve's initial willingness to instruct Vincent always remained an important token of support despite the fact that the two artists later became estranged. In a letter to Theo, Vincent indicates Mauve's importance to him: "Mauve has been kind to me and has helped me thoroughly and well, but— it lasted only a fortnight—*that is too short.*" L 190. Roland Dorn also quotes this passage as an indication of Mauve's significance for van Gogh in Vienna 1996, p. 63.

13. For discussion of the importance of these masters of the Hague School on van Gogh, see J. Sillevis in Vienna 1996, pp. 24–26. Also see Murray 1980, pp. 413–14, and G. Pollock, Review of "London, Royal Academy, The Hague School," *The Burlington Magazine* 125, no. 963 (June 1983): pp. 375–77. Van der Weele is mentioned repeatedly in Vincent's letters to his friend and fellow Dutch artist Anton van Rappard.

14. That these masters had made an indelible impression on the young van Gogh is clearly evident in a letter that he wrote to Theo from the Borinage in 1879 (L 130), in which he states, "A picture by Mauve or Maris or Israëls says more, and says it more clearly, than nature herself."

15. Pollock 1980, p. 42, stresses the significance of the writings of the Dutch critic J. van Santen Kolff, which appeared in *De Banier* in 1877. See also Amsterdam 1980, pp. 23–27.

16. E. van Uitert in The Hague 1990, pp. 158–60.

17. For further discussion of this material, see London 1992. Pollock 1980, p. 108, notes that this kind of imagery was intended for the middle-class British reading public, a group analogous to the Dutch citizens to whom van Gogh himself hoped to appeal.

18. In selected letters written to his friend, Anton van Rappard, from The Hague, Vincent elaborated on this subject. See LR 12, 14, 15, 20, 22, 23, and 24. In LR 12 van Gogh refers to these illustrators as the "black and white artists of the people," whereas in LR 20 he mentions the swift and spontaneous effects of this black and white medium and admires its virility.

19. L 240 (1 November 1882).

20. Pollock 1980, p. 435.

21. Ibid., pp. 29–31, 214–16, 352–54, 367–69, 372–76.

22. L 251. See also Pollock 1980, p. 139.

23. L 181. Van Gogh projects an analogous attitude in his early representations of coal miners of the Borinage trudging to work and of their wives bearing their burdens. See Amsterdam 1980, pp. 33–34, no. 44 (ill.).

24. This observation has already been made by J. van Lindert in The Hague 1990, p. 128.

25. The fishermen are, in fact, "orphan men" (wards of the state) posing in Vincent's atelier in sou'westers that he had acquired as costumes for this purpose.

26. For a detailed analysis of the charitable institutions in The Hague devoted to maintaining the indigent, see Pollock 1980, pp. 109–10 and p. 129, n. 75. For further discussion of the complex psychological impact of these drawings and the degree to which they transgress the conventional distinction between genre and portraiture, see Pollock 1983, pp. 351–53.

27. Pollock 1980, p. 109, and Zemel 1997, p. 17. Zemel 1987, p. 360, maintains that instead of representing the exaggerated rhetorical gestures associated with much Victorian imagery, van Gogh created starkly depicted figures in minimal settings. His pronounced graphic technique with its emphasis on angular contours, harsh lines, and gaunt facial features emphasized by physical scoring of the paper creates a disconcerting, palpable presence.

28. Roland Dorn has made an extensive study of the lithographs resulting from these drawings. See Vienna 1996, pp. 41–42, 105–7, 114, 131–32.

29. Amsterdam 1980, p. 57.

30. L 331. In L 330 he also describes the impact that the Drenthe landscape has on him: "I see no possibility of describing the country as it ought to be done; words fail me, but imagine the banks of the canal as miles and miles of Michels or Th. Rousseaus, Van Goyens or Ph. De Konincks."

31. Van Gogh read Carlyle's *Sartor Resartus* in March 1883 and *On Heroes, Hero-Worship, and the Heroic in History* in October of the same year. For discussion of the impact of Carlyle on van Gogh, see Pollock 1980, pp. 166–68, 170–71, and Amsterdam 1980, pp. 89–91.

32. L 337.

33. In a letter to Theo (L 299), he states, "Speaking of a Jules Dupré . . . It expresses that moment and that spot in nature where one can go alone without company. Ruysdael's 'Buisson' also has it very strongly."

34. Pollock 1980, p. 169. For an assessment of peasant subject matter in nineteenth-century French painting, see Herbert 1970.

35. Pollock 1980, p. 181. In Drenthe he had already become fascinated by the peasants. In one letter to Theo (L 330), he states, "There are a lot of Ostade types among them, physiognomies reminding one of pigs or crows . . ."

36. Although the French impressionists initially eschewed peasantry as a fitting subject within their repertory, by the 1880s Camille Pissarro became extremely interested in the theme. Gauguin and other painters of the Pont Aven school treated peasant themes as one of the key components of their repertoire.

37. As stated to Theo in L 384 (late 1884).

38. As noted by S. van Heugten in van Tilborgh et al. 1993, p. 103.

39. Pollock 1980, pp. 471, 508–9, n. 72, itemizes all the probable paintings by Hals that van Gogh saw in museums and exhibitions. In van Gogh's day *Isaac Massa and His Wife* was believed to represent Hals and his wife.

40. L 431.

41. L 427.

42. Pollock 1980, p. 435.

43. His defense of Hals's use of black may have served to justify his own use of dark, earth-toned colors. In a letter to Theo (L 428), he states, "But tell me, *black* and *white,* may they be used or may they not, are they forbidden fruit? I don't think so; Frans Hals has no less than twenty-seven blacks."

44. L 371.

45. As noted by L. van Tilborgh in van Tilborgh et al. 1993, p. 19.

46. R.R. Brettell and C.B. Brettell were the first to call attention to the girl standing before the table who lacks a chair to sit on (see *Painters and Peasants in the Nineteenth Century* [Geneva and New York, 1983], pp. 94–95). This curious detail in *The Potato Eaters* may, even quite subconsciously, reflect van Gogh's recollection of the standing servant figures in Hals's two representations of the governors of the old men's almshouse or the servant standing at the right in Rembrandt's *Pilgrims at Emmaus.*

47. L 597. As Pollock 1980, pp. 327–73, notes, van Gogh's enthusiasm for this painting was doubtlessly influenced by Fromentin's high estimation of it. Fromentin focused on the central significance of Rembrandt's use of light—by which he could fuse the visible and visionary, finite and infinite, the material and the spirit.

48. Van Uitert 1981–82, p. 231.

49. Pollock 1980, p. 263. Ostade produced hundreds of representations of peasants and was arguably the leading seventeenth-century Dutch painter of these low-life subjects. Early in his career Ostade's peasants were rowdy and often brawling. As his art evolved they became more gentrified. Ostade's most celebrated pictures represent either peasants gathered before the entrance of a house or tavern or within rustic interiors.

50. Stark 1982.

51. Boime 1966 was the first to point out the connection to Israëls. Subsequently this link has been cited by many authors, see Pollock 1980, p. 274, and van Tilborgh in Tilborgh et al. 1993, p. 29. E. van Uitert in The Hague 1990, pp. 153–55, points out that Israëls's painting was exhibited in the Paris Salon in 1876 and reproduced by Goupil in 1884. At the same time Goupil also reproduced a sketch by Israëls that is closely related to another painting by Israëls, *Family at a Table,* which van Uitert argues is even more closely related to van Gogh's *The Potato Eaters.* Van Uitert concludes that Israëls was the primary source of inspiration for van Gogh in creating this work. Pollock 1988, pp. 408–32, stresses the degree to which *The Potato Eaters* subverts the conventional bourgeois appreciation of sanitized peasant imagery associated with the work of artists such as Jules Breton or Léon Lhermitte, or even certain images by Jozef Israëls, to create a psychologically disconcerting image. *The Frugal Meal,* dated 1882, was acquired by the Van Gogh Museum in 1987; see "Nieuwe aanwinsten: Twee werken van Jozef Israëls," *Van Gogh Bulletin* 5, no. 2 (1990): unpaginated.

52. Pollock 1980, pp. 388–89, describes Rembrandt, Millet, and Israëls as harmonists who used chiaroscuro and a tonality based on warm black and browns in comparison to a second triad composed of Hals, Delacroix, and Dupré who, as colorists, produced symphonies of color.

53. L 181. These two paintings were displayed together in Paris. See Paris 1998, pp. 108–9, cat. nos. 49, 50.

54. Zemel 1993, introduction (unpaginated).

55. Zemel 1997, p. 137. Rubens and van Dyck also produced self-portraits on more than one occasion, but they were hardly preoccupied with self-imagery to the degree that Rembrandt was.

56. For an exhaustive analysis of Rembrandt's self-portraits, see H.P. Chapman, *Rembrandt's Self Portraits: A Study in Seventeenth-Century Identity* (Princeton, N. J., 1990)

57. LB 12. In his letter van Gogh actually conflates two paintings by Rembrandt in the Louvre, the *Self-Portrait* and *Saint Matthew and the Angel,* painted in 1661. Rembrandt was not the sole source of inspiration for van Gogh's *Self-Portrait as an Artist.* As the organizers of the exhibition at the Musée d'Orsay indicate, van Gogh must also have been aware of Cézanne's *Self-Portrait Holding a Palette* of about 1885–87, now in the collection of the Bührle Foundation in Zurich. See Paris 1998, p. 174, no. 68.

58. Pollock 1980, pp. 465, 517–18.

59. Ibid., p. 464.

60. Ibid., p. 450–51.

61. Van Lindert and van Uitert 1990, p. 65, figs. 45, 46.

62. L 496. For further discussion of his representations of

La Crau, see Roskill 1966, pp. 14–15. In another letter to Theo (L 502), Vincent states, "Here, except for an intenser coloring, it reminds one of Holland: everything is flat, only one thinks rather of the Holland of Ruysdael or Hobbema or Ostade than of Holland as it is." This evocation of the past is tinged by strong emotions as a passage from another letter (L 512) indicates: "Involuntarily—is it the effect of this Ruysdael country?—I keep thinking of Holland, and across the twofold remoteness of distance and time gone by these memories have a kind of heartbreak in them." In one of his last letters to Theo from Auvers (L 644), the artist reasserts his essential Dutchness: "The Dutchman works quite diligently, but he still has quite a few illusions about the originality of his way of seeing things. He is doing studies almost what Koning [Koninck] did, a little gray, a little green, with a red roof and a whitish road."

63. Pollock 1980, p. 491.

64. Although acquired by the Louvre in 1880 as by Hals, the portrait of *Catharina Both van der Hem* is now generally considered to be by Pieter Soutman (ca. 1580–1657).

65. Pollock 1980, pp. 484–85.

66. Ibid., p. 490.

67. Ibid., p. 492.

68. Ibid., p. 491, n. 98. This painting was formerly in the Suermondt Collection in Aachen along with Hals's *Malle Babbe.* Whereas van Gogh could have seen *Malle Babbe* when it was exhibited in Brussels in 1880, he may only have known the other Hals from reproductions. See Pollock 1980, pp. 428–29. This type of double portrait representing an adult woman holding a small child was common in The Netherlands. The Philadelphia Museum of Art possesses a characteristic example by Jan Anthonisz. Ravesteyn, where the child is actually seated on a table next to the woman. See *Paintings from Europe and the Americas in the Philadelphia Museum of Art* (Philadelphia, 1994), p. 89.

69. This comparison was first noted by van Lindert and van Uitert 1990, p. 88.

70. Pollock 1980, pp. 464, 518.

71. L 531.

Fantasy and Reality in The Hague Drawings

References to van Gogh's letters are to the English translation; see van Gogh 1958. The original Dutch or French texts are contained in van Gogh 1974. For the dates of the letters I have relied upon the chronology published in Hulsker 1993, pp. 29–33. My thanks to my Carleton College colleague Alison Kettering for helpful suggestions.

1. LW 5 (31 July 1888), L 517 (ca. 3 August 1888), LB 14 (ca. 4 August 1888).

2. LB 14. In L 516 (31 July 1888), van Gogh calls Roulin a "républicain enragé." In LW 5, writing in Dutch, van Gogh calls him a "fameus republikein."

3. L 261, 262, 267, and LR 22 discuss the heads using the Dutch word *koppen.* Regarding Roulin, LW 5, written in Dutch, uses the word *portret.* LB 14 and L 518, written in French, use the word *portrait.*

4. *Dictionary of Art* (1996), s.v. "trony." See also A. Blankert, *Rembrandt: A Genius and His Impact,* exh. cat.

(Melbourne, National Gallery of Victoria, 1997 [Sidney and Zwolle]), pp. 71–73; and F. Schwartz, "'The Motions of the Countenances': Rembrandt's Early Portraits and the Tronie," *Res* 17/18 (1989): 89–116. I am grateful to Alison Kettering for referring me to these, and to our former student Paul Crenshaw for discussion of the tronie.

5. L 141.

6. L 261. I accept Sjaar van Heugten's argument that this letter is not a separate missive but a postscript to L 260 and therefore dated ca. 13 January 1883. See van Heugten 1996, p. 197. Hulsker 1996 dates L 261 as ca. 21 January 1883. The drawing van Gogh mentions as having already made is lost, or possibly it was transformed into one of the existing drawings of a fisherman with a sou'wester.

7. L 300 (ca. 13 July 1883).

8. L 267 (ca.15 February 1883).

9. Van Gogh's teacher was Adriaan Johannes Madiol (1845–1927). See Hulsker 1990, p. 92.

10. L 173 and 181. Mauve was a distant cousin by marriage of van Gogh.

11. A line incised in the pigment extends from the boat in the direction of two horses at the water's edge. The horses, however, are linked to a cart. Such horse-drawn carts were used to collect shellfish on the beach—another subject depicted by painters of the Hague School. Perhaps not quite comprehending, van Gogh seems to have merged the two distinct subjects: horses pulling fishing boats onto shore and horses pulling carts full of shellfish.

12. LR 22 (ca. 15 January 1883).

13. LR 22. Also L 257 (3 January 1883): "Het zijn een paar 'heads of the people,' en mijn voornemen zou wezen door veel dergelijke dingen te zoeken een soort geheel te vormen, dat den titel 'heads of the people' meit geheel onwaardig zou zijn."

14. Visser 1973, pp. 58–65; van Heugten 1996, pp. 128–29.

15. L 235 (ca. 1 October 1882).

16. Besides JH 243, they are JH 241 and JH 271.

17. Visser 1973, p. 64, discovered that eight veterans were living in the Home while van Gogh was in The Hague.

18. ". . . een Zondagschen lap voor zijn blinde oog." LR 37 (ca. 14–15 June 1883). Another reference is in L 256 (31 December 1882–2 January 1883): "The model who sat for this really had a head injury and a bandage over his left eye." Van Gogh makes no mention of the medal, but he did have some sense of his sitter's military background, for he continues, "Just like a head, for instance, of a soldier of the old guard in the retreat from Russia."

19. L 264 (5 February 1883). Heyerdahl (1857–1913) was living in Paris and knew Theo, who probably reported his comment to Vincent.

20. Upset that *The Graphic* would replace its series of illustrations, "Heads of the People," with another, "Types of Beauty," he wrote "I cannot make 'Types of Beauty'; I do try my best to make 'Heads of the People.'" L 252 (ca. 11 December 1882).

21. Visser 1973, pp. 62–63, identified Zuyderland by collating the number, 199, that appears on his jacket sleeve in JH 287 with the registry of the Old People's Home. None of the other sitters from the Home has been identified.

22. "There is something very pleasant in the intercourse with the models." L 262 (ca. 25–29 January 1883).

23. LR 14 (22 or 23 September 1882); L 235 (ca. 1 October 1882).

24. L 251 (ca. 3–5 December 1882).

25. LR 14, L 235, L 236 (8 October 1882), L 238 (ca. 10 October 1882), L 254 (ca. 21 December 1882), L 258 (5 or 6 January 1883).

26. "Here they call them very expressively *orphan men* and *orphan women* [*weesmannen en weesvrouwen*]," van Gogh's emphasis (L 235). The terms actually referred only to residents of another Old People's Home in The Hague, as Visser 1973, p. 62, pointed out, but van Heugten 1996, p. 129, is undoubtedly correct in asserting that this distinction was lost on van Gogh.

27. "Vindt gij die expressie weesman en wessvrouw niet echt." LR 14 (22 or 23 September 1882). The English edition of van Goth's letters translates "echt" as "characteristic"; van Heugten 1996, p. 129, uses "superb." I think "the real thing," although slangy, more accurately conveys the quality of genuineness van Gogh saw in the pensioners.

28. L 117 (9 January 1878).

29. L 178 (3 March 1882). Also L 205 (3 June 1882): "Her mother is a little old woman exactly like Frère paints them."

30. For information on Sien and her family based upon archival research, see Zemel 1987. A revised version of this article appears as chapter 1 in Zemel 1997.

31. Two other children had died in infancy.

32. LR 8 (28 May 1882).

33. Zemel 1987, p. 355.

34. L 178 (3 March 1882).

35. One of the drawings is the "woman in a black merino dress" van Gogh mentions in L 195 (1 May 1882). He refers to the unfinished chair (JH145) in L 192 (3–12 May 1882). In the same letter he mentions the "bent figure of a woman" (either JH 143 or JH 144r), which is done on paper that van Gogh refers to as "double Ingres." All four sheets were originally in the Hidde Nijland collection and are now in the Kröller-Müller Museum in Otterlo.

36. L 205 (3 June 1882): "But my work clothes are not untidy at all, just because I have Sien to take care of them and make the necessary repairs." When van Gogh grew alienated from Sien, it was her negligence in "mending the clothes and making clothes for the children" that he cited in justification. See L 284 (9 or 10 May 1883). For the significance of the seamstress image in van Gogh's art, see Soth 1994.

37. L 215 (15–16 July 1882).

38. The identification of these sitters as Sien's sister and mother is likely but not definite (for discussion of this question, see van Heugten 1996, pp. 184–92). Nor is it certain that the shawl Sien's sister wears is the same one van Gogh refers to in L 178. When Sien appears in a head covering, it is usually a scarf.

39. Adrianus Zuyderland is recognizable in JH 287 and 288; the orphan man with the eye patch is represented in JH 285 and 289; a third orphan man is represented in JH 284 and 286.

40. I am grateful especially to Griselda Pollock and Susan Wolverton, and also to Carol Zemel and Stephane Houy-Towner for discussion on the cap Sien is wearing.

41. A term used by Griselda Pollock (1980, p. 109). Pollock does acknowledge that the "virtual portraits" were at base figure studies.

Van Gogh in Paris: Between the Past and the Future

1. L 450.

2. L 459.

3. The basic study of Vincent's period in Paris is Rewald 1956 (rev. ed. 1978), especially pp. 11–72. The first exhaustive study of the period is the doctoral dissertation of Bogomila Welsh-Ovcharov (Welsh-Ovcharov 1976), which was the groundwork for her exhibition "Van Gogh à Paris" (Paris 1988). Like every author who studies this period, I am indebted to both of these scholars.

4. For a summary of Theo's activity as a dealer, see R. Thomson, "Theo van Gogh: An Honest Broker," in *Theo van Gogh 1857–1891: Art Dealer, Collector, and Brother of Vincent*, exh. cat. (Amsterdam, Van Gogh Museum, 1999), pp. 61–151.

5. See L 27 and 29. The sale of ninety-five drawings by Millet from the collection of Emile Gavet took place at the Hôtel Drouot on Friday and Saturday, 11 and 12 June, 1875. There van Gogh saw in the original such works as *Noonday Rest* (lot no. 60), which he was later to copy from a reproduction. I am grateful to Alexandra R. Murphy for providing me with a copy of the annotated sale catalogue. See also Amsterdam 1989, pp. 99–102 and Paris 1998, pp. 145–51.

6. L 30.

7. L 28 and 43.

8. C. Bargue, with J.-L. Gérôme, *Cours de dessin* (Paris, 1868–70).

9. See L 115 (4 December 1877): "Today while I was sitting at my work I had before me a page from the 'Cours de Dessin Bargue' (the drawing examples) 1st part No. 39, Anne of Brittany. It was hanging in my room in London [i.e., in 1874], together with No. 53, and 'A Young Citizen [of the Year V]' was hanging between; what I liked and admired in the beginning I like and admire still."

10. L 136 (24 September 1880).

11. L 135 (7 September 1880): "I cannot tell you the pleasure Mr. Tersteeg gave me in letting me have for a while the 'Exercises au Fusain,' and the 'Cours de Dessin Bargue.' On the first I worked almost a whole fortnight, from early morning until night, and from day to day I seem to feel that it invigorated my pencil." His first copy after the *Daughter of Jacob Meyer,* almost certainly drawn in 1880, is F 847; de la Faille 1970 and Hulsker 1996 date the Kröller-Müller sheet to his time in Etten, in 1881. For more on van Gogh's interest in Bargue, see Koslow 1981.

12. Ibid.

13. A. Sensier, *La vie et l'oeuvre de Jean-François Millet* (Paris, 1881).

14. See also London 1974 and London 1992.

15. L 299 (ca. 11 July 1883); as translated in van Gogh 1996.

16. For Millet, see L 402; for Delacroix and color, see L 401.

17. See note 10 above.

18. L 402.

19. L 404 (30 April 1885).

20. L 443.

21. L 439.

22. Ibid. See also L 546 (written in early October 1888): "I write in haste, I am working on a portrait. That is to say, I am doing a portrait of Mother for myself [fig. 118]. I cannot stand the colorless photograph, and I am trying to do one in a harmony of color, as I see her in my memory."

23. L 447.

24. L 442: "I've done the portrait about which, as I told you, I'd been negotiating, and a study of the same head for myself." As translated in van Gogh 1996.

25. Ibid. See also Zemel 1997, chapter 3.

26. See L 427 (October 1885); for further references to Chardin and/or the Goncourts, see L 395, L 428, L 431, and L 442. The artist had likened Sien Hoornik to "some curious figure by Chardin or Frère" in L 164 (written in Etten in December 1881).

27. L 443.

28. Ibid.

29. See L 452.

30. The most important letters written from Paris are L 459a, to Horace Livens, L 461, to Theo, LB 1, to Emile Bernard, and LW 1, to the painter's sister Wil. Letters written in Arles in the spring and summer of 1888 reveal Vincent's continuing fascination with Paris and its artists. See, for example, L 468, L 471, L 476, L 480, and L 481.

31. For landscape, compare *Lane with Poplars* (F 45, JH 969, 1885, Rotterdam, Museum Boijmans Van Beuningen), *Houses Seen from the Back* (F 260, JH 970, 1885, Amsterdam, Van Gogh Museum), and *View of Roofs and Backs of Houses* (F 231, JH 1099, 1886, Amsterdam, Van Gogh Museum). For still life, compare *Still Life with Two Baskets of Potatoes* (F 107, JH 933, 1885, Amsterdam, Van Gogh Museum) and *Still Life with a Plate, Glasses, and a Wine Bottle* (F 253, JH 1121, 1886, Amsterdam, Van Gogh Museum).

32. L 248. For an almost identical study, see F 1354a, JH 997 (Amsterdam, Van Gogh Museum).

33. See Sensier 1881 (note 13 above), p. 182, n. 1. Sensier describes Millet as sending drawings of blades of wheat to women who asked for such a souvenir, and drawings of his clogs to men: "Aux dames, c'étaient des épis; aux hommes, c'était presque toujours une paire de sabots. Il m'en fit parvenir cinq ou six paires pour des admirateurs éloignés. C'étaient ses armes parlantes et comme un salut de politesse qu'il rendait." See also L. van Tilborgh, "Van Gogh, disciple de Millet," in Paris 1998, p. 36. De la Faille 1970, p. 130, entry for no. 255, notes that Carl Nordenfalk proposed another source of inspiration for the shoe still lifes in the work of the painter Nils Kreuger. See also Paris 1988, pp. 64–67, and Amsterdam 1990, pp. 70–71, where it is noted that one of Millet's drawings was shown in the retrospective exhibition of his work held in Paris in 1887.

34. The dating of the *Still Life of Shoes* is contested. Welsh-Ovcharov, in Paris 1988, pp. 64–65, cites Vincent's

comrade François Gauzi's description of the still lifes to date them to the period of Vincent's study in Cormon's atelier, which she places in the autumn of 1886. Roland Dorn, in Essen 1990, dated the painting to the Nuenen period, that is, before November 1885. According to Louis van Tilborgh (verbal communication), an X-radiograph of the painting confirms that Vincent painted the still life over an urban view, suggesting a post-Antwerp date for the picture.

35. See Rewald 1956 (rev. ed. 1978), pp. 16–18, 30–33; Welsh-Ovcharov 1976, pp. 41–43, 218–20; and Paris 1988, chronology.

36. L 459a. See Paris 1988, pp. 379–84.

37. The self-portraits in question are F 180, JH 1194; F 181, JH 1090; F 208, JH 1195; F 208a, JH 1089; and F 263a, JH 1199 (all Amsterdam, Van Gogh Museum).

38. See Paris 1988, pp. 278–79.

39. See Paris 1988, pp. 35–37, for a useful list of addresses and a map of Vincent's Paris.

40. Bing was himself to organize, in 1890, an extremely important exhibition of Japanese prints at the Ecole des Beaux-Arts. See *Exposition de la gravure japonaise: à l'Ecole nationale des beaux-arts à Paris du 25 avril au 22 mai: Catalogue* (Paris, 1890). Van Gogh was not able to see this exhibition during his brief visit to Paris in 1890. See New York 1986, p. 75.

41. Welsh-Ovcharov in Paris 1988, p. 322 (author's translation). It should be noted that Vincent thought *Poudre de riz* would be an admirable pendant to his portrait of the shepherd Patience Escalier (see fig. 193, JH 1548); see L 520. See also Toronto 1981, p. 133, and C.F. Stuckey, *Toulouse-Lautrec: Paintings,* exh. cat. (The Art Institute of Chicago, 1979), p. 121.

42. For the 1886 paintings, see note 37 above. For the other 1887 self-portraits, see F 268, JH 1299 (Hartford, Wadsworth Atheneum); as well as F 179v, JH 1300, F 269v, JH 1301, F 61v, JH 1302, F 109v, JH 1303, and F 77v, JH 1304 (all Amsterdam, Van Gogh Museum).

43. L 439. See also note 22 above.

44. L 501b.

45. L 514.

46. For Vincent's *japonaiseries*—paintings after Japanese prints—see F 371, JH 1296, F 372, JH 1297, and F 373, JH 1298 (all Amsterdam, Van Gogh Museum).

47. Welsh-Ovcharov, in Paris 1988, p. 164, cites the commentary of A.S. Hartrick, who proposed the relationship between Vincent's striated brushwork and the *crépons* in Vincent's collection in his *A Painter's Pilgrimage through Fifty Years* (Cambridge, 1939), p. 46.

48. Welsh-Ovcharov 1976, pp. 198–99, relates the skull to "the famous and definitive statement about his portrait aims . . . in Vincent's letter of early September, 1888, concerning his portrait of Eugène Boch" (i.e., L 531, in which Vincent writes, "I want to paint men and women with that something of the eternal which the halo used to symbolize, and which we seek to convey by the actual radiance of our coloring").

49. See Welsh-Ovcharov 1976, pp. 158–59.

50. See also Welsh-Ovcharov 1976, p. 173, for Vincent's adaptation of Degas's hatched pastel technique. For more on van Gogh and Degas, see the forthcoming essay by

Richard Kendall, to be published in the journal of the Van Gogh Museum.

51. ". . . il atteint à la vérité et à l'illusion de la carnation avec des coups de rouge vif, de bleu pur, de jaune d'or, avec des couleurs entières et absolues qui sembleraient devoir outrer la vie et forcer le ton de la réalité." See E. and J. de Goncourt, *L'art du XVIIIe siècle* (Paris, 1880–82), pp. 145–46; for the translation, see *French XVIII Century Painters,* trans. R. Ironside (London, 1948), p. 143.

52. L 431, October 1885: "I should like to tell you a great deal more, especially about what Chardin made me think about color and . . . not painting the local color. I think it splendid." Then, quoting Goncourt, "Comment surprendre—comment dire de quoi est faite cette bouche démeublée, qui a d'infinies délicatesses. Cela n'est fait que de quelques trainées de jaune et de quelques balayures de bleu!!!'" For the translation, see *French XVIII Century Painters* (note 51 above), p. 144.

53. L 431. Goncourt had made the comparison to Rembrandt: ". . . the drawing of the entire head, the planes of the face and their transitions . . . take shape and substance under his broad, abrupt handling in the same fashion as forms emerge from the impasto of Rembrandt." See *French XVIII Century Painters* (note 51 above), p. 143. I am grateful to Pierre Rosenberg for confirmation that the pastels were exhibited in the late nineteenth century.

54. LW 4.

55. See Zemel 1997, chapter 4, and Hamburg 1995.

56. See Paris 1988, p. 174. For the earlier self-portrait of this type, see F 181, JH 1090 (Amsterdam, Van Gogh Museum).

57. LW 7.

58. L 562.

59. LW 22.

60. L 636.

61. See LW 22.

62. See Zemel 1997, chapter 3, and Sund 1988 and 1992.

63. L 489; as translated in van Gogh 1996.

The Arles Period: Symbolic Means, Decorative Ends

Unless otherwise noted, quotations from van Gogh's letters are taken from the facsimile edition; see van Gogh 1977.

1. L 464, 571, 573, and 574. Both self-portraits show him with a bandaged ear; one of these (F 527) was for Theo, while the other (F 529) was evidently given to the Ginoux.

2. L 480, 535, 537, 544–47, 565, 571, et al.

3. L 481, 482.

4. In van Gogh's terminology, "figure" points to a complete representation, at least "with the hands" or "down to the knees," whereas "portrait" normally indicates not more than the "bust, head and shoulders." As van Gogh worked at close to life size, this implies a difference in the size of the canvas: his "figures" are larger than his "portraits." See L 517.

5. Theo to Willemina van Gogh, 6 December 1888: "Vincent . . . heeft onlangs portretten geschilderd waarover hij vooral tevreden schijnt te zijn. In figuur vind

hij de hoogste uiting van zijn kunst." (Amsterdam, Van Gogh Museum, inv. b916 v/1962; partially published in Hulsker 1974, pp. 14–15).

6. For works included in the earliest group, referred to by van Gogh simply as "la série des figures," see note 37 below, and for those in the second, the Roulin Family, see note 49. The third group comprises the "repétitions" of *La Berceuse* (F 505–8) and *L'Arlésienne* (F 488), the portrait of Dr. Félix Rey (F 500), and the two self-portraits with bandaged ear (F 529, F 527).

7. See especially L 519, 524, 526, 529, 537.

8. L 531 (3 September 1888): "Ah, mon frère quelquefois je sais tellement bien ce que je veux . . . Je voudrais peindre des hommes ou des femmes avec ce je ne sais quoi d'eternel dont autrefois le nimbe était le symbole et que nous cherchons par le rayonnement même par la vibration de nos colorations."

9. Hammacher and Hammacher 1982, p. 161. Also Hammacher 1968.

10. Gauguin to van Gogh, about 19 March 1890: "Je vous fais mon sincère compliment, et pour beaucoup d'artistes vous êtes dans l'exposition le plus remarquable. Avec des choses de nature vous êtes là le seul qui pense." See Cooper 1983, Letter 40.

11. Information from van Gogh's correspondence needs to be checked carefully: for example, at one point he thought that the *Pietà* by Delacroix (which he was at the time copying) was in the possession of Carmen Sylva. In fact, he had simply associated the print he had at hand with a statement by Pierre Loti in *Le Figaro supplément littéraire,* 28 April 1888, mentioning "une grande et superbe toile de Delacroix, la mise au tombeau du Christ" hanging in Carmen Sylva's studio. In no way does van Gogh's conclusion form a serious basis on which to reconstruct the provenance of the rather small-sized *Pietà* by Delacroix in the Nasjonalgalleriet, Oslo (see L. Johnson, *The Paintings of Eugène Delacroix: A Critical Catalogue* [Oxford, 1981 and 1986], p. 443); see Dorn 1990, p. 16.

12. L 615 (26 November 1889): "J'ai écrit à Bernard et aussi à Gauguin que je croyais que la pensée et non le rêve était notre devoir . . ."

13. L 507 (about 2 July 1888): ". . . je me vois revenir moi même d'un travail mental pour equilibrer les 6 couleurs essentielles rouge—bleu—jaune—orange—lilas—vert travail et calcul sec et où on a l'esprit tendu extrêmement comme un acteur . . . dans un rôle difficile—ou l'on doit penser a mille choses à la fois dans une seule demi heure."

14. For more on this topic, see Vienna 1996, pp. 31–48.

15. The first portrait of Madame Roulin (F 503) forms part of The Roulin Family, a set of five portraits conceived in late November 1888; see note 49 below. The first version of *La Berceuse,* the last painting of 1888 and referred to by the artist as a "study" (L 578), is most probably the one in the Kröller-Müller Museum (F 504). *Augustine Roulin with Her Baby* (F 490) is among the few size 30 canvases executed in December 1888 and not mentioned in van Gogh's correspondence; see Dorn 1990, pp. 414–16, 428–32, 451–52.

16. See Vienna 1996, pp. 105–29.

17. See V. Hugo, *William Shakespeare* (Paris, 1864), pp. 267–71.

18. See van Tilborgh et al. 1993, pp. 99–101, 105–7.

19. See van Heugten 1995, pp. 63–85: X-rays of versions nos. 4–6 reveal large figure paintings of 1884.

20. LB 15 (about 20/24 August 1888): "Je veux faire de la figure, de la figure et encore de la figure."

21. See especially L 501a, 505, 540.

22. See L 405, referring to A. Sensier, *La vie et l'oeuvre de Jean-François Millet* (Paris, 1881), p. 127; for materials and metaphors, see LR 13, L 371, 415, 451 and Vienna 1996, p. 39.

23. For van Gogh's metaphorical approach, see Vienna 1996, pp. 38–39.

24. L 533 (8 September 1888): "Le café de nuit continue le semeur ainsi que la tete du vieux paysan et du poète . . . C'est une couleur alors pas localement vraie au point de vue realiste du trompe l'oeil. mais une couleur suggestive d'une emotion quelconque d'ardeur de tempérament." The paintings van Gogh is referring to are *The Night Café* (fig. 117), *The Sower* (F 422), *The Old Peasant* (F 444), and *The Poet* (fig. 140).

25. L 520 (18 August 1888): "Je voudrai faire le portrait d'un ami artiste qui rêve de grands rêves qui travaille comme le rossignol chante parceque c'est ainsi sa nature / Cet homme sera blond. Je voudrai mettre dans le tableau mon appréciation mon amour que j'ai pour lui / Je le peindrai donc tel quel aussi fidèlement que je pourrai— pour commencer— / Mais le tableau n'est pas fini ainsi Pour le finir je vais maintenant être coloriste arbitraire / J'exagère le blond de la chevelure j'arrive aux tons oranges aux cromes au citron pale / Derrière la tête—au lieu de peindre le mur banal du mesquin appartement—je peins l'infini / je fais un fond simple du bleu le plus riche le plus intense que je puisse confectionner et par cette simple combinaison la tête blonde eclairée sur ce fond bleu riche obtient un effet mysterieux comme l'étoile dans l'azur profond."

26. L 531 (3 September 1888): "Exprimer l'amour de deux amoureux par un marriage de deux complémentaires leur melange et leurs oppositions les vibrations mystérieuses des tons rapprochés. Exprimer la pensée d'un front par le rayonnement d'un ton clair sur un fond sombre. Exprimer l'espérance par quelqu'étoile. L'ardeur d'un être par un rayonnement de soleil couchant."

27. L 503 (29 June 1888): "[Delacroix] parle un langage symbolique par la couleur même . . . Mais allez-y et on tombe en pleine métaphysique de couleurs à la Monticelli, gâchis d'où sortir à son honneur est bougrement incommode."

28. L 526 (ca 22/24 August 1888): "Je voudrais peindre de façon qu'à la rigueur tout le monde qui a des yeux puisse y voir clair."

29. For a full analysis of this *Décoration*, see Dorn 1990.

30. L 531 (3 September 1888): "hier j'ai encore passé la journée avec ce Belge . . . Tu le verras sous peu ce jeune homme a mine Dantesque car il va venir à Paris . . . ."

31. See H. Belting, *Das unsichtbare Meisterwerk: Die modernen Mythen der Kunst* (Munich, 1998), pp. 218–24. In this author's opinion, Belting's interpretation demands readjustments. Van Gogh's concept of decoration supplies the rational framework for production, while Belting's interest is directed toward the emotional components.

Thus, van Gogh's musical inspirations are extensively discussed, while his literary sources do not receive the attention they deserve.

32. L 609 (about 6/12 October 1889): "Quand je serai de retour à la rigueur cela formera un espèce d'ensemble 'Impressions de la Provence.'"

33. L 503 (see note 27 above) and L 504.

34. See P. Loti, *Madame Chrysanthème* (Paris, 1888), chapters 3 and 4; Kodera 1990, pp. 54–56, and Dorn 1990, pp. 128–29.

35. *L'Italienne* (F 381) was given this title and placed with the Arles period in the handwritten "Catalogue des oeuvres de Vincent van Gogh" of autumn 1890 (Amsterdam, Van Gogh Museum, inv. B3055 V/1962). Later, the model was thought to be Agostina Segatori and the portrait therefore dated to Paris. But its style clearly indicates Arles. Therefore, it would better be connected with the "petite Arlésienne," described in L 521 ("une jeune fille à teint café du lait . . . cheveux cendrés, yeux gris, *corsage d'indienne rose pâle, sous lequel on voyait les seins droits durs et petits*" [my italics]) and mentioned again in L 529 ("je crains que la petite Arlésienne me posera un lapin pour le reste du tableau . . .") and therefore datable to September 1888; see Dorn 1990, p. 248.

36. F. Champsaur, "La rue, par Jean-François Raffaelli," *Le Figaro supplément littéraire*, 3 March 1888; see L 501.

37. With the exception of *La Mousmé* (F 431), which is painted on a size 20 canvas, the "figures" of *The Zouave* (F 424), *The Postman* (F 432), and *L'Italienne* (F 381) are size 25. The "portraits" of the Zouave (F 423), Roulin (F 433), and Escalier (F 443, F 444) are size 15 (*figure* and *paysage!*); the one of Boch (F 462) is size 12 *paysage*; the portrait of Milliet (F 473) and self-portrait for Gauguin (F 476) are size 12 *figure*; the portrait of van Gogh's mother (F 477) is size 6; and *The Mudlark* (F 535) even smaller, size 5.

38. In 1888, Alphonse Daudet's *L'Arlésienne*, in a dramatic adaptation set to the music of Georges Bizet, was the success of the day at the Odéon Theater in Paris; van Gogh was probably acquainted with the original version in prose, published in *Lettres de mon moulin* (1872); see Dorn 1990, pp. 152–53.

39. For a discussion of the chair pendants in relation to the "empty chair" metaphor, see Dorn 1988, pp. 380–82.

40. L 520, 590.

41. L 560 (about 2 December 1888): "Mais j'ai fait les portraits de *toute une famille* celle du facteur dont j'ai déjà précédemment fait la tête—l'homme la femme le bébé le jeune garcon et le fils de 16 ans tous des types et bien francais quoique cela aie l'air d'être des russes. Toiles de 15. Cela tu sens combien je me sens dans mon élément et que cela me console jusqu'a un certain point de n'être pas un medecin. J'espère insister là dessus et pouvoir obtenir des poses plus sérieuses payables en portraits. Et si j'arrive a faire encore mieux *toute cette famille* là j'aurai fait au moins une chose à mon goût et personelle."

42. For the reconstruction of this set of portraits, see Roskill 1970, pp. 77–81, and Dorn 1990, pp. 446–54.

43. See L 520, 533, 629.

44. See L 330, 410.

45. See L 572 and Dorn 1990, p. 222, n. 71.

46. Isaiah 53:3: "a man of sorrow and acquainted with grief," was one of young Vincent's favorite Bible verses, to which he referred in his 1885 "portrait" of his father's Bible (F 117); see Nordenfalk 1947, pp. 141–42.

47. On September 11, 1888, Vincent sent "ce petit article sur Dostoievsky" to Theo (L 535). The article was by Dom Blasius (i.e., Jules Prével) and appeared in *L'Intransigéant* on 10 September 1888: "Le visage de Dostoïevsky était celui d'un paysan russe: le nez écrasé, de petits yeux clignotants, le front large, bossué de plaies et de protubérances, les tempes renfoncées comme au marteau. 'Jamais, dit M. de Vogüé, je n'ai vu sur un visage humain pareille expression de souffrance amassée.'" Merlhès 1989, p. 130, was the first to establish the connection between this article and the Roulin portraits mentioned in L 560.

48. "To stick to truth" was the maxim of French artist Paul Gavarni (1804–66), which van Gogh shared throughout his lifetime; see J. and E. de Goncourt, *Gavarni, l'homme et l'oeuvre* (Paris, 1873), p. 67, and L 177.

49. In canvas sizes varying from 5 to 30, van Gogh's portrait studies of December 1888 include three each of Joseph Roulin (F 435, F 436, F 439) and of the baby Marcelle (F 440, F 441, F 441a), two each of Armand (F 492, F 536), of Camille (F 537, F 538), and of Madame Roulin (F 490, F 504). There are three other December portraits, the one which Ronald Pickvance (Arles 1989, p. 76) has convincingly identified as Joseph Ginoux (F 533), the small study for a portrait of Gauguin painting (F 546), and the self-portrait for Laval (F 501).

50. For Zola's "experimental" approach, which implied "scientific" analysis and procedures, see Dorn 1990, pp. 174–86.

Famine to Feast: Portrait Making at St.-Rémy and Auvers

1. These two paintings, which hang in the Museum of Modern Art, New York, and the Van Gogh Museum, Amsterdam are—along with *The Night Café* (fig. 117)—the artist's most mythologized.

2. L 516 (translations are from van Gogh 1958 [1978 ed.], unless otherwise noted).

3. See, for instance, LW 4, in which van Gogh—writing from Arles in the summer of 1888—notes, "And today I am a landscape painter, whereas in reality portrait painting would suit me better."

4. LW 22 (written at Auvers).

5. J. Woodall, "Introduction: Facing the Subject," in *Portraiture: Facing the Subject* (Manchester, England, 1997), p. 7.

6. Although he lived with his brother Theo from March 1886 to February 1888—a period during which he made several portraits (some of people whose identities remain unknown) van Gogh never assayed Theo's likeness. In September 1888 he chided Emile Bernard for failing to paint a portrait of their mutual friend Gauguin, yet during his own two-month cohabitation with Gauguin (23 October to 23 December 1888) van Gogh never painted his colleague's features (though Gauguin made a portrait of him)—instead rendering his empty seat in *Gauguin's Chair* (fig. 152).

7. Portraits undertaken as commercial transactions between artists and patrons usually privilege external appearance and are expected to be "accurate" and/or flatter; images of artists' intimates, in addition to capturing likeness, are generally intended/assumed to render some inner essence as well, so that, as Woodall writes (note 5 above), "a lived intimacy between painter and sitter [is] imaginatively reproduced in the viewer's relationship to the painting."

8. See L 531 (Arles, September 1888): "Ah! portraiture, portraiture with the thoughts, the soul of the model in it, that is what I think must come."

9. See note 5 above.

10. In a letter to Bernard (LB 19a, autumn 1888), van Gogh declared: "It is often so difficult for me to imagine the painting of the future theoretically as something other than a new succession of powerful, simple [portraits], comprehensible to the general public."

11. At the end of his life, in June 1890, van Gogh told his sister, (LW 22) "I should like to paint portraits which would appear after a century to the people living as apparitions . . . using our knowledge of and our modern taste for color as a means of arriving at the expression of and intensification of the character." In his last letter to her (LW 23, also written in June), he remarked, "There are modern heads which people will go on looking at for a long time to come, and which perhaps they will mourn over after a hundred years."

12. The most thoughtful assessment of the origins and impact of van Gogh's ideas about Hals remains Griselda Pollock's unpublished doctoral thesis (Pollock 1980); see especially chapters 5 and 6. As Pollock demonstrates, van Gogh's sense of Hals's achievements was very much influenced by the writings of nineteenth-century French critics Charles Blanc and Théophile Thoré, both of whom were ardent republicans.

13. LB 13.

14. See, for instance, L. Nochlin, "Impressionist Portraits and the Construction of Modern Identity," in C.B. Bailey, with the assistance of J.B. Collins, Renoirs's Portraits: Impressions of an Age, exh. cat. (Ottawa, National Gallery of Canada, 1997), pp. 64–66

15. C.B. Bailey, "Portrait of the Artist as a Portrait Painter," in Renoir's Portraits (see note 14 above), p. 7.

16. As Linda Nochlin (see note 14 above, p. 64) points out, Manet's Déjeuner (1863, Paris, Musée d'Orsay) includes portraits of his brothers and his well-known, and often portrayed model Victorine Meurent; Renoir's La Loge (1874, London, Courtauld Institute Galleries) is a portraitlike genre scene posed by the artist's brother Edmond and the model known as Nini.

17. Pollock, having noted van Gogh's difficulties in representing "complexities of class and social change" in early paintings like The Potato Eaters (fig. 23), describes his portraits of 1888–89—which seek to present randomly encountered individuals as examples of general types— as bourgeois constructions that, in their mystification of socially determined distinctions, serve the utopian fiction of a classless society. Pollock (1980, p. 466) writes that "the individual presented without elaboration of context may represent a strategy for not only evading the recognition and representation of immediate class relations, but evacuating the individual from any real social location whatever, in favour of an ideal or imaginary abstraction."

18. Van Gogh consistently referred to Trabuc as "the head attendant" and described him (in L 604) as having "a very interesting face; there is a fine etching by [Alphonse] Legros, representing an old Spanish grandee . . . that will give you an idea of the type . . . There is a sort of contemplative calm in his face, so that I can't help being reminded of Guizot's face . . . But he is of the people and simpler." Ronald Pickvance (New York 1986, p. 127) identifies the portrait etching by Legros as Le Grand Espagnol, ca. 1870 (and reproduces the New York Public Library's version of it).

19. L 482.

20. See L 602, L 605, L 640a.

21. See L 604, L 605.

22. L 595.

23. L 602.

24. L 614.

25. See, for instance, L 610, LW 15, LB 19.

26. L 592.

27. See L 595, L 606, L 609.

28. See LB 19, LB 21.

29. L 605.

30. Ibid.

31. L 604.

32. Ibid.

33. C. Bollas, "Aspects of Self Experiencing," in Being a Character: Psychoanalysis and Self Experience (New York, 1992), pp. 11–32.

34. L 605.

35. L 601.

36. L 604.

37. Ibid.

38. Of the forty-odd self-images in van Gogh's oeuvre, only four show him bearing painter's apparatus, and one of those, The Artist on the Road to Tarascon (formerly Magdeburg, Kaiser Friedrich Museum, now destroyed; fig. 221) shows him as a plein-airist trekking the open road with a canvas under his arm rather than the more traditional studio-bound artist referenced in the other three.

It is notable that van Gogh did not include a painter in the panorama of modern types made at Arles in 1888; he pointedly chose to label his portrait of artist friend Eugène Boch "the poet" rather than "the painter," and in his own self-portrait of that era (fig. 129) van Gogh enacts a monkish ascetic rather than displaying his artist's paraphernalia. The painting was sent to Gauguin as part of an artists' exchange of self-portraits; as Carol Zemel (1997, p. 161) notes, none of the self-portraits produced for this exchange—by van Gogh, Gauguin, Emile Bernard, and Charles Laval—shows its maker as a painter at work.

39. See B. Welsh-Ovcharov in Paris 1988, p. 174. In August 1888, van Gogh wrote from Arles (LB 15) of the Rembrandt self-portrait, which he described as showing its maker as an "old lion" with "toothless smile . . . a piece of white cloth around his head, his palette in his hand!"

40. He describes his attire thus in a retrospective description of this self-portrait; see LW 4.

41. In a letter written to Gauguin some months later (L 544a), van Gogh described himself, at the end of his Parisian sojourn, as "seriously sick at heart and in body, and nearly an alcoholic because of my rising fury at my strength failing me . . . I shut myself up within myself, without having the courage to hope!"

42. See Pickvance (New York 1986, p. 39), who attributes Dr. Peyron's reluctance to van Gogh's ingestion, during his breakdown, of poisonous paints.

43. See Self-Portrait with Bandaged Ear and Pipe (frontis. in this volume) and Self-Portrait with Bandaged Ear (London, Courtauld Institute Galleries); van Gogh's authorship of the latter has been disputed.

44. LW 4.

45. L 604.

46. L 605.

47. L 607. Despite his remarks upon the vagueness of this self-image, Vincent offered it to Theo as a document of his improved state, declaring, "When you put the portrait with the light background . . . next to the self-portraits from Paris . . . I look saner now than I did then, even much more so" (L 604).

48. Ibid.

49. Douglas Cooper (1955, p. 105) noted that the self-portrait on swirling ground is "more suavely painted and in a different tonality" than other pictures from September 1889 and wrote, "Both its flammèches and its tonality accord stylistically with pictures painted at the end of April and beginning of May 1890."

50. L 612.

51. Ibid.

52. Although van Gogh considered the life of the agrarian laborer "a world apart" that was "in many respects so much better than the civilized world," he did not see it as superior "in every respect, for what do they know about art and many other things?" (L 404).

53. In L 604, van Gogh wrote, "They say—and I am very willing to believe it—that it is difficult to know yourself— but it isn't easy to paint yourself either."

54. L 604.

55. Van Gogh had made the woman's acquaintance "when doing some olive trees behind their little house" (L 605).

56. L 604.

57. L 605.

58. L 604.

59. L 605.

60. Ibid.

61. Ibid.

62. See, for instance, the Goncourts' preface to Germinie

Lacerteux (1865)—the in-depth portrayal of a love-starved housemaid with a secret life—wherein the authors write, "Living in the nineteenth century, in a time of universal suffrage, of democracy, of liberalism, we asked ourselves if those whom one calls 'the lower classes' didn't have the right to a Novel." Edmond de Goncourt later claimed, in his preface to *Chérie* (1884), that *Germinie Lacerteux* had launched the naturalist movement, countering Zola's assertion, in the preface to the 1877 edition of *L'Assommoir* (first published serially in 1876), that that book—the squalid tale of a hardworking laundress's drunken decline—was "the first novel about the people that doesn't lie and that has the smell of the people."

Although naturalist attitudes toward the proletariat often were condescending, they were not condemnatory; Zola, for instance, reminds the (probably middle-class) reader of *L'Assommoir* that "one must not conclude that the whole working class is bad, because my characters aren't bad, they are only ignorant, and spoiled by the environment of harsh labor and poverty that they inhabit."

63. LW 1. For a thorough discussion of van Gogh's literary interests, see Sund 1992.

64. On the occasion of Wil's birthday in 1888, van Gogh set aside two pictures for her. He had dozens of works on hand at the time, yet both of the paintings he chose for his sister included modern novels: "As I should very much like to give you something of my work that will please you, I have set aside a little study of a book for you and also, on a somewhat larger scale, a flower with a lot of books with pink, green and red bindings . . . Parisian novels" (LW 3).

65. Theo considered naturalist novels "forbidden fruit" for women; see LT 1a.

66. LW 14. With patronizing patience, and a sarcastic undertone, van Gogh wrote, "It's a very good and fortunate thing that you are not quite enthusiastic about the masterly book by de Goncourt [sic]. All the better that you should prefer books by Tolstoi, you who read books in the first place to draw from them the energy to act . . . But I, who read books to find the artist who wrote them, should I for my part be in the wrong if I like the French novelists so much?"

67. LW 14. Although by 1889 Joris-Karl Huysmans had notoriously defected from the naturalist school (his quintessentially "decadent" novel, *A Rebours,* was published five years earlier), van Gogh, a fan of Huysmans's *En ménage* (1881), continued to see him as the follower of Zola he once had been.

68. Van Gogh made duplicates of each of the Trabucs' portraits, so that the couple might have the originals, yet he and Theo could have records of his work. Of the four paintings made, the whereabouts of only two (figs. 171 and 175) are known.

69. Although he would, by fall 1889, paint a fellow patient (see L 612), van Gogh didn't consider that a viable option in September.

70. L 607.

71. In L 607, van Gogh writes, "Many people do not copy, many others do—I started on it accidentally . . ."

72. Ibid. Freudians might question the "accidental" nature of an incident that defaced the work of a patriarchal

figure whose work van Gogh sought both to emulate and to rival in his own.

73. Ibid. The translation here is Jan Hulsker's (1996, p. 408), which seems to me in better keeping with the original French-language text than that given in *The Complete Letters* (van Gogh 1958).

74. L 605.

75. L 607.

76. L 605. In addition to variants on works by Delacroix and Jean-François Millet, van Gogh at St.-Rémy made pictures based on compositions by artists as varied as Rembrandt and Honoré Daumier, Gustave Doré, and Virginie Demont-Breton; see Homburg 1996.

77. In L 607, van Gogh writes that "making copies interests me enormously, and it means that I shall not lose sight of the figure, even though I have no models at the moment." He adds, "Mostly because I am ill at present, I am trying to do something to console myself, for my own pleasure."

78. L 607. In affirming his decision to "let the black and white by Delacroix or Millet or something made after their work pose for me as a subject," van Gogh remarks, "It is not a hard and fast rule that only the composer should play his own composition."

79. In L 607, van Gogh writes that when formulating color improvisations on other artist's works, he is not "altogether myself, but searching for memories of their pictures . . . 'the vague consonance of colors which are at least right in feeling'—that is my own interpretation." Some months later the artist referred to himself as "a musician in colors" (L 626).

80. See Homburg 1996, p. 71.

81. In a letter to his sister (LW 14), van Gogh noted the play of violet and yellow in the clouds of his *Pietà*. Moreover, an interplay of blue and orange animates the sky, and in the body of Christ pinks are offset by green—a contrasting of complementary hues van Gogh also employed in the flesh tones of his contemporaneous self-portraits.

82. Although van Gogh had probably seen examples of Delacroix's work during his youthful stint as an art dealer, he first became intently interested in Delacrucian color theory in 1884, while living in isolation from the art world, at his parents' home in rural Holland. Though his introduction to Delacroix's use of complementary colors was theoretical rather than actual, van Gogh made attempts to amplify complementary color contrast in his own work after reading Charles Blanc's essay on Delacroix in *Les artistes de mon temps* (Paris, 1876). He came to a better understanding of Delacroix's application of color theory by reading Théophile Silvestre's *Eugène Delacroix: Documents nouveaux* (Paris, 1864), but only after his move to Paris in 1886 did van Gogh's grasp of Delacroix's practice become complete—presumably through visual examination of paintings on view in the city and experimentation based on visual experience rather than verbal description. See Homburg 1996, pp. 46–53.

83. Both van Gogh's Protestant upbringing and his reluctance to paint without models made him uneasy with religious subject matter. In the summer of 1888, he had tried, on two separate occasions, to paint Christ in the Garden of Olives but destroyed both attempts because

"I will not paint any more without models" (L 540). In the fall of 1889 he wrote, "With me there is no question of doing anything from the Bible" (apparently his copy after Delacroix's biblical subject did not count) and expressed distress that Gauguin and Bernard were making pictures of Christ in the Garden (L 615). To van Gogh's mind, "the figure of Christ, as I feel it, has been painted only by Delacroix and Rembrandt" (LB 8). Delacroix's *Pietà* thus provided a "model" not just for figuration but for figuration of a particularly daunting sort, enabling van Gogh to undertake a subject to which he himself felt inadequate.

84. See, for instance: Hulsker 1996, p. 408; Washington 1998, p. 121; Lubin 1972, p. 102; Maurer 1998, p. 94.

85. Van Gogh acknowledged, in this era, that his thoughts sometimes took "an absurd religious turn" (L 605) and wrote of his suspicion that his "perverted and frightful ideas about religion" (L 607) were fueled by living in a one-time monastery (St.-Paul-de-Mausole had been built by a religious order in the Romanesque era). He characterized himself as the "prisoner" of an administration that "very willingly fosters these sickly religious aberrations, whereas the right thing to do would be to cure them" (L 605).

86. Van Gogh had not seen his mother since 1885, but he often wrote to her from St.-Rémy.

87. LW 14.

88. Ibid.

89. In July 1889, after revisiting Arles (and just prior to his first bout of illness at St.-Rémy), van Gogh noted, "You get very fond of people who have seen you ill, and it has done me a world of good to see people who were kind and gentle with me then" (L 600).

90. L 605.

91. Ibid. Van Gogh writes, "And then do you know why the pictures of Eug. Delacroix—the religious and historical pictures, the 'Bark of Christ,' the 'Pietà,' the 'Crusaders,' have such a hold on one? Because when Eug. Delacroix did a 'Gethsemane,' he had first gone to see firsthand what an olive grove was, and the same for the sea whipped by a strong mistral, and because he must have said to himself—These people whom history tells us about, doges of Venice, Crusaders, apostles, holy women, were of the same character and lived in a manner analogous to that of their present descendants."

92. Renan's *Vie de Jésus*—the first installment of a seven-volume opus, *Les origines du Christianisme*—is ostensibly an objective account of a powerful and charismatic man who changed the course of history, but who, according to the author, was neither divine nor a miracle worker. Van Gogh read *Jésus* in 1875, and it remained vivid in his mind for years thereafter.

93. In L 587 (spring, 1889), van Gogh asked, "Isn't Renan's Christ a thousand times more comforting than the so many papier maché Christs they serve up to you in . . . churches?"

94. Taking the reader back to a time when Christianity constituted "an immense social revolution," Renan notes that Christ's first followers were "not rich people, not scholars, not priests, [but] women and men of the people . . . humble, simple folk who would triumph by their very humanity." The author asserts that Jerusalem in those days was "pretty much as it is today: a town of acrimony,

disputes, hatred and small-mindedness" and notes that the Galileans felt like fish out of water there; their "corrupt patois" led to laughable misunderstandings, and their religious beliefs were derided for being not just unorthodox, but uninformed. (See Renan, *Vie de Jésus,* chapter 7; and J. Sund, "Van Gogh's *Berceuse* and the Sanctity of the Secular," in Masheck 1996, pp. 220–21).

95. See also LB 21, in which van Gogh describes a tiny panel by Giotto, showing "the death of some good holy woman." "The expression of pain and ecstasy in it is so utterly human," he writes, "that however nineteenth-century one may be, one feels as though one were present."

96. This revision of a black and white print in a coloristic oil may be compared to a series of paintings van Gogh made after drawings and woodcuts by Jean-François Millet. Van Gogh insisted that his work based on Millet "is not purely and simply copying. Rather it is translating —into another language—that of color—the impressions of light and shade in black and white" (L 623; see also L 625).

97. The radical reduction of the composition's figures is also at odds with van Gogh's assertion that his copies were motivated by a desire to paint the human form in the absence of living models, and thus seems particularly freighted.

98. Van Gogh's oblique denial of Christ's resuscitative role here may hark back to Renan, who discredits scriptural accounts of Christ's miracle working.

99. See L 630, L 631.

100. Freud uses the term *dramatization* to refer to a dreamer's transformation of thoughts into situations.

101. L 632.

102. In his writings on dreams, Freud labels this sort of overlay "condensation" and in one instance notes that "the alternative 'either-or' is never expressed in dreams, both of the alternatives being inserted into the text of the dream as though they were equally valid" (see "On Dreams" in P. Gay, *The Freud Reader* [New York, 1989], pp. 158–59).

103. Bollas (see note 33 above, p. 13) writes that in one's dream one is simultaneously "an actor inside a drama and an offstage absence directing the logic of events," a split that "mirrors an important feature of self experience." During the day, Bollas notes, "we nominate persons, objects and events as psychically significant" and through "projective identification" transform "material things into psychic objects . . . furnishing a matrix for dreams, fantasies, and deeper reflective knowings" (pp. 22–23).

104. Van Gogh made five versions of this image, one of which was lost almost as soon as it was made (it remains unaccounted for).

105. Van Gogh fondly recalls Ginoux's "merit" as a model in L 595.

106. Van Gogh later wrote in a letter to Gauguin that he "paid for doing [*L'Arlésienne* of 1890] with another month of illness, but I also know that it is a canvas that will be understood by you and by a very few others, as we would wish it to be understood" (L 643).

107. Hulsker (1996, p. 440) dates all five versions of this portrait to February, and though Pickvance (New York 1986, p. 175) believes van Gogh may have started work on

the series in January, I believe Hulsker is correct. As I note below, it seems likely that a major impetus for his project was van Gogh's receipt at St.-Rémy of a letter Gauguin wrote at Pont-Aven, dated 28 January. Moreover, a letter van Gogh himself wrote to his brother on 1 February (congratulating Theo on the birth of his son the day before) mentions Mme Ginoux as "the one whose portrait I did in yellow and black" (i.e., *L'Arlésienne* of November 1888) and does not refer to any new portrait of that sitter.

108. It seems likely that the version now in the Museu de Arte, São Paulo, was the first of van Gogh's improvisations, since Ginoux's expression there is closest to that of Gauguin's drawing. The version now owned by the Kröller-Müller Museum, Otterlo, is known to have been the one given to critic Albert Aurier, and since the variant Vincent presented to Theo was described by the artist as showing the model in a pink dress and posed against a "yellowish white" ground (LW 22), it can be identified as the version now in a private collection in New York. The remaining known version, now in the Galleria Nazionale d'Arte Moderna, Rome, was given to Gauguin after Vincent directed Theo to do so in late April 1890 (L 629).

109. L 643. In his word choice, van Gogh doubtless alludes to "synthetism," the label Gauguin devised for his own way of working in this era.

110. LB 20.

111. L 605.

112. L 625; see also LW 19.

113. LW 622a.

114. See Cooper 1983, p. 297.

115. See Sund 1988.

116. L 587.

117. It should be noted that the colors van Gogh used in his 1890 portraits of Ginoux, especially the pink, have faded; the edges of the Otterlo version—formerly covered by a frame—give glimpses of the deeper hue originally applied in its background (Amsterdam 1990, p. 246). The instability of some of the pigments van Gogh used in the last months of his life is explored in detail by Jean-Paul Rioux, "The Discoloration of Pinks and Purples in Van Gogh's Paintings from Auvers," in New York 1999, pp. 104–13.

118. LW 22.

119. L 540.

120. LW 14.

121. LW 22.

122. LW 16. Van Gogh went on to acknowledge that "some of my pictures certainly show traces of having been painted by a sick man, and I assure you I don't do this on purpose. It's against my conscious will that all my calculations end in broken tones" ("broken tones" being Van Gogh's way of designating the coloristic grays that result from a mix of complementary colors). Some months earlier, Vincent told Theo that he was living "soberly" at St.-Rémy and asserted that "very deliberate sobriety" helped him think more clearly. He added, "It is a difference like painting in gray or in colors. I am going to paint more in gray, in fact" (L 599).

123. LW 17.

124. LB 21.

125. L 643; this letter, unfinished and unmailed, was found among van Gogh's papers after his death. In it, he tells Gauguin that he had used "the medium of color" to connote "the sober character and style of the drawing." Nearly a year before, he had drawn a link between sobriety and grayed tones; see note 122 above.

126. Offerings of the Charpentier publishing house are identifiable by their yellow covers; Hachette's paperbacks were red. Van Gogh referred to such contemporary books as "Parisian novels" and painted two still lifes littered with multiple books in varied hues (F 358, JH 1612, Amsterdam, Van Gogh Museum, and F 359, JH 1332, Private Collection). J.K. Huysmans creates a textual image of brightly colored paperbacks in one of his own "Parisian novels," *En ménage* (1881), and Henry James writes, in *The Ambassadors* (1903), of "lemon-colored volumes, fresh as fruit on the tree" and of the "sharp initiation" they represented for the book's American protagonist, who returns home "with lemon-colored volumes in general on the brain, as well as with a dozen . . . in his trunk."

127. The version of this portrait now in Rome is the only one in which the included books bear their original, English-language titles rather than French translations.

128. Van Gogh once noted that as a young man he read Dickens's *Christmas Stories* every year; he initially read *Uncle Tom's Cabin* in the period of lonely wandering that followed his dismissal from a preaching post in Belgium (L 130, L 131).

129. L 582.

130. LW 11; van Gogh's emphasis.

131. Ibid. In a letter written to Theo in April 1889, van Gogh wrote of Dickens's *Christmas Stories,* "There are things in them so profound that one must read them over and over again" (L 583).

132. L 605.

133. Whereas van Gogh's letters to his siblings, friends, and colleagues are replete with references to books and authors, the letters he wrote to Ginoux and her husband (L 622a, L 626b, LW 634a, L 640a) make no mention of books or reading, which they probably would have, had either of them been a fellow aficionado of the writings of Beecher Stowe and Dickens.

134. LW 11.

135. An account of one man's search for happiness, Rod's book struck van Gogh as trite and pretentious (L 596); "The moral of the story," he wrote, "is that under certain circumstances a gentleman prefers ultimately to live with a sweet and very devoted wife and his child, rather than to live in the restaurants and cafés of the boulevard . . . That is undoubtedly very nice" (LW 13).

136. See LW 13, LW 14. Even as he suggested to his sister that she read books "to draw from them the energy to act" (LW 14), van Gogh remarked to Theo that "good women and [good] books are two different things" (L 596).

137. De Haan's portrait had as its companion piece Gauguin's *Self-Portrait with Halo* (Washington, D.C., National Gallery), which shows its artist as an angelic figure beset by temptation (in the forms of a serpent and dangling apples). De Haan himself is presented by Gauguin as a bestial creature (head supported by a hoof/paw) confronting a still life that emblematizes civilization's

power to corrupt: the lamp (enlightenment) and books (erudition) adjoin a plate of apples that recall those in Gauguin's self-portrait, and, by extension, those that tempted Eve. Temptation is a leitmotif in Milton's oeuvre, and *Paradise Lost* (1667) recounts the fall from grace of Satan, the rebel angels, and humanity. While *Sartor Resartus* (1831) touches on a variety of issues (including the importance of vocation, the human need for heroes, the division of modern society into opposed economic camps of poor and rich), two of its themes seem particularly applicable here: the crisis induced by loss of faith and the clash of nature and culture. It is perhaps notable that van Gogh, in the spring of 1889, had written of the "tremendously close connection with Carlyle" he found in Dickens's *Christmas Stories* (L 583).

138. Gauguin mentions the project in a letter to van Gogh which dates from October 1889 and notes that he is including a drawing of it. According to Cooper (1983, p. 273), the sketch to which Gauguin alludes apparently was lost at some later date.

139. In contrast to Ginoux, however, de Haan is said to have shared his portrayer's interest in the books displayed (see D.L. Paul, "Willumsen and Gauguin in the 1890s," *Apollo* 91, n.s., no. 215 [January 1980]: p. 36). Indeed, Françoise Cachin, (*The Art of Paul Gauguin*, exh. cat. [Washington, D.C., National Gallery of Art], 1988, p. 169, n. 8) believes de Haan may have introduced Gauguin to the ideas expressed in *Sartor Resartus*, which was not translated into French until 1899. It is seems possible, however, that van Gogh (who read *Sartor Resartus* in 1883 and praised it as anti-dogmatic [LR 30]) had already discussed the book with Gauguin at Arles; writing to Theo in the fall of 1888 of his desire to work with Gauguin there, Vincent cited Carlyle on the nature of fame and success (L 524).

The copy of Milton's epic that is included in de Haan's portrait is a French translation, and given Cachin's assertion that "de Haan spoke terrible French" (p. 169), it seems unlikely that he chose to read this English-language work in that tongue. The book labeled *Paradis Perdu* more likely was Gauguin's.

140. See, for instance, L 595, L 632, L 634a. In LB 15, van Gogh referred to Ginoux and Roulin as "the woman with black hair and white skin [and] the woman with yellow hair and a sunburned brick-red face."

141. Unlike the repetitions produced by Monet and Cézanne in the 1890s and beyond, van Gogh's multiple reprises of these compositions do not reflect dissatisfaction with his attempts to capture the motif (see S. Z. Levine, "Monet's Series: Repetition, Obsession," *October* [Summer 1986]: 65–75) but rather the opposite. Van Gogh's belief in the absolute rightness of *La Berceuse* and the later *L'Arlésienne*, along with the satisfaction he derived from producing them, fueled his desire to remake and to disperse his portrayals to those he felt would benefit from and "understand" them (see L 643). In this practice, van Gogh more closely resembles an icon-maker of old than contemporaries who engaged in seriality.

142. LW 19.

143. L 629.

144. LB 21.

145. Ibid.; van Gogh cited *La Berceuse* (fig. 125) as one such "abstraction."

146. Van Gogh later described this "very romantic . . . memory of Provence" in a letter intended for Gauguin but never sent; see L 643.

147. Given the palette used for the female figure in *Evening Promenade,* it is perhaps significant that van Gogh thought of his *L'Arlésienne* of 1888 (fig. 181) as "the woman's figure in black and yellow," (L 595) and of Ginoux herself as "the one whose portrait I did in yellow and black" (L 625).

148. L 635. For a detailed portrayal of Auvers in 1890, see Zemel 1997, chapter 6, "'The Real Country': Utopian Decoration in Arles," especially pp. 214–19.

149. See Cooper 1955.

150. For detailed biographical information on Gachet, including descriptions of his activities as a physician, collector, and amateur artist, see New York 1999.

151. See LT 18, LT 19, L 609.

152. Gachet's thesis for the Université de Montpellier (1858) was titled "Etude sur la mélancholie." As Cynthia Saltzman (1998, pp. 32–40) has noted, Gachet's approach was more anecdotal than scientific, though he did make case studies at La Salpêtrière in Paris.

153. Zemel 1997, p. 207.

154. See, for example, L 638, L 646, L 648.

155. The toddler shown holding an orange was the daughter of a carpenter named Levert who lived near the inn where van Gogh lodged at Arles. Levert later built van Gogh's coffin. See A. Ravoux-Carrié, "Recollections on Vincent van Gogh's Stay in Auvers-sur-Oise," *Les cahiers de Van Gogh* (1956); reprinted in Stein 1986, p. 216.

156. L 646.

157. L 649.

158. L 645.

159. Ibid.

160. L 646.

161. Ibid.

162. L 520; see also LB 15.

163. L 520.

164. Ibid.

165. Theo saw Toulouse-Lautrec's "excellent portrait of a woman at the piano" at the Salon des Indépendants in the spring of 1890 (LT 29). Although Zemel (1997, pp. 231, 279, n. 43), noting that "it hardly seems accidental that van Gogh's image is almost identical in design" to Toulouse-Lautrec's *Mlle Dihau*, claims Vincent saw that portrait at the Indépendants as well; that exhibition ran from 19 March to 27 April (that is, while he was in St.-Rémy), and Vincent apparently did not see the portrait until 6 July, when he made a day trip to Paris from Arles. On that day, Toulouse-Lautrec lunched at Theo's apartment, and while John Rewald (1956, p. 375) writes that the former "then took van Gogh to his studio to see *Woman at the Piano*," it seems more likely that Toulouse-Lautrec brought the painting with him to Theo's, since—according to Johanna van Gogh-Bonger's recollection—Vincent's July visit (the last time she saw him) was rushed (van Gogh 1958, p. LII). Upon returning to Auvers, van Gogh wrote a letter to Theo and Jo in which he remarked that though "the hours I shared with you . . . were a bit too difficult and trying for us all . . . I retain many pleasant memories of that journey

to Paris . . . I had hardly dared hope to see my friends again . . . Lautrec's picture, portrait of a musician, is amazing. I saw it with emotion" (L 649). Rewald suggests that this painting's seemingly fortuitous resemblance to *Mademoiselle Gachet at the Piano* occasioned van Gogh's amazement.

166. As a novice painter, van Gogh had mused upon the possibility of painting "respectable" women, "girls such as our sister, for instance," but despaired of ever "getting on sufficiently intimate footing with girls of that sort for them to be willing to pose for me. Especially . . . my own sisters" (L 395). Now, at Auvers, he described Marguerite Gachet as someone "with whom I imagine Jo would soon be good friends" (L 638).

167. Van Gogh's image of Marguerite Gachet is notable in its lack of emphasis upon the model's face; in contrast to the subjects of more traditional portraits, this sitter—chin lowered and eyes on the keyboard—turns away from the viewer, an indication that, in the artist's mind, the type she embodied took precedence over the specifics of individual likeness.

168. The prevailing pink and green color scheme of this portrait recalls that of the 1890 portraits of Marie Ginoux.

169. For a discussion of the domestic piano recital as a stereotypical marker of middle-class femininity, see Eyerman 1997.

170. L 644.

171. Although he soon came to pair Mlle Gachet's portrait with a landscape painting rather than *Peasant Woman in Wheat Field,* the vista ultimately chosen to partner the pianist's image was one of wheat fields (F 775, JH 2038). Van Gogh wrote of pairing these pictures on the basis of their shared double-square dimensions (approximately 40 by 20 inches) and opposed orientations (vertical vs. horizontal) and color schemes: "one canvas is vertical and in pink tones, the other pale green and greenish yellow, the complementary of pink" (L 645). Evert van Uitert (1981–82, p. 236) believes their opposition was not merely formal and writes that "comments in this same letter indicate that the combination of the two works has to do with the relationship between man [sic] and nature. Van Gogh had encountered that subject in Puvis de Chavannes's *Inter artes et naturam,* of which he had seen a sketch while traveling through Paris . . . [and] later copied . . . from memory in a letter." The artist's own comments are more suggestive than explicit: "We are still far from the time when people will understand the curious relation between one fragment of nature and another, which all the same explain each other and enhance each other. But some certainly feel it, and that's something" (L 645).

172. L 626.

173. An etching Dr. Gachet made of his wife, Blanche, playing piano by candlelight in 1873 (some two years before her death) may have been a specific inspiration for van Gogh's somewhat anomalous portrayal of Marguerite Gachet. Zemel (1997, p. 232) notes this connection and illustrates Gachet's image, which shows Mlle Gachet from behind in a shadowy space, and lays emphasis on the act of music making (and the mood that music evokes) rather than particulars of the pianist's appearance.

174. Adeline Ravoux—by then Adeline Ravoux-Carrié—recalled her father's most famous lodger some years after the fact. She wrote that "Vincent never had a conversation with me before doing my portrait, except for several words out of sheer politeness. One day he asked me, 'Would it please you if I were to do your portrait?' He seemed very keen on it . . . and he asked my parents' permission . . . He did my portrait one afternoon in one sitting. As I posed he did not speak to me; he smoked his pipe continually" (Stein 1986, p. 213).

175. Stein 1986, p. 213: "[Van Gogh] found me very well behaved and complimented me on not having moved."

176. Since the fifteenth-century rise of the three-quarters view, profile portraits have become vastly outnumbered in Western art by the "eye and a half" presentation. See L. Campbell, *Renaissance Portraits: European Portrait-Painting in the 14th, 15th and 16th Centuries* (New Haven, 1990), pp. 75–86.

177. See J. Pope-Hennessy, *The Portrait in the Renaissance* (Washington, D.C., 1966), p. 35. Pope-Hennessy asserts that the profile view is also the most flattering presentation of feminine physiognomy. Ravoux-Carrié and her family, however, were disappointed with her portrait (her father later sold it off cheaply) and did not find it "true to life"—though the sitter recalled that on one occasion, "a person who came to interview me about van Gogh, in meeting me for the first time, recognized me from the portrait that Vincent had executed" (Stein 1986, p. 213).

178. "Mousmé" was Loti's transcription—in his novel of Japan, *Madame Chrysanthème*—of what he called "one of the prettiest words in the Japanese tongue." It denoted, he wrote, the "droll little pout" and "rumpled, roguish little face" of the teenage girl and had no French equivalent. Taking up the term himself after reading *Madame Chrysanthème* and encountering the model he painted as *La Mousmé*, van Gogh told Theo that the term indicated "a Japanese girl—Provençal, in this case—12 to 14 years old" (L 514).

179. Van Gogh associated oleanders—which grew in abundance at Arles—with love and sensuousness (see L 539, L 541, L 587). In a bust-length, three-quarters view portrait of Adeline Ravoux (Cleveland Museum of Art)—apparently done outside the model's presence (Stein 1986, p. 213)—the young model is flanked by floral buds and blossoms that appear to be roses and may also suggest figurative "flowering."

180. L 635.

181. A comprehensive and fully illustrated account of Gachet's collection may be found in New York 1999. In May 1890, van Gogh remarked specifically on Gachet's "very fine Pissarro . . . and two fine flower pieces by Cézanne" (L 638).

182. LW 21.

183. L 638.

184. Ibid.

185. Ibid.

186. LW 22. Theo van Gogh noted the resemblance as well; after his first meeting with Gachet, Theo reported to his brother: "I met Dr. Gachet, the physician Pissarro mentioned to me. He gives the impression of being a man of understanding. Physically he is a little like you" (LT 31).

187. Van Gogh later remarked that Gachet's portrait and the self-portrait he took with him to Auvers had "the same sentiment" (L 638).

188. Meyer Schapiro (1950, p. 120) has long since noted that the self-portrait Gachet admired and the doctor's own depiction by van Gogh are linked by the combination of "two modes of portrayal": "the probing of the features in their tiniest inflections, and the free creation of an expressive structure of lines, colours, and areas which convey a sensed mood of the person."

189. Perhaps the best-known instance of this pose occurs in Albrecht Dürer's engraving of *Melancholia* (1514), a female personification of the melancholic disposition associated with artistic genius. (Significantly, the emblems of science and art that surround Dürer's brooding figure are presented as useless in the absence of divine inspiration.)

Bogomila Welsh-Ovcharov (Toronto 1981, p. 163) has noted the resemblance between Gachet's pose and that which Delacroix used in *Tasso in the Hospital of St. Anna* (1839, Winterthur, Switzerland, Oskar Reinhart Foundation) and suggests that "the one was a consciously employed source for the other." Torquato Tasso (1544–95) was a poet plagued by mental illness and twice confined to an asylum; Van Gogh's interest in Delacroix's portrayal of him predated the artist's own hospitalization. As Welsh-Ovcharov notes, van Gogh asked Theo to send him a lithograph of "Tasso in the Madhouse" shortly after visiting the Alfred Bruyas collection at the Musée Fabre in Montpellier with Gauguin in mid-December 1888. There van Gogh admired Delacroix's *Portrait of Bruyas*, a man who struck him as both "heartbroken" and "frustrated" (L 601) and "with red hair and beard, uncommonly like you or me" in appearance (L 564); he believed Delacroix's image of Tasso "must have some affinity with this fine portrait of Brias [sic]" (L 564). As it turned out, Gachet (who was of the same physical type) had pursued medical studies in Montpellier and had encountered Bruyas there—a fact that van Gogh found striking and which he mentioned to Theo in conjunction with a description of his portrait of Gachet (L 638).

190. LW 22. Evert van Uitert (1980, pp. 97–98) remarks that Gachet's facial expression—particularly its downward slanting eyelids—bears comparison to a physiognomic diagram found in Humbert de Superville's *Essai sur les signes inconditionelles dans l'art* (Leiden, 1827, p. 23) and notes the popular dispersal of Humbert's theories by Charles Blanc (whose work van Gogh knew and assimilated early in his painter's career).

191. In Gauguin's painting of *Christ in the Garden of Olives* (1889, West Palm Beach, Florida, Norton Gallery of Art), Jesus wears the artist's own face.

192. L 643.

193. See L 505: "I have scraped off a big painted study, an olive garden, with a figure of Christ in blue and orange, and an angel in yellow . . . I scraped it off because I tell myself I must not do figures of that importance without models." A few weeks later, van Gogh recounted a second failed attempt to paint Christ in the Garden of Olives; see L 540.

194. LB 21.

195. L 643; van Gogh's emphasis.

196. In his last letter to his sister, van Gogh remarked that his portrait of Gachet gave "an idea of the extent to which, in comparison to the calmness of the old portraits, there is an expression in our modern heads, and passion—like a waiting for things as well as a growth. Sad yet gentle, but clear and intelligent—that is how one ought to paint many portraits" (LW 23).

197. L 617. The role of Puvis's portrait in the formulation of van Gogh's image of Gachet was first suggested by Aimée Brown Price (1975).

198. The table shown is a garden table upon which van Gogh later painted a still life of roses and anemones that was given to Gachet; see New York 1999, pp. 82–83.

199. See Paris 1954, p. 41.

200. LW 22. "His hands, the hands of an obstetrician, are paler than his face."

201. Van Gogh had long admired Meissonier's images of readers (many of which are costume pieces evoking another era) and continued to esteem that facet of Meissonier's oeuvre even when his general admiration for that artist diminished (see L 130, L 542, L 590, L 594, L 623). In the summer of 1889—just before his first breakdown at St.-Rémy—van Gogh labeled Meissonier "first rate" and asked Theo, "Have many things been done which give the nineteenth-century note better than the portrait of [Jules] Hetzel? When [Albert] Besnard . . . made the modern man a reader he had the same idea" (L 602). In fact, Meissonier had made two portraits of Hetzel, one dating from 1870 (current whereabouts unknown), the other to 1879 (Meudon, Musée d'Art et de Histoire de la Ville). It is not clear how van Gogh knew either portrait (probably through reproduction), but Constance Cain Hungerford (source: personal communication with the author) believes it more likely that he saw the later portrait, since Meissonier left the image of 1870 unfinished. On the other hand, the catalogue of the Meissonier retrospective held at the Galerie Georges Petit in 1893 describes (p. 245) the red-bearded Hetzel of the 1870 portrait with a book in his right hand, index finger holding his place—much as Besnard's *Modern Man* does in the panel to which van Gogh compared it—while the later portrait has no book. I am most grateful to Professor Hungerford for her generous assistance in sorting through these issues.

202. Besnard's paired images of primitive and modern man figure prominently in a suite of panels he made for the Ecole de Pharmacie in Paris (ca. 1883). Whereas the primitive, in a swampy landscape, hunches over a crude sketch, his modern counterpart slumps against the column of a loggia overlooking a bustling port. Besnard's "modern man" appears to ignore the woman and child before him and, with a melancholic air, to mull over the contents of a yellow book held in his right hand, the index finger of which holds his place (Besnard's panel is illustrated in Sund 1992, pl. 11, fig. 49).

203. L 602.

204. It has been suggested that Gachet, like van Gogh, may have admired naturalist literature (see Hulsker 1996, p. 460), while Paul Gachet *fils* later insisted that this was not the case; he recalled van Gogh's eagerness to share his

literary enthusiasms with the doctor but noted that the books included in his father's portrait bore "no relation to [the sitter's] literary tastes" (Gachet 1928, n. p.). The argument that these volumes meant little to Gachet is strengthened by the fact that they do not appear in the second version of his portrait, which van Gogh apparently made for Gachet to keep (Paris, Musée d'Orsay).

205. Vincent often related the Goncourts to himself and Theo in letters to his brother (see L 442, L 450, L 550) and was more generally drawn to the Goncourts' work together as an exemplar of the sort of male collaboration for which he longed.

206. L 638. In addition to describing Gachet himself as "something like another brother," van Gogh associated the doctor with Alfred Bruyas, an art lover who, on the basis of the portraits of him hanging at the Musée Fabre, was described by Vincent to Theo as "uncommonly like you and me" (L 564).

207. *Manette Salomon,* chapter 106.

208. Theo's recent fatherhood may also have recalled this novel to Vincent, who seems to have believed that his brother's duty to his wife and child would force both brothers to downplay professional ambition in favor of familial concerns (see, for example, L 648).

209. *Manette Salomon,* chapter 120. This passage has been cited in connection with Gachet's portrait by Evert van Uitert (1980, p. 96).

210. Ibid.

211. L 635.

212. L 638. Gachet warmed to Ginoux's portrait gradually; it may have taken him some time (and some prompting by the artist) to sense the complex emotions behind this deceptively simple composition, but by early June, van Gogh told Theo, the doctor "has got so far as to understand the last portrait of the Arlésienne." Gachet linked *L'Arlésienne* to the self-portrait he admired, and van Gogh noted, "He always comes back to these two portraits when he comes to see the studies, and he understands them exactly, exactly, I tell you, as they are." Writing to Gauguin of the work he considered their collaboration, van Gogh noted: "My friend Dr. Gachet here has taken to [*L'Arlésienne*] altogether after two or three hesitations, and says, 'How difficult it is to be simple'" (L 643).

213. See Sund 1988.

214. L 635.

215. L 622a.

216. See LW 11. *Germinie Lacerteux* was the one naturalist novel Wil van Gogh is known to have disliked enough to say so to her brother; this may well have marked it, in her mind, as a "man's book," unappreciated by women and thus particularly appropriate to a masculine portrait.

217. In the same letter to his sister in which he writes of "books written by men for men," van Gogh writes warmly of *Uncle Tom's Cabin* and *Christmas Stories* (LW 11).

218. In June 1889, van Gogh had written to Theo, "Unfortunately we are subject to the circumstances and maladies of our time, whether we like it or not" (L 595).

219. LW 23.

220. LW 22.

221. L 643.

222. Ibid.

The Modern Legacy of van Gogh's Portraits

1. LW 22 (Auvers, first half of 1890).

2. J.K. Varnedoe in the foreword to *Modern Portraits: The Self and Others* (Wildenstein Gallery, New York, 1976), p. xi.

3. See Kodera 1993, Feilchenfeldt 1988, and Essen 1990.

4. One of the paintings is in the collection of the Norton Simon Museum of Art in Pasadena, California; the other is in a private collection.

5. Matisse would have seen either the *L'Arlésienne* presently in Rome or the one in São Paulo (fig. 184).

6. H. Spurling, *The Unknown Matisse* (New York, 1998), p. xix.

7. L. Vauxcelle, *Gil Blas* (October 17, 1905).

8. J. Rewald, *Les Fauves,* exh. cat. (New York, Museum of Modern Art, 1952), p. 9.

9. J. Leymarie, *Fauvism,* trans. J. Emmons (Geneva, 1959), p. 48. See also Essen 1990, p. 287, and M. Vlaminck, *Tourant dangereux* (Paris, 1929), p. 229.

10. Leymarie (see note 9), p. 48.

11. Ibid., p. 27.

12. See Essen 1990, Fuchs and Hoet 1999, and the essay by George Keyes in this volume.

13. R. Rosenblum, *Modern Painting and the Northern Romantic Tradition, Friedrich to Rothko* (New York, 1975).

14. Feilchenfeldt 1988.

15. The exhibition was organized by the Galerie Cassirer in Berlin and was shown in Hamburg and Vienna (in part) before opening in November 1905 at the Galerie Arnold in Dresden.

16. The early German fascination with van Gogh could be said to have ended with the confiscation by the Nazis in 1933 of his portrait of Dr. Gachet. This work had been in the collection of the Städelisches Kunstinstitut und Städtische Galerie in Frankfurt since 1911 but had been off view, along with all the museum's expressionist works, since shortly after Hitler came to power. See Saltzman 1998, p. 161.

17. F. Whitford, *Expressionist Portraits* (New York, 1987).

18. M.M. Moeller, "Van Gogh and Germany," in Essen 1990, pp. 312–408.

19. Essen 1990, p. 313.

20. Kodera 1993, p. 46.

21. J. Richardson, with the collaboration of M. McCully, *A Life of Picasso,* vol. 2 (New York, 1991), p. 56.

22. Ibid., p. 211.

23. P. Guillaume, "Soutine," *Les arts à Paris* (January 1923): 6; quoted in K.E. Silver, "Where Soutine Belongs: His Art and Critical Reception in Paris Between the Wars," in N.L. Kleebatt and K.E. Silver, *An Expressionist in Paris: The Paintings of Chaim Soutine,* exh. cat. (New York, The Jewish Museum, Los Angeles County Museum of Art, and Cincinnati Art Museum, 1998), p. 21.

24. Ibid., pp. 21–22.

25. Essen 1990, p. 426.

26. Ibid.

27. R. Heller, "Ferdinand Hodler: A Unique Note in the Birch Bartlett Collection," *Art Institute of Chicago Museum Studies* 12, no. 2 (1986): 178. Reinhold Heller notes the ironic parallel that both artists were interested in Albrecht Dürer's thesis on perspective, wherein he describes an image of the subject being projected, in a very flattened manner, onto a sheet of glass. Heller suggests that Hodler used this device, the so-called *Dürerscheibe,* in the making of the Vibert portrait. Van Gogh describes his own similar experiments in translating three dimensions into two in a letter to Theo (L 223) that dates from 1882, well before one can logically connect Hodler to the late portraits.

28. J.J. Sweeney, *Joan Miró,* exh. cat. (New York, The Museum of Modern Art, 1941), p. 15.

29. Quoted in R.S. Lubar, "Joan Miró before 'The Farm,' 1915–1922: Catalan Nationalism and the Avant-garde," Ph. D. diss. (New York University, 1988), p. 74, n. 35.

30. Besides New York, the exhibition traveled to the California Palace of the Legion of Honor, San Francisco; the Pennsylvania Museum of Art (now the Philadelphia Museum of Art); and the Cleveland Museum of Art. See Barr 1935.

31. Pach 1936, p. 9.

32. Artaud's essay, *Van Gogh le suicidé de la société,* initially published in 1947 (Paris, 1947; reprint 1990), is in many ways the literary equivalent of Bacon's series.

33. J. Russell, "A Private Mythology," *The Sunday Times* (London), March 24, 1957.

34. A. Bowness (1985), quoted in A. Sinclair, *Francis Bacon: His Life and Violent Times* (New York, 1993), p. 314.

35. O. Kokoschka, "Van Gogh's Influence on Modern Painting," in Stein 1986, p. 375.

36. R. Storr, with essays by J.K. Varnedoe and D. Wise, *Chuck Close,* exh. cat. (New York, The Museum of Modern Art, 1998).

37. *Tate: The Art Magazine,* no. 18 (summer 1999): 7.

228. *The Old Peasant Patience Escalier* (F 1460, JH 1549) 11 August 1888
Graphite and ink, 49.4 x 38 cm
Cambridge Massachusetts, Fogg Art Museum, Harvard University

References

Amsterdam 1980
Amsterdam, Rijksmuseum Vincent van Gogh. *Vincent van Gogh in zijn Hollandse jaren*. Exh. cat., 1980.

Amsterdam 1987
The Rijksmuseum Vincent van Gogh. Art Treasures of Holland. Amsterdam, 1987.

Amsterdam 1989
Amsterdam, Rijksmuseum Vincent van Gogh. *Van Gogh & Millet*. Exh. cat., 1989.

Amsterdam 1990
Amsterdam, Rijksmuseum Vincent van Gogh. *Vincent van Gogh: Paintings*. Exh. cat., 1990.

Arles 1989
Arles, Ancien Hôpital Van Gogh. *Van Gogh et Arles: Exposition du centenaire*. Exh. cat., 1989.

Barr 1935
Barr, A.H., Jr., ed. *Vincent van Gogh: With an Introduction and Notes Selected from the Letters of the Artist*. New York, The Museum of Modern Art, 1935.

Boime 1966
Boime, A. "A Source for Van Gogh's Potato Eaters." *Gazette des beaux-arts* 67, no. 1167 (April 1966): 249–53.

Cooper 1955
Cooper, D. "The Painters of Auvers-sur-Oise." *The Burlington Magazine* 97, no. 625 (April 1955): 100–106.

Cooper 1983
Cooper, D. *Paul Gauguin: 45 Lettres à Vincent, Théo et Jo van Gogh*. The Hague and Lausanne, 1983.

Dorn 1988
Dorn, R. "Vincent van Gogh's Concept of 'Décoration.'" In *Vincent van Gogh International Symposium: Tokyo, October 17–19, 1985*. Tokyo, 1988, 375–84.

Dorn 1990
———. *Décoration: Vincent van Goghs Werkreihe für das Gelbe Haus in Arles*. Hildesheim, Zurich, and New York, 1990.

Essen 1990
Essen, Museum Folkwang. *Vincent van Gogh and the Modern Movement, 1890–1914*. Exh. cat., 1990 (Freren, Germany).

Eyerman 1997
Eyerman, C.N. "The Composition of Femininity: The Significance of the Woman at the Piano Motif in Nineteenth-Century French Culture from Daumier to Renoir." Ph.D. diss. University of California, Berkeley, 1997.

de la Faille 1970
Faille, J.-B. de la. *The Works of Vincent van Gogh, His Paintings and Drawings*. Amsterdam, 1970 [first published in 1928 under the title *L'oeuvre de Vincent van Gogh, catalogue raisonné*].

Feilchenfeldt 1988
Feilchenfeldt, W. *Vincent van Gogh & Paul Cassirer, Berlin: The Reception of Van Gogh in Germany from 1901 to 1914*. Zwolle, 1988.

Fuchs and Hoet 1997
Fuchs, R., and J. Hoet, eds. *Flemish and Dutch Painting: From Van Gogh, Ensor, Magritte, and Mondrian to Contemporary Artists*. New York, 1997.

Gachet 1928
Gachet, P. *Souvenirs de Cézanne et van Gogh à Auvers, 1873–1890*. Paris, 1928.

van Gogh 1958
Gogh, V. van. *The Complete Letters of Vincent van Gogh: With Reproductions of All the Drawings in the Correspondence*. Ed. J. van Gogh-Bonger. 3 vols. Greenwich, Conn., 1958; 2nd ed., 1978; 3rd ed., 1988.

van Gogh 1974
———. *Verzamelde Brieven van Vincent van Gogh*. 4 vols. Amsterdam and Antwerp, 1974.

van Gogh 1977
———. *Letters of Vincent van Gogh 1886–1890: A Facsimile Edition*. 2 vols. London and Amsterdam, 1977.

van Gogh 1996
———. *The Letters of Vincent van Gogh*. Ed. R. de Leeuw, trans. A. Pomerans. London, 1996.

The Hague 1990.
The Hague, Haags Historisch Museum. *Vincent van Gogh en Den Haag*. Exh. cat., 1990.

Hamburg 1995
Hamburg, Hamburger Kunsthalle. *Van Gogh: Die Pariser Selbstbildnisse*. Exh. cat., 1995 (Stuttgart).

Hammacher 1968
Hammacher, A.M. *Genius and Disaster: The Ten Creative Years of Vincent van Gogh*. New York, 1968.

Hammacher and Hammacher 1982
Hammacher, A.M., and R. Hammacher. *Van Gogh: A Documentary Biography*. London, 1982.

Herbert 1970
Herbert, R. "City vs Country—The Rural Image in French Painting from Millet to Gauguin." *Art Forum* 18, no. 6 (February 1970): 44–55.

van Heugten 1995
Heugten, S. van. "Radiographic Images of Vincent van Gogh's Paintings in the Collection of the Van Gogh Museum." *Van Gogh Museum Journal* (1995): 63–85.

van Heugten 1996
———. *Vincent van Gogh: Drawings*. Vol. 1, *The Early Years, 1880–1883*. Amsterdam, 1996.

van Heugten 1997
———. *Vincent van Gogh: Drawings*. Vol. 2, *Nuenen, 1883–85*.
Amsterdam, 1997.

van Heugten and Pabst 1995
Heugten, S. van, and F. Pabst. *The Graphic Work of Vincent van Gogh*. Cahier
Vincent 6. Zwolle, 1995.

Homburg 1996
Homburg, C. *The Copy Turns Original: Vincent van Gogh and a New Approach
to Traditional Art Practice*. Amsterdam and Philadelphia, 1996.

Hulsker 1974
Hulsker, J. "What Theo Really Thought of Vincent." *Vincent* 3, no. 2
(1974): 2–28.

Hulsker 1990
———. *Vincent and Theo van Gogh: A Dual Biography*. Ann Arbor, Mich.,
1990.

Hulsker 1993
———. *Vincent van Gogh: A Guide to His Work and Letters*. Amsterdam,
1993.

Hulsker 1996
———. *The New Complete Van Gogh: Paintings, Drawings, Sketches*. Revised
and Enlarged Edition of the Catalogue Raisonné of the Works of Vincent van Gogh.
Amsterdam and Philadelphia, 1996.

Kodera 1990
Kodera, T. *Vincent van Gogh: Christianity versus Nature*. Amsterdam and
Philadelphia, 1990.

Kodera 1993
Kodera, T., ed. *The Mythology of Vincent van Gogh*. Tokyo and Amsterdam, 1993.

Koslow 1981
Koslow, S. "Two Sources for Vincent van Gogh's 'Portrait of Armand
Roulin': A Character Likeness and a Portrait Schema." *Arts Magazine* 56,
no. 1 (September 1981): 155–63.

Leymarie 1951
J. Leymarie. *Van Gogh*. Paris, 1951.

van Lindert and van Uitert 1990
Lindert, J. van, and E. van Uitert. *Een eigentijdse expressie: Vincent van Gogh
en zijn portretten*. Amsterdam, 1990.

London 1974
London, Arts Council of Great Britain. *English Influences on Vincent
van Gogh*. Exh. cat., 1974.

London 1992
London, Barbican Gallery. *Van Gogh in England: Portrait of the Artist as a
Young Man*. Exh. cat., 1992.

Lubin 1972
Lubin, A.J. *Stranger on the Earth: A Psychological Biography of Vincent
van Gogh*. New York, 1972.

Masheck 1996
Masheck, J.D, ed. *Van Gogh 100*. Westport, Conn., 1996.

McQuillan 1989
McQuillan, M. *Van Gogh*. New York and London, 1989.

Maurer 1998
Maurer, N.M. *The Pursuit of Spiritual Wisdom: The Thought and Art of Vincent
van Gogh and Paul Gauguin*. Madison, Wisc., 1998.

Merlhès 1989
Merlhès, V. *Paul Gauguin et Vincent van Gogh 1887–1888: Lettres retrouvées,
sources ignorées*. Taravao, Tahiti, 1989.

Murray 1980
Murray, A. "'Strange and Subtle Perspective . . .': Van Gogh, The Hague
School and the Dutch Landscape Tradition." *Art History* 3, no. 4 (December
1980): 410–24.

New York 1976
New York, Wildenstein and Company. *Modern Portraits: The Self and Others*.
Exh. cat., 1976.

New York 1984
New York, The Metropolitan Museum of Art. *Van Gogh in Arles*. Exh. cat.,
1984.

New York 1986
New York, The Metropolitan Museum of Art. *Van Gogh in Saint-Rémy and
Auvers*. Exh. cat., 1986.

New York 1999
New York, The Metropolitan Museum of Art. *Cézanne to Van Gogh:
The Collection of Doctor Gachet*. Exh. cat., 1999.

Nordenfalk 1947
Nordenfalk, C. "Van Gogh and Literature." *Journal of the Warburg and
Courtauld Institutes* 10 (1947): 132–47.

Pach
Pach, W. *Vincent van Gogh 1835–1890* (New York, 1936).

Paris 1954
Paris, Musée de l'Orangerie. *Van Gogh et les peintres d'Auvers-sur-Oise*.
Exh. cat., 1954.

Paris 1988
Paris, Musée d'Orsay. *Van Gogh à Paris*. Exh. cat., 1988.

Paris 1998
Paris, Musée d'Orsay. *Millet / Van Gogh*. Exh. cat., 1998.

Pollock 1974
Pollock, G. "Vincent van Gogh, Rembrandt and the British Museum."
The Burlington Magazine 116, no. 860 (November 1974): 671–72.

Pollock 1975
———. Review of *Anthon van Rappard: Companion and Correspondent of
Vincent van Gogh, His Life and All His Works*, by J. Brouwer, J.L. Siesling, and
J. Vis. *The Burlington Magazine* 117, no. 872 (November 1975): 743–44.

Pollock 1980
————. "Vincent van Gogh and Dutch Art: A Study of the Development of van Gogh's Notion of Modern Art with Special Reference to the Critical and Artistic Revival of Seventeenth Century Dutch Art in Holland and France in the Nineteenth Century." Ph.D. diss. Courtauld Institute of Art, University of London, 1980.

Pollock 1983
————. "Stark Encounters: Modern Life and Urban Work in Van Gogh's Drawings of The Hague 1881–3." *Art History* 6, no. 3 (September 1983): 330–58.

Pollock 1988
————. "Van Gogh and the Poor Slaves: Images of Rural Labour as Modern Art." *Art History* 11, no. 3 (September 1988): 408–32.

Pollock and Orton 1978
Pollock, G., and F. Orton. *Vincent van Gogh, Artist of His Time*. New York, 1978.

Price 1975
Price, A.B. "Two Portraits by Vincent van Gogh and Two Portraits by Pierre Puvis de Chavannes." *The Burlington Magazine* 117, no. 872 (November 1975): 714–18.

Rewald 1956
Rewald, J. *Post Impressionism: From Van Gogh to Gauguin*. New York, 1956.

Roskill 1966
Roskill, M. "Van Gogh's 'Blue Cart' and His Creative Process." *Oud Holland* 81 (1966): 3–19.

Roskill 1970
————. *Van Gogh, Gauguin and French Painting of the 1880s: A Catalogue Raisonné of Key Works*. Ann Arbor, Mich., 1970.

Saltzman 1998
Saltzman, C. *Portrait of Dr. Gachet, The Story of a Van Gogh Masterpiece: Modernism, Money, Politics, Collectors, Dealers, Taste, Greed and Loss*. New York and London, 1998.

Schapiro 1950
Schapiro, M. *Vincent van Gogh*. New York, 1950.

's Hertogenbosch 1987
's Hertogenbosch, Noordbrabants Museum. *Van Gogh in Brabant: Schilderijen en tekeningen uit Etten en Nuenen*. Exh. cat., 1987.

Soth 1994
Soth, L. "Van Gogh's Images of Women Sewing." *Zeitschrift für Kunstgeschichte* 1 (1994): 105–10.

Soth 1995
————. "Van Gogh's *Sorrow* and Millet's *The Shepherdess*." *Source* 14, no. 3 (spring 1995): 9–12.

Stark 1982
Stark, D. "Charles de Groux's *Le Bénédicité*: A Source for Van Gogh's Les mangeurs de pommes de terre." *Gazette des beaux-arts* 124, nos. 1360–61 (May–June 1982): 205–8.

Stein 1986
Stein, S.A., ed. *Van Gogh: A Retrospective*. New York, 1986.

Sund 1988
Sund, J. "Favoured Fictions: Women and Books in the Art of Van Gogh." *Art History* 11, no. 2 (June 1988): 255–67

Sund 1992
————. *True to Temperament: Van Gogh and French Naturalist Literature*. New York, 1992.

van Tilborgh et al. 1993
Tilborgh, L. van. *The Potato Eaters by Vincent van Gogh*. With contributions by D. Dekkers, S. van Heugten, I. Hummelen, and C. Peres. Cahier Vincent 5. Zwolle, 1993.

Toronto 1981
Toronto, Art Gallery of Ontario. *Vincent van Gogh and the Birth of Cloisonnism*. Exh. cat., 1981.

van Uitert 1978–79
Uitert, E. van. "Vincent van Gogh in Anticipation of Paul Gauguin." *Simiolus* 10, no. 3/4 (1978–79): 182–99.

van Uitert 1980
————. "Van Gogh and Gauguin in Competition: Vincent's Original Contribution." *Simiolus* 11, no. 2 (1980): 81–106.

van Uitert 1981–82
————. "Van Gogh's Concept of His *Oeuvre*." *Simiolus* 12, no. 4 (1981–82): 223–44.

Vienna 1996
Vienna, Bank Austria Kunstforum. *Van Gogh und die Haager Schule*. Exh. cat., 1996 (Milan).

Visser 1973
Visser, W. J. A. "Vincent van Gogh en 's-Gravenhage." *Geschiedkundige Vereniging Die Haghe. Jaarboek* (1973): 1–125.

Washington 1998
Washington, D.C., National Gallery of Art. *Van Gogh's Van Goghs: Masterpieces from the Van Gogh Museum, Amsterdam*. Exh. cat., 1998 (New York).

Welsh-Ovcharov 1976
Welsh-Ovcharov, B. "Vincent van Gogh: His Paris Period, 1888-1888." Ph.D. diss. University of Utrecht, 1976.

Zemel 1987
Zemel, C. "Sorrowing Women, Rescuing Men: Van Gogh's Images of Women and Family." *Art History* 10, no. 3 (September 1987): 351–68.

Zemel 1993
————. *Vincent van Gogh*. New York, 1993.

Zemel 1997
————. *Van Gogh's Progress: Utopia, Modernity, and Late-Nineteenth-Century Art*. Berkeley, Calif., Los Angeles, and London, 1997.

Acknowledgments

The Detroit Institute of Arts, the Museum of Fine Arts, Boston, and the Philadelphia Museum of Art are deeply indebted to the many lenders to "Van Gogh: Face to Face." To part with a major work by Vincent van Gogh is an extraordinary act of generosity, and we wish to express our profound thanks to all the lenders who have made this exhibition possible. In particular, the Van Gogh Museum in Amsterdam has been extraordinarily generous and has, to a unique degree, assured the breadth, scope and importance of this exhibition. John Leighton and his staff have been a pillar of support. Sjraar van Heugten, curator of drawings, and Louis van Tilborgh, curator of paintings, have been extremely willing to offer their time and expertise. Likewise we wish to acknowledge the helpful assistance of Andreas Blühm, curator of special exhibitions; Fieke Pabst, head archivist, and Aly Noordermeer, registrar, and their staffs; and Melchert Zwetsman and Josette van Gemert of the reproductions department.

By the same token, the Kröller-Müller Museum in Otterlo has been equally generous in sharing its rich collection. We are deeply indebted to Evert J. van Straaten, the director, and members of his staff, Jaap Bremer and Toos van Kooten, who facilitated the loan of a splendid series of drawings and paintings from this world-famous collection of van Gogh material.

At the Rijksmuseum, Amsterdam, we wish to thank Ronald de Leeuw, general director, Jan Piet Filedt Kok, director of the collections, and Wouter Kloek, senior curator of the paintings department.

We are also much obliged to the following people for their kind assistance: Katharina Schmidt, Kunstmuseum Basel; Ernst Beyeler, Beyeler Foundation, Basel; Rudolf Staechelin, Rudolf Staechelin Foundation, Basel; Toni Stooss and Henriette Mentha, Kunstmuseum Bern; Eliane De Wilde, Koninklijke Musea voor Schone Kunsten van België, Brussels; James Cuno, Ivan Gaskell, and Marjorie Cohn, Harvard University Art Museums, Cambridge; Edmond Charrière, Musée des Beaux-Arts, La Chaux-de-Fonds; James Wood, Douglas Druick, Peter Zegers, and Barbara Mirecki, the Art Institute of Chicago; the late Robert Bergman and Diane de Grazia, the Cleveland Museum of Art; Timothy Clifford and Michael Clarke, National Galleries of Scotland, Edinburgh; Georg Költzsch, Museum Folkwang Essen; Charles F. Stuckey, Kimbell Art Museum, Fort Worth; Mark Neill and Vivien Hamilton, Glasgow Museums; Eddy de Jonge, Groninger Museum, Groningen; J.L. Locher, Mariette H. Josephus Jitta, Jonieke van Es, and Titus M. Eliëns, Haags Gemeentemuseum, The Hague; A.C.M. Grondman, Hannema-de Stuers Fundatie, Heino; Thomas Gibson, Thomas Gibson Fine Arts, London; S. Martin Summers, The Lefevre Gallery, London; Christopher Riopelle, National Gallery, London; John Walsh, Jr., and Lee Hendrix, the J. Paul Getty Museum, Los Angeles; Graham W.J. Beal, former director, Los Angeles County Museum of Art; Léonard Gianadda, Fondation Pierre Gianadda, Martigny; Timothy Potts, former director, and Sonja Dean, National Gallery of Victoria, Melbourne; Irina Antonova and Mikhail A. Kamensky, Pushkin State Museum of Fine Arts, Moscow; Thomas Krens and Lisa Dennison, Solomon R. Guggenheim Museum, New York; Philippe de Montebello and George R. Goldner, the Metropolitan Museum of Art, New York; Laurence B. Kanter, Robert Lehman Collection, the Metropolitan Museum of Art; Glenn Lowry, the Museum of Modern Art, New York; Leonard Lauder, New York; Philip Niarchos and Rupert Burgess, the Niarchos Family collection, New York and Switzerland; Anne-Birgitte Fonsmark, Ordrupgaard; Henri Loyrette, Musée d'Orsay, Paris; Sara Campbell, Norton Simon Museum, Pasadena; Bianca Alessandra Pinto and Gianna Piantoni, Galleria Nazionale d'Arte Moderna e Contemporanea, Rome; Erik W. Wentges, Rotterdam; Chris Dercon, Piet de Jonge, and Bram Meij, Museum Boijmans Van Beuningen Rotterdam; Christoph Vögele, Kunstmuseum Solothurn; Edmund Capon, Art Gallery of New South Wales, Sydney; Earl A. Powell III and Philip Conisbee, National Gallery of Art, Washington, D.C.; Dieter Schwarz, Kunstmuseum Winterthur; Verena Steiner-Jaeggli and Ursula Perruchi-Petri, Villa Flora, Winterthur. Our gratitude also goes to Alexander Apsis, Betsy Z. Cohen, Robert Light, Martha and Edward Snider, Jayne Warman, and Max Weitzenhoffer.

Many other people have provided invaluable assistance. Of these we first wish to thank Walter and Maria Feilchenfeldt, whose interest in this project matches our own. Walter's vast knowledge of the provenance of van Gogh's paintings was tremendously helpful to the organizers. Willem Rappard and Martha op de Coul at the Rijksbureau voor Kunsthistorische Documentatie in The Hague were most generous of their time and expertise. We also wish to thank the many art history libraries that facilitated our research and met constant requests for interlibrary loans.

The organizers have benefited from the expertise of van Gogh specialists throughout the world, and we are most grateful to the three who prepared essays for the book: Roland Dorn, Lauren Soth, and Judy Sund. Their contributions add greatly to our understanding of van Gogh's fascination with character likeness and his determination to make a unique contribution to portraiture. We thank them for participating in this project with its demanding time constraints. We also wish to thank Evert van Uitert, Andrea Gaston, Carol Zemel, and other specialists who kindly discussed our project with us. We are indebted to the scholars whose work on van Gogh has provided the context for our own research. Chief among these are the late Jacob Baart de la Faille and the late John Rewald, as well as Jan Hulsker, Tsukasa Kodera, Ronald Pickvance, Griselda Pollock, Susan Alyson Stein, and Bogomila Welsh-Ovcharov.

The organizers are deeply indebted to Alice M. Whelihan, the indemnity administrator, and the members of the indemnity board of the National Endowment for the Arts.

At the Detroit Institute of Arts we gratefully acknowledge Julia P. Henshaw, Cynthia Newman Bohn, Maya Hoptman, Tanya Pohrt, Kelli Carr, Simone Sobel, and Maria Santangelo, whose enormous efforts have resulted in the production of this splendid book. Their enthusiasm for the project remained undiminished through thick and thin. Working with our copublishers, Thames & Hudson, in London and New York has resulted in a fruitful collaboration. The book design by Sarah Praill provides a fresh and highly attractive context for the exploration of the subject matter. We also thank the museum's Publications Department for editing the exhibition label and brochure copy. This they have done hand-in-hand with Linda Margolin and Jennifer Czajkowski of the Education Department, whose enormous efforts have provided our public stimulating and effective educational access to this exhibition. With tremendous dedication, registrar Pamela Watson and her department have assumed huge responsibilities in overseeing all aspects of organizing the packing, insurance, and transportation of all the objects lent to the show. Working together with the registrar, Aimée Marcereau, assistant curator in the European Paintings Department, has played a pivotal role in generating all the correspondence pertaining to the loan requests. Her patience and good humor have proven to be a Rock of Gibraltar for the curator who cannot adequately express his thanks for her inestimably important contribution. Annmarie Erickson, Barbara van Vleet, and other members of the Communications and Marketing Department have effectively promoted this project with great success. They have maintained gusto and enthusiasm for van Gogh despite the daunting logistical consequences of staging such a major exhibition. Ross Pfeiffer and his staff in the Development Department have effectively worked closely with our generous corporate sponsor in Detroit. Jennifer L.S. Moldwin and Kraig A. Binkowski of the museum's research library have provided invaluable assistance. Louis Gauci and his staff have created an outstanding installation design for this exhibition. Robert Hensleigh, Randal Stegmeyer, and Eric Wheeler of the Visual Resources Department worked against the clock to accommodate the myriad photographic demands of this project. Virtually all members of the staff of the DIA have contributed a huge amount of time and energy to this project, and we wish to acknowledge their important role.

Finally, we in Detroit are all most grateful for the unstinting encouragement we received from Maurice D. Parrish, interim director of the Detroit Institute of Arts, and the guidance of David W. Penney, chief curator. Our recently appointed director, Graham W.J. Beal, has been a most helpful supporter of this project. Having overseen the Los Angeles venue of the exhibition "Van Gogh's van Goghs," he well understands the enormous potential "Van Gogh: Face to Face" will have in expanding our audience.

However, one person deserves special praise for guiding this project from its beginnings to its final realization—Tara Robinson, curator of exhibitions. She determinedly kept all the organizational aspects of this exhibition on track and also coordinated the nuts and bolts aspects of the show in Detroit. Her tremendous dedication, and that of her assistant, Amy Hamilton Foley, assured that this project went from being a dream to becoming a reality.

At the Museum of Fine Arts, Boston, we are indebted to many for their dedication to the success of this exhibition. We are grateful to Malcolm Rogers, Ann and Graham Gund Director, for his enthusiastic support and to Katherine Getchell, deputy director for curatorial affairs, who has overseen myriad aspects of the organization of the exhibition; and in their offices we thank Jennifer Bose, Carol Fredian, and Catherine East. Patricia Jacoby, Paul Bessire, and Linda Powell of External Relations are to be thanked for their unstinting work in assuring funding here in Boston. Registrar Patricia Loiko's seamless efforts ensured the safe transportation of the exhibition and guided colleagues through other critical stages of planning. She was assisted by Kim Pashko, Jill Kennedy-Kernohan, and Adelia Bussey. We are grateful to Clifford S. Ackley, Ruth and Carl J. Shapiro Curator of Prints and Drawings, head of the Department of Prints and Drawings, for a generous loan from his collection. Gilian F. Shallcross and Barbara T. Martin in the Division of Education inspired and informed our Boston audience. Cynthia Purvis and Janet O'Donoghue and their colleagues in Creative Services expertly presented the exhibitions with style in print. Also to be recognized are the efforts of Dawn Griffin, Sylvia Sukop, and their staff, who have promoted the exhibition with great success, and those of Thomas Lang, Nicole Luongo,

Kristin Bierfelt, Leah Ross, Nicole Salamone, Phil Getchell, Jonathan Delgazio, and Sean Westgate, who provided visual, research, and technological support.

We acknowledge with gratitude Paintings Conservation staff members Jean Woodward, Irene Konefal, Rhona MacBeth, Lydia Vagts, Andrew Haines, Leane Delgaizo, and particularly Jim Wright, Eyk and Rose-Marie van Otterloo Conservator of Paintings, head of Paintings Conservation, who insured that the museum's two portraits look magnificent. We extend our thanks to Roy Perkinson and Gail English, who offered their assistance with works on paper. Thanks also go to the expert team of Susan Wong, Valerie McGregor, and their staff in Exhibitions and Design. The curator acknowledges with gratitude the support of Erica E. Hirshler and Amy M. Benns in the Art of the Americas Department. And in the Art of Europe Department, the invaluable efforts of Deanna M. Griffin, Kathleen A. McDonald, and Erika M. Swanson have contributed to the successful realization of the exhibition and this book. A special note of thanks goes to research fellow Alexandra Ames Lawrence, whose patience, perspicacity, and perseverance have been appreciated by all who have worked with her. Finally, we acknowledge the many unnamed colleagues and friends, all of whom have worked tirelessly to present these works by van Gogh in their full glory.

At the Philadelphia Museum of Art, we must thank our corporate sponsors, who have generously supported the Philadelphia venue. Anne d'Harnoncourt, the George D. Widener Director and chief executive officer, has been an exemplar of support, guidance, and enthusiasm for this project from the beginning. Alexa Q. Aldridge and Kim Sajet have devoted themselves to all matters of development, funding, and sponsorship. In Special Exhibitions, Suzanne Wells, with the help of Krista Mancini, has performed her customary magic. We thank Robert Morrone in Operations for his assistance with numerous details and Jack Schlechter and Andrew Slavinskas in Installation Design for giving their customary elegance and functionality to the exhibition design. In the Department of Twentieth Century Art, Ann Temkin and Michael R. Taylor have contributed their curatorial and scholarly talents to help shape the exhibition. Invaluable research support has come from Allen Townsend, Lila Mittelstaedt, and Josephine Chen in the Museum Library, while Lynn Rosenthal, Conna Clark, Terry Fleming-Murphy, and Holly Gallagher have provided exemplary help from Photography and Rights and Reproductions. In Conservation, Mark Tucker, Teresa Lignelli, Faith Zieske, and Nancy Ash have all devoted themselves to the success of the exhibition. Sandra Horrocks, former director of marketing and public relations, and Laura Coogan, former assistant director of marketing devoted themselves to the exhibition with their customary zest; they have been matched in this by Kris Batley, Rene Firman, Sacha Adorno, and Matt Singer. In the Department of European Painting, Jennifer Vanim and William Rudolph have each provided day-to-day assistance with all things van Gogh and not van Gogh, while Lauren K. Chang was especially instrumental in getting the van Gogh exhibition off to a smooth start. Against a particularly dense exhibition calendar, Irene Taurins, senior registrar, has seemingly effortlessly coordinated loans for the Philadelphia venue.

List of Illustrations

Index

Page numbers in italics refer to illustrations